DATE DUE

Twayne's United States Authors Series

Sylvia E. Bowman, *Editor*

INDIANA UNIVERSITY

J. E. Spingarn

J. E. SPINGARN

By MARSHALL VAN DEUSEN

University of California, Riverside

 182

Twayne Publishers, Inc.   ::   New York

Preface

J. E. Spingarn was the first consistent and the most persistent spokesman in twentieth-century American criticism for the idea that the work of the literary artist was a primary imaginative activity which resisted reductive analysis. Though related to life, it was in some sense autonomous with respect to ordinary, moral, political, sociological, and rhetorical categories; superior to, or anterior to, conceptual discourse; but of central importance in human experience.

Spingarn began his work at the turn of the century under the guidance of his mentor, George Edward Woodberry, whose gentle (if not "genteel") idealism played an important part in encouraging Spingarn's early critical interests. But, by the time of Spingarn's famous lecture at Columbia in 1910 on "The New Criticism," he was in full rebellion against the "genteel tradition" of the polite literary world—presided over by E. C. Stedman, Hamilton Wright Mabie, and Richard Watson Gilder—and in rebellion against most varieties of academic criticism as well. In that lecture he announced his allegiance to the idealistic esthetic of Benedetto Croce and attempted to "make use of" Croce's theories in working out the difficult implications of his own conviction that art was an expression of the creative "spirit" that virtually called into being its own terms of reference. Spingarn continued to urge this view during the 1920's, directly opposing, on the one hand, the moralism of the neo-Humanists led by Irving Babbitt, and indirectly skeptical, on the other hand, of the sociological apologists for Naturalism. His most ambitious, and his final, statement of his position came in 1931 in a series of six lectures (only one of which has been published) on *Literature and the New Era,* delivered at the New School for Social Research in New York just as American criticism was entering a decade in which the Marxists and the new "new critics" were to share the spotlight.

Spingarn's insistence throughout his career on a kind of autonomy for art was really a version of a central epistemological paradox much emphasized in our time: we know what we know only in the act of knowing it. In such circumstances, criticism is extraordinarily difficult. Spingarn's difficulty was compounded because he argued his convictions with polemical fervor during the years of what he himself characterized as the "guerilla warfare" of American criticism—a warfare which began in the first decade of the twentieth century and which continues today. H. L. Mencken gleefully welcomed this warfare—and the name-calling and sloganeering which accompanied it—as "one of the most hopeful symptoms of the new *Aufklärung* in the Republic"; but among the critics of criticism there has been little enlightenment concerning what Spingarn himself was fighting for, and his "influence" has remained problematical at best.

Spingarn's "importance," however, has always been admitted on all sides, though it has been, in the hands of different writers, many contradictory things. His good friend Van Wyck Brooks hailed him as a "patron of aesthetic radicalism"; but Henri Peyre and William Van O'Connor have agreed to class him with the neo-Humanists or with the "traditionalists."[1] Others have grouped him with that prince of American iconoclasts, Mencken himself, or with James Huneker. And still others, variously responding to his idealism, or his estheticism, or his modernism, or his traditionalism, have coupled his name with that of Emerson, Poe, Hawthorne, Melville, Dreiser, Sherwood Anderson, O'Neill, Sandburg, Amy Lowell, or T. S. Eliot. Allen Tate, though denying "intrinsic merit" to Spingarn's writing, put him at the head of the whole modern critical movement in America because he had urged the claims of the alienated artist in an increasingly unsympathetic society.[2]

These estimates, confusing and contradictory, usually come from critics involved in literary battles of their own. Because Spingarn's manner was combative, they have naturally supposed he must have been a partisan in this camp or that; but the truth seems to be that, though he was *in* the critical wars of the pre- and post-World War I era, he was not *of* them. His primary allegiance was to a Romantic literary doctrine of "inspiration" and "genius" largely out of fashion in the twentieth century, devoted as it has been to sociological or rhetorical analysis. For Spingarn, analytical categories had only a minimal or marginal usefulness in describing the dialectical unity of "spirit." Certainly party labels are not helpful in describing *his* spirit. The common notion, for example, of Spingarn's rebellious "radicalism" (based largely on his "New Criticism" of 1910) and its apparently contradictory counterpart—that he was a "conservative," even a "reactionary" (based largely on his "The Younger Generation" of 1922)—may be, from the point of view of the Romantic idealist, complementary rather than contradictory.

Because Spingarn became, as John Chamberlain put it, "a guerilla on the cultural front,"[3] the central motive of his theory of literature is not easily evident in his published writings. His championship of spirit against the unexamined materialistic assumptions that he considered the besetting evil of pragmatic America emerges best when we have some sense of the interesting and versatile career of the man behind the writings. Lewis Mumford wrote of his friend that Spingarn's "final testament to us is the book that he lived, but never lived to write."[4]

Nor has anyone else ever published a substantial study of Spingarn's life or his theory, though a book on his work in the field of race relations has been announced by Miss Barbara Joyce Ross. If we can put together some sense of "the book of Spingarn's life" and the animating principles of his theory, we may see in the interpenetration of act and principle the development of a position that is a little apart from, and a little above, the guerilla warfare—a position out of sympathy with much of twentieth-century American thought, but a viewpoint not the less advantageous from which to estimate that thought. We may see from this vantage point an independent rehearsal of many of the recurrent problems of modern American criticism. We may see, for example, the concern for "content" on the part of the literary radicals, the Marxists, and the neo-Humanists, and the concern for "form" on the part of the "new critics," defined by Spingarn's own demand for a fusion of form and content in a structuring act of the imagination, derived from a Romantic esthetic modernized by Crocean doctrine. And to see such rehearsals of such problems may give the problems an unfamiliar clarity that will help enlighten the work of other American critics as well as Spingarn's own.

In recent years such diverse investigations as Noam Chomsky's studies in psycho-linguistics and the studies of many scholars concerning the literary uses of myth have alerted us to unsuspected or forgotten dimensions of the human spirit not easily explained by orthodox behaviorist theory. In this context there may be a special timeliness in recognizing that Spingarn, despite his old-fashioned vocabulary, was centrally concerned to defend literature as a fundamental manifestation of the freedom of spirit, as virtual creation. And we may also be interested to follow his philosophy of the spirit a little way into such practical areas of experience as race relations, academic freedom, political reform, and military service, areas which posed for Spingarn, as they have for many of us, pressing problems both personal and public.

The biographical material of Part I of this study does not pretend to be a "life" of Spingarn. But Spingarn's scholarly work, the dispute with Nicholas Murray Butler that preceded his dismissal from Columbia University, his candidacy for public office, his service in the army during World War I, his pioneer editorial work for Harcourt, Brace and Company, and his part in forming the National Association for the Advancement of Colored People are important in understanding the versatile personality behind the criticism and the real intention of the criticism itself. And so in the first four chapters, which comprise Part I, I have attempted to bring into focus certain "moments" of Spingarn's life in order to enlighten his critical theory, which is the subject of Part II. I hope especially that these moments may help illuminate his conception of the "spiritual" nature of "practice." Such illumination should make clearer his conception of the "life of theory," which included the world of literature; for "theory" was to Spingarn the dialectical counterpart of "practice" in the whole "life of the spirit." The meaning of such terms as these emerges best, I think, if they are allowed to develop without formal definition in Part I. But at the beginning of Part II general definitions are provided in an effort to project these emergent concepts into the different but related world of ideas and to protect them from being wholly lost in the smoke of the guerilla warfare which they quickly enough became a part of.

My procedure has no doubt led to some repetition. But my

aim has been to provide detailed analyses of many of the facets of Spingarn's thought, while yet preserving through occasional repetition and recapitulation some sense of its unity. In this way I hope I may have prepared the way for my general conclusions.

For valuable advice and counsel in the preparation of this study I wish to thank Professors Robert E. Spiller, University of Pennsylvania; Leon Howard, University of California, Los Angeles; Milton Miller, University of California, Riverside; and Mr. Harry Lawton of the University of California, Riverside. Professor Arthur Collins of the State University of New York, Albany, kindly made available to me his translations of many of Croce's letters to Spingarn. I also wish to acknowledge the assistance given me by Frederick J. Hoffman, late Research Professor in the Department of English at the University of Wisconsin, Milwaukee. And I acknowledge the financial help of the Intramural Research Committee of the University of California, Riverside.

Special thanks are due Mr. Arthur B. Spingarn, who gave me the important benefit of his keen recollections of persons, places, and events. Most important of all has been the help of Mrs. J. E. Spingarn, who gave me access to all the letters and other unpublished material cited in this book and answered my questions with fairness and patience. Her generosity has been of very great assistance to me in more ways than one.

MARSHALL VAN DEUSEN

University of California, Riverside

Contents

Chronology

1875   Joel Elias Spingarn born to Elias Spingarn and Sarah
       Barnett Spingarn May 17, 1875, in New York. Spingarn's
       father was from Austria; his mother from England.
1890   Ran away from home to Philadelphia; returned after
       a month.
1892   First of several trips to Europe.
1893   Admitted to junior class at Columbia College.
1894   Notes on Lyly's *Endimion* in *The Athaneum*, August 4.
1895- Bachelor's degree from Columbia with honors. Studied
1896   English and comparative literature in graduate school at
       Harvard. Enrolled for work in comparative literature in
       graduate school at Columbia.
1899   Doctorate from Columbia. Published *A History of Liter-*
       ary Criticism in the Renaissance, his dissertation done
       under George Edward Woodberry. Appointed assistant
       in comparative literature at Columbia under Woodberry.
1900   Address to International Congress of Comparative Histo-
       ry in Paris on American scholarship, published following
       year in the *Proceedings*. Made tutor in comparative
       literature at Columbia.
1901   Read "The New Hesperides," his most ambitious poem
       to date before Phi Beta Kappa Society at Columbia in
       June.
1902   Summer trip to Breathitt County, Kentucky, to investi-
       gate Hargis-Cardwell-Cockrill feud. Review in *The Nation*
       (April 24) of Opdycke's translation of Castiglione's
       Cortegiano, first public clue to Spingarn's interest in the
       history of the gentleman. Review in *The Nation* (Sep-
       tember 25) of Croce's *Estetica*.
1903   Founding editor of *Journal of Comparative Literature*.
1904   Resignation of Woodberry; Spingarn appointed Adjunct

Professor of Comparative Literature.

1905   Published revised and enlarged edition of *Literary Criticism in the Renaissance* in Italian. Married Amy Einstein.

1908-   Ran for Congress. Published three volumes of *Critical*
1909   *Essays of the Seventeenth Century.* Appointed Professor of Comparative Literature.

1910   "The New Criticism" delivered in March as public lecture at Columbia; published the following year. Department of Comparative Literature abolished. Dismissal of Harry Thurston Peck.

1911   Spingarn fired from Columbia, March 6, 1911. Issued *A Question of Academic Freedom.* Bought *Amenia Times,* published in Amenia, N. Y., near Troutbeck, Spingarn's country house.

1913   Chairman of the directors of National Association for the Advancement of Colored People till 1919; treasurer till 1930; president till his death.

1915   Went to Plattsburgh military training camp in August; first of several Spingarn attended before his enlistment.

1916   Convened the Amenia Conference on racial problems at Troutbeck.

1917   Published first edition of *Creative Criticism.* Enlisted in the army; graduated as major in the Infantry from Madison Barracks, N. Y. After assignment to 78th Division at Camp Dix, N. J., followed by a physical collapse, Spingarn served in Military Intelligence in Washington, D. C., where he pressed for training of Negro officers.

1918   Brief service in France; discharged as lieutenant-colonel.

1919   One of the founders of Harcourt, Brace and Co., editor of European Library, 1920-1924.

1922   Published "The Younger Generation: A New Manifesto" in *The Freeman* (June), giving the "other side" of the argument of "The New Criticism."

1924   Published anthology of modern American criticism, *Criticism in America: Its Function and Status.* Recurrence of old illness caused Spingarn to go on inactive status at Harcourt, Brace. Publication of *Poems.* Began private printing of *Troutbeck Leaflets.*

1926   Review of Magendie's *La politesse mondaine* in *Romanic*

Review (January-March) initiated controversy about methods of social and literary history.

1931   New and enlarged edition of *Creative Criticism.* Lectured on *Literature and the New Era* at New School for Social Research in New York. Growing interest in comparative religion.

1932   Address on "Racial Equality" at National Association for the Advancement of Colored People Conference May 17, 1932.

1933   Second Amenia Conference at Troutbeck.

1934   Published "American Clematis for American Gardens," in *National Horticultural Magazine* (January), first of several articles on clematis and landscape gardening.

1936   Article on Woodberry in *Dictionary of American Biography.*

1939   Death of Spingarn July 26, 1939.

1942   Posthumous publication of "Politics and the Poet," with an introductory note by Lewis Mumford, the *Atlantic Monthly* (November).

Part I: The Practice of Life

CHAPTER 1

Amateur of Action

JOEL ELIAS Spingarn was born May 17, 1875, at 215 East Fifty-ninth Street in New York City. He was the first of six boys (two of whom died in infancy) born to Elias Spingarn and Sarah (Barnett) Spingarn. His parents were both born abroad, his father in Austria and his mother in the north of England. In a series of unpublished autobiographical fragments, Spingarn recounts with pride how his father, "swept from his Austrian home as a mere boy by the political and economic upheaval of 1848," settled, after a short period of "wandering" with his two older brothers, in New York City; how the three brothers then showed their "mettle" by sending for still another, younger, brother; and how they put this younger brother through Harvard Law School (where, it is noted, "he was a classmate of Justice Holmes of the Supreme Court") and started him on a promising legal career.

Spingarn's admiration in his autobiographical notes for his father's abilities as a practical man seems mixed with pride that success had come as part of a ceremonial American *rite de passage.* This penchant for idealizing the practical seems closely associated with the "profound" influence he attributed to his mother, whose "fondness for poetry" encouraged in her son the imaginative bent that shaped his own career, whether in the realm of action or of thought.

As a youth Spingarn also became aware of Europe, where he later discovered the "idealism" he felt was the necessary complement for American pragmatism. He explained in his autobiographical notes that his father's business, that of wholesale tobacco merchant, put him in touch with American "dirt farmers" and also took him on travels to the richer, more complicated world across the Atlantic. He had, as it were, "advantages"; for his father, though "never a millionaire or a captain of industry . . . was well-to-do," and the "happy, well-to-do, but not overly-rich household is one of the best of all in which to be born."

I   *The Incurable Romantic*

These autobiographical fragments, written as they are in the quaint formality of the third person, reveal as much about Spingarn the man as about Spingarn the boy. They show his admiration of distinction and of the idea of responsible devotion to duty. Along with these traits, which, in the jargon of the 1920's, would, ironically enough, have been called "the traits of the Puritan," these fragments show Spingarn's incurable Romanticism. They reveal his faith in the ability of the individual to prove himself in spite of adversity, and they hint at the same romantic idealization of America that Spingarn expressed in his Phi Beta Kappa poem on "The New Hesperides."

One of the incidents Spingarn selected for his autobiographical record confirms the suspicion that, both as boy and man, he habitually thought of "actual" experience as interpenetrated with "ideal" events that were every bit as "real" as "facts." He tells of his running away from home at the age of fifteen. He walked, he says, to Philadelphia, where he assumed the name of Juan de Lara, a name he had already used for one of the characters in some of his juvenile efforts at writing fiction. He also invented a biography to go with the name—a wild story about an orphan who had been cheated out of his rights. In Philadelphia he met an alcoholic writer by the name of George E. Richards, who was, according to Spingarn's account, really the scion of a wealthy old Southern family, and "one of the only two men whose personality impressed me as the personality of a man of genius."

Richards, apparently impressed in turn by Spingarn's tale of woe, and convinced by his imitation of a Spanish accent, hired him as a secretary and became interested (in his lucid moments) "in going to Spain and getting back the castles out of which I had been cheated." He "even proposed," wrote Spingarn years later, "to marry me off to one of these Southern relatives of his." Neither of these projects was realized, but according to

Spingarn's account (which apparently includes some fictional interpolations), the Philadelphia adventure did include a trip to Sea Island City and an encounter with two of Richards' elderly female relatives in a Rittenhouse Square apartment, where Spingarn had gone to collect Richards' semiannual allowance, Richards himself being too drunk to put in an appearance. Spingarn's parents, who had hired private detectives in their effort to find him, finally recovered their boy by tracing a letter he had written home asking, prosaically enough, for more clothes.

The effort to distinguish the fictional elements in Spingarn's account of the whole episode is perhaps not as important as it is to mark his somewhat melodramatic concluding comment: the adventure was, he says, his "real introduction to life." Spingarn's whole manner in describing his escapade suggests that he often thought of life as a kind of drama created by the actors.

After a preliminary education, chiefly at private schools, and some work at the College of the City of New York, Spingarn was admitted, in 1893, to the junior class of Columbia College. His juvenile stories—romantic, exotic, and improbable—and his diaries attest to his early interest in imaginative literature. At Columbia he continued to write, contributing frequent verses to the *Columbia Monthly*. As an undergraduate at Columbia, he also gave evidence of his scholarly ambitions. His brother Arthur reports that Joel and he, with the boldness and confidence of youth, planned to edit the complete works of John Lyly.

Whatever the fate of this project, Joel did engage in a minor scholarly skirmish in 1894, at the age of nineteen, with R. Warwick Bond and F. G. Fleay about the dating of Lyly's *Endimion*. He conjectured, in a letter to the London *Atheneum* (August 4, 1894), that Lyly's three allusions in *Endimion* to seven years waiting (II, i; III, iv; IV, ii) referred to the period of time Lyly had waited since Queen Elizabeth's hint in 1579 that he might be made Master of the Revels. Hence Spingarn dated *Endimion* in 1586. One week after his letter appeared, the *Atheneum* carried replies from both Bond and Fleay. Bond later summarized the exchange in a footnote in the third volume of his edition of Lyly's *Works* (1902).

After receiving his bachelor of arts degree with honors from Columbia in 1895, Spingarn attended graduate school at Harvard

University, where he took courses in English and in comparative literature from F. J. Child, George Pierce Baker, Barrett Wendell, J. B. Fletcher (later a colleague of Spingarn's on the faculty at Columbia), George Lyman Kittredge, Arthur Richmond Marsh, and Charles Eliot Norton. He also had a course at Harvard with Lewis Gates on "English Literature in its Relation to German Literature, from 1790 to 1830," which presumably included some study of the German Romantic literary theorists and philosophers whom Spingarn later credited with laying the foundations of modern esthetic thought. But there is no evidence that Gates' own theories[1] influenced Spingarn directly, either while he was at Harvard or later. It is reported that Spingarn himself asserted that the only thing he got from Gates was the address of the best French restaurant in Boston, and it is certain that Spingarn never mentioned Gates in his published writings.

The similarity between the theories of the two men—a similarity remarked by both Robert Spiller and Morton Zabel[2]— hardly needs the explanation of cause and effect: it can be accounted for by Spingarn's and Gates' common inheritance of the attenuated Romanticism of the late nineteenth century and by their common opposition to "philological" scholarship as the sole end of literary interest. As we shall see, Spingarn agreed with Gates that critics need both the sensitivity of the Impressionist and the objectivity of the scholar; but he rejected the implied "psychologism" of Gates' theory as well as Gates' emphasis on pleasure as the end of poetry.

After only one year at Harvard, Spingarn transferred to the graduate school of Columbia. And there is no doubt that George Edward Woodberry, Spingarn's mentor there, influenced him profoundly. Spingarn acknowledged the debt in the first of his New School lectures when he coupled Woodberry with the great Italian philosopher Benedetto Croce: these "two inspiring teachers," he said, were truly the men who "educated" him. In fact, "I have been so profoundly influenced by them," he continued, "especially in my early youth, that what I am going to say is, I hardly know whether theirs or mine."[3]

It is clear that what Spingarn got from Woodberry was not

specific doctrine. Woodberry himself devoted a good part of one of his essays to a refutation of what he considered the irresponsible iconoclasm of his protégé's theories.[4] And Spingarn, in a biographical sketch that he prepared for the *Dictionary of American Biography,* noted that Woodberry's concrete judgment, although "characterized by a certain detached insight, . . . exhibits a narrowness of sympathy which brushes aside the racier writers like Walt Whitman, Thoreau, Mark Twain, and Herman Melville. . . ." In his critical writings, Spingarn mentioned Woodberry only once. In "American Criticism Today" he grouped Woodberry with the "older critics" and explained that these critics "have scarcely concerned themselves" with modern problems, have preferred instead to think of themselves as above transitory and local issues, as "citizens of a Republic of Letters in which geographical boundaries seemed almost literary accidents." Of Woodberry individually, he said: he "is an inheritor of the Lowell tradition, in whom, despite many new influences, New England idealism carries on its appointed task of illuminating the meeting-point of art and life."

This is the verdict (somewhat muted by affection for the subject) of the progressive, the revolutionary Spingarn, denying the "genteel tradition" in literature. But Spingarn himself was little interested in "geographical boundaries," and his own writings contain virtually no mention of contemporary American authors. Though his tone was certainly more vigorous than Woodberry's and his vocabulary more modern, he was less interested in "local issues" than in the large issue of combating the "materialism" which he saw closing in on men's minds all around him, and his own life seems a continuing effort to discover the actual as a function of the ideal. It was Woodberry's "idealism" that made Spingarn, when writing to Croce in December, 1899, in the full enthusiasm of his discovery of Croce's early critical writings, call Woodberry "the most distinguished of American critics," and to recommend to Croce (in a letter of February 18, 1900) "Pr. Woodberry's recent *Heart of Man* . . . , which contains . . . a defence of poetry by an idealist who does not sympathize with realism in literature or with materialism in life."[5]

Unfortunately, Woodberry's "idealism" seems pale and mere-

ly genteel in his published essays. Spingarn felt the deficiency
and in 1923 wrote Stuart Sherman to ask if he would not do an
appreciation of Woodberry in answer to the "half-truths" contained in an extremely sarcastic article by John Macy.[6] Macy,
following the fashion of the 1920's, had accused Woodberry of
being a "Puritan" and had argued that Woodberry "can not help
demoralizing poetry by moralizing it into pseudo-philosophical
prose" filled with "abstract phrases, which on pressure yield nothing." Sherman declined Spingarn's invitation to reply to Macy,
but his letter (July 1, 1923) shows that he had "divined"
Woodberry's essential virtues quite well. He called Woodberry a
"spirit and a kindling torch" who cast a "spell" over those who
had sat at his feet; and he lamented that Woodberry's "bright
youth in the classroom," his "fire and . . . radiance," "cool
somehow and lose their quickening immediacy on the printed
page."[7]

It was, in fact, such an influence as Sherman described that
Woodberry wielded over his disciple. It was a moral influence
too, as much as a strictly literary one. Spingarn once wrote to
Woodberry (September 5, 1900): "I have learnt—in no small
way thro' the guidance you have given me—that to do one's
duty is the main thing, and to that, as a man, I hope to conse-
crate myself more and more." He wrote to Croce upon the
occasion of Woodberry's resignation from Columbia (March 11,
1904): "No one else among my countrymen had quite the same
power to fill and fire the mind and imagination of youth; a re-
served man himself, he still had an influence in the class room
and outside, that makes one think of Guarino or Poliziano." In
his article in the *Dictionary of American Biography* Spingarn
noted that in Woodberry's poetry "the Platonic tradition of European poetry mingles with a deep American patriotism." And
he remarked that in Woodberry's best critical work there is "a
subtle intuition of the emotional experience that produced the
work of literature and a deep sense of its relation to the spiritual
background of western man." Spirituality, sensitivity, idealism, patriotism—these are the things that Spingarn praised in
Woodberry; these things—of the character and not of the mind—
are the "influences" of the master on the disciple.

II   *Theory and Practice*

Lewis Einstein, Spingarn's brother-in-law, and himself a good scholar as well as a distinguished diplomat, called attention to a further complication in Woodberry's character. In an unpublished reminiscence, Einstein described Woodberry as a "deeply patriotic man," "more cultivated than scholarly," a curious mixture of "dreamy somnolence" and inspired brilliance (especially when he spoke of Shelley), a man whose "idealism" was "not particularly calculated to fit his disciples for the rougher competition of American life," and yet a man with "an unexpected strain of New England practical judgment."

The incongruity which Einstein felt between Woodberry's idealism and his practicality raises also a problem central to Spingarn's life: in Crocean terms, it is the problem of mediating between theory and practice. We can note here that the first step in the resolution of the problem, the assertion of the primacy of "spirit" in *all* experience, is the main point of Spingarn's extended tribute to Woodberry in his first New School lecture. Woodberry, he said, "taught us to look inside the spirit of man rather than nature for the real secret of man's life." For Woodberry, who "had actually . . . talked with Emerson," knew that life itself came into being through an act of the constructive imagination, an act which creates "our conception of life," an act of "reaction against the hegemony of the natural sciences" which places them in a dependent relation to the realm of the spirit. These ideas were the central "inspiration" Spingarn drew from Woodberry. They were the ideas most needed in the "rougher competition of American life," and Spingarn's sense of America's needs was a patriotic, moral conviction as much as an esthetic one. To confront the roughness and to refine it, to make practice a function of spirit, was the problem set by Woodberry; and, in one form or another, it was a problem Spingarn wrestled with throughout his life.

It was Woodberry, of course, who guided Spingarn through his doctoral dissertation on Renaissance literary criticism, but Spingarn had apparently discovered the subject for himself. His early interest in Lyly had led him to do special research in the origins of Elizabethan prose style.[8] This research led him, in turn, to investigate the Italian literary theorists of the Renaissance. The result of these investigations was his *A History of Literary Criticism in the Renaissance,* first published in 1899 (the year Spingarn received his doctorate) as volume I of the *Columbia University Studies in Literature.* This work, the product of a man only twenty-four years old, was hailed by scholars both at home and abroad as a pioneer work of first-rate importance. It brought personal letters of praise from such different people as Giosuè Carducci and S. H. Butcher, Gustave Lanson, Giovanni Gentile, George Saintsbury, G. Gregory Smith, L. P. Getz, Karl Vossler, Aloïs Brandl, and many others praised it publicly. In 1905 it became perhaps the first work of American scholarship to be translated into a foreign language since George Ticknor's *History of Spanish Literature.* In that year a revised and enlarged Italian edition appeared with a commendatory preface by Benedetto Croce. In 1908 a second American edition came out; there have been seven printings of this edition, and in 1963 Harcourt, Brace and World published it as a Harbinger Book with an introduction by Bernard Weinberg.[9]

Upon the completion of his graduate work, Spingarn became the chief assistant to Woodberry in the Department of Comparative Literature in 1900. When Woodberry resigned in 1904, Spingarn was made Adjunct Professor of Comparative Literature; in 1909 he became full professor; and in 1910 he became the chairman of the Division of Modern Languages and Literature.

But Spingarn did not retreat to the library to rest upon his scholarly and academic laurels. He was interested in the world of action as well as the world of the mind. In the summer of 1902, for example, he took time out to go to Breathitt County in Kentucky to investigate the notorious Hargis-Cardwell-Cockrill feud, one of the bloodiest vendettas in the history of the state; for he hoped to write an account of the feud for magazine publication. He roomed with Curtiss Jett, later convicted of murder and, in fact, became so friendly with him that Jett apparently confided in him. But Spingarn characteristically felt that he was honor-bound to respect what Jett had told him as the confidences of a friend; consequently, he never made any public record of his adventure.[10]

Spingarn's interest in public affairs was intense in these early years too. On September 30, 1901, after the assassination of President McKinley, he wrote to Croce of his fear that "the reaction against anarchistic license may result in legislation unfavorable to free speech." His anxiety about civil liberties and his faith in the new president's ability combined to bring Spingarn "under the spell of Theodore Roosevelt," as Lewis Mumford put it, and to make him "ambitious to serve his country politically."[11] Lewis Einstein wrote in his reminiscence that Spingarn's "craving for action" was in part a reaction against the influence of Woodberry and an unfortunate rebellion "against his own natural academic inclinations." But it may be that this hunger for experience was only the logical outcome in a forceful personality of the Romantic urge for excitement which the gentler Woodberry himself had taught Spingarn to value in literature. And Woodberry, as Spingarn knew, had in his own way been something of a political radical; he had early rejected New England "Whiggery" for a kind of "liberalism" not so very different from the liberalism Spingarn saw in Theodore Roosevelt.[12] And he had even been a Democratic candidate (from an overwhelmingly Republican district) for the Massachusetts legislature.

Einstein gives an amusing sketch of Spingarn's activities in "a small Republican organization known as the Freedom Club in which he tried to initiate the methods of Tammany Hall by combining social pleasures with politics":

He tried to form a library for this club and wrote to Theodore Roosevelt who was then governor to ask for one of his books. He sent one but the gift met with some criticism on the ground that the edges of the pages of this book were rough so that some of the members thought that as our club was of small importance, the Governor had sent us a defective copy. The situation was saved when one of the members remarked that rough edges were "the latest fashion in London; they call it uncut" [deckle edge?].

In 1908 Spingarn ran for Congress as the Republican candidate from New York City's traditionally Democratic Eighteenth District. He lost, though he substantially increased the Republican share of the total vote, and he apparently enjoyed the experience tremendously. In a letter to Woodberry (November 18,

1908), he described his feelings at length:

> But surely you will want to hear something of the "crowded hour of glorious life" which he only knows in our peaceful democracy, who is a candidate for office. The sense of life which the experience gave me is beyond my academic style to picture. Be a candidate, I abjure you, dear Mr. Woodberry, before you die! Defy your "illusionaries," break faith with Nietzsche and Anatole France, send rainbows shooting through their mists, by being a candidate!
>
> . . . I spoke every evening, scarcely ever less than four or five times, once as many as eight, whirling from place to place as fast as gasolene could speed me. I attended Catholic bazars, German literary societies, colored mass-meetings, and every other function in my district where I was wanted or tolerated. I received delegations and individuals, and expounded my views on the universe to them. In a word, I did everything that every other candidate for office does in very much the same way. (. . . I am now sharing the first heritage of all candidates in a kaleidoscopic sense of the mere experience.) I have felt no results from this unusual burden of work, except possibly a heightened sense of physical well-being, and a temporary ennui at the contrasting tameness of the academic life.

Four months later, in a letter to Croce (March 14, 1909), Spingarn repeated his comparison of the political and academic world, concluding that "the experience [of running for Congress] was a vital one for me, with its many opportunities of meeting types of men not found in the monastic atmosphere of a University."

Spingarn's lifelong devotion to what he called *"the political sense"* never lapsed. He defined this sense as "a spiritual gift quite as distinct as the poetic gift," and though he conceded that the attempt to deal with political fact from the point of view of spirit may have led him to undertake many tasks "for which I was unfitted,"[13] he always insisted that practice and theory were not incompatible. A winning example of his concern for the quality of American political life, which is also an example of his academic manner, appeared in a report of an interview with Spingarn in the *Cincinnati Post* for January 22, 1909. Spingarn had visited the University of Cincinnati to give a speech on comparative literature; but apparently his views on politics were solicited too. In the *Post* he is credited with saying: "The day of the 'low-brow' as a political boss will soon be a thing of the past." He followed this statement, it is true, with the opinion that most reform movements needed to emphasize

party organization and the ward worker as much as abstract
principles. And he insisted that he "wouldn't want to be
governed by my co-professors at Columbia. That would be
too much theory and too little practical." He concluded, however, with a rhetorical question: "It is not at all extraordinary in
England to see college professors sitting in Parliament. Why not
in America?"

In 1912, and again in 1916, Spingarn was a delegate to the
national conventions of the Progressive party in Chicago; but his
interest in entering politics directly as a candidate did not re-
vive, though he made a number of speeches in support of Franklin D. Roosevelt's presidential candidacy in 1932. It may be
that his sense of service, his patriotism, and his youthful, romantic desire to be the complete man, to have a full experience
of life, to "make" life, had led him into politics; and it may be
that his sense of honor, his sense of "quality," and his inflexi-
bility in the face of compromise led him out.

III   *A Study of Manners: Freedom and Decorum*

During these early years Spingarn continued to write verses—
verses which had to do with art, beauty, love, and knowledge.
Some of them appeared in 1899 and 1900 in *East and West,* a
short-lived magazine edited and published by Spingarn's friend,
William Aspenwall Bradley, and by George Sidney Hellman. In
June, 1901, Spingarn read his "The New Hesperides," a romantic profession of faith and an optimistic poetic forecast of America's role in the world of ideas and action, before the Society of
Phi Beta Kappa at Columbia University. In 1900 Edmund
Clarence Stedman, America's leading poetry anthologist, published one of Spingarn's poems in his *American Anthology, 1787-
1900.* And in April, 1902, the *Atlantic Monthly* published Spingarn's "Prothalamion." But in December, 1905, the poet, suit-
ing deed to word, turned from writing bridal hymns to taking a
bride. She was Amy Einstein, the daughter of David L. Einstein
of New York, and the sister of Lewis Einstein.[14]

Spingarn's life at this stage in his career must certainly have
seemed full of promise. His various public activities were beauti-
fully complemented by the devotion and seriousness with which

he assumed the private roles of husband and father. Some idea of his ideal of the complete man, "equally at home in a garden, a library, an office, or on a battlefield," as his friend Lewis Mumford put it,[15] can be glimpsed in another of Spingarn's projects in these early years, the writing of a history of the gentleman. To this "magnum opus" of his "youthful dreams," as he called it, Spingarn "sometimes gave the fanciful title of 'The Birth and Death of the Gentleman' "; it "was to be a history of social ideals, as summed up in the word 'gentleman,' from the days of chivalry to the days of American democracy, . . . but," said Spingarn sadly in 1926, "the project is recorded only in a few fragmentary and negligible studies, beginning with a review of L. E. Opdycke's translation of Castiglione's *Cortegiano* in the *Nation* in 1902 and ending with the editing of an Elizabethan version of Della Casa's *Galateo* in 1913. Of all the fifteen years of study which I devoted to this subject," he added, "nothing remains except the two hundred volumes, more or less, which still gather dust in my library. . . ."[16]

Spingarn's successful scholarly career and his ideas on the place of scholarship and the university in the national life will be described in a later chapter, but here it may be useful to glance at his unfulfilled scholarly ambition of writing a history of the ideal of the gentleman, in order to gain some notion of a problem central to all his life and thought: the problem of mediating between external rules and inner meaning in an effort to define the indefinable, to express the inexpressible. In his famous lecture in 1910 on "The New Criticism" the problem was raised, as we shall see later in our analyses of his literary theory, in an especially troublesome form; and it was to plague him in his various subsequent efforts to correct the misunderstandings growing out of that lecture. We may be able to follow these later developments more sympathetically and to understand better the rejection in that lecture of almost all critical formulas in favor of the central idea that the art work has a kind of autonomy that virtually renders null and void the treaties we make with it and the treatises we write on it, if we recognize that earlier, and in other connections, Spingarn had come to the conclusion that the most important meanings, in practice as well as in theory, in life as well as in art, always escape our efforts to formulate them, however necessary it is to keep trying.

In Spingarn's studies of the gentleman, we can sense what we have already seen manifested in his political activities: that a conservative regard for an elite is not incompatible with a genuine enthusiasm for democracy. If we think of history as a process of spiritual exploration, as Spingarn did, we may even see in his study of the gentleman an attempt at a synthesis of Renaissance *sprezzatura* and Romantic humanitarian democracy. And, if such a synthesis seems bizarre, we may remember that the fusion of opposites, the wedding of form and fact, art and life, theory and practice, is a basic theme in all Spingarn's activity, whether he is running for Congress or writing of Della Casa's *Galateo of Manners*. Insofar as manners themselves are a kind of esthetic ritual fusing subject and object, private conduct and public performance, individuality and convention, Spingarn's fragmentary remarks about manners are an important clue to his ideas on art and literature.

In the review of Opdycke's book, Spingarn began to sketch out his ideas by describing the change from the medieval knight to the Renaissance courtier. The courtier added to the "martial virtues of chivalry" "the further grace of culture," and he "fused the ideal of honor with the classical ideal of glory." Such a fusion of personal grace and individual integrity with public glory and fame resulted in the "ideal man of the Renaissance": "A man in the universal cultivation of his accomplishments, like Castiglione himself—soldier, poet, courtier, and diplomat."

It is clear that Spingarn was describing not only the courtier, but, in part at least, his own "ideal of perfect manhood." And it is clear also that the change from the courtier to the French "gallant" of the seventeenth century was not, for Spingarn, a change for the better; for it tended to elevate preciosity over manliness, self-indulgence over discipline. But "after dominating social life for two centuries, the gallant succumbed to the democratic influences of the Revolution, and in the new conception of the 'gentleman' England added to the ideal of honor, which expresses what is due to ourselves, the nobler ideal of duty, or what is due to others."

The ideal of duty was early a noble one to Spingarn. He wrote to Woodberry (September 5, 1900) at the age of twenty-five: "I can see how much of my life has been spent in subjecting desire to duty, and how duty has become more and more

the master." For Spingarn, duty did not mean simply devotion
to a cause, or loyalty to the prince, or submission to fate. Instead, duty was compounded of the liberal democratic humanitarianism of the Romanticist, the *noblesse oblige* of the aristo-
crat, and the stoicism of the soldier. The dutiful man was to
attend to "the universal cultivation of his [own] accomplishments"; but one of his chief accomplishments should be his skill
in service to others. Or stated another way, the performance of
democratic "duty" was a warrant of individual dignity. As Spingarn explained in the first New School lecture, the democratic
ideal must be "an ideal of excellence, an ideal of quality, not an
ideal of averages." The question of the critical measure of
personal "accomplishment," or of "service," is presumably
resolved in the actual ritual of performance. For Spingarn, as for
Henry James, the esthetic and the moral sense lay very close
together.

As we shall see, Spingarn's sense of duty, his sense of his
"role," was partly defined in his military service and in his service to the National Association for the Advancement of Colored
People. In both cases Spingarn's performance had some of the
characteristics of moral and esthetic ritual. Thus it was not the
result of simple patriotism or simple humanitarianism. But neither was it simply a matter of individual self-expression. For the
individual could find identity only through what Spingarn called
"the political sense," the "sense of relation to a *civitas.*"[17] And
this sense, in turn, led back again, as Spingarn explained in an
unpublished fragment of his dream of the gentleman, to the
problem of manners, which is a problem of "social ideals," "the
eternal problem of the individual's relation to his social environment." The circle is perhaps unbroken, but so, in a sense, is all
experience a constant passage from self to society and back
again. "Self-love and Social" *are* intertwined.

In his "Introduction" to a Renaissance translation of Della
Casa's *Galateo of Manners and Behaviours* (1914), Spingarn gave
a glimpse of the kind of dialectic which may help to explain
his own peculiar combination of aristocratic *hauteur,* which
relied on a code, and romantic zeal, which relied on individual
invention. In trying to explain how a sense of social duty was
rooted in a sense of personal manners, he argued that "the serious preoccupation with manners, characteristic of the Middle

Ages and the Renaissance, made it possible for modern European society to form an organic social whole, with a model of the finished gentleman, more or less the same in all countries and all periods." Here is the conservative Spingarn, the defender of tradition. But there is another side to the matter, and Spingarn did it full justice. He wrote: "Codes and rules have no more justification in the art of life than in the arts of poetry and painting. Each individual soul must express its past and its present, its inheritance and its aspiration, in its own way; and it is as futile and as vulgar to apply 'rules' in the estimate of a life as it is in the criticism of a poem or a picture. . . ." The other side is the rebellious, proud, individualistic, romantic side of Spingarn —the man who said (in this same "Introduction") "moderation is as often a vice as a virtue." Here is a hint of incipient relativism. But also, though unstressed, a principle of reconciliation is suggested in the sentences which conclude this passage. "Empirical observations," codified into rules by those of experience, have a disciplinary or educative value for the novice without experience. They are instruments of discovery, necessary but not final. The modern democratic individualist, like the creative artist or the literary critic, must finally "reach the point where the very rules that nurtured [him] no longer apply."

Spingarn thought of himself as "a moralist before anything else."[18] But his attitude toward "duty" suggests that morality was for him a kind of esthetic ritual. This is not to say that Spingarn's conception of duty was soft or self-indulgent; manliness was for him *the* cardinal virtue—and manliness was rooted in discipline. Discipline was terribly important, but it was a means to freedom, not to slavery. In a fragmentary unpublished "introduction" to his proposed work on the gentleman, Spingarn summed up the problem. He proposed to investigate codes of gentlemanly conduct, but he would refuse to be committed to a single definition; "for a definition is an epitaph which describes not the living but the dead—the lifeless within the living." He expected that he would be able to find "no single ideal . . . , but a series of ideals which are constantly at odds with each other and yet which have something in common in the hearts of men. . . . For life," he concluded, "by definition, escapes defining."

CHAPTER 2

Scholar

SPINGARN'S conception of the gentleman suggests that he thought of the practice of life as an art. His early apprenticeship in the art shows him trying out, or testing, various romantic roles of action: the run-away adventurer, the investigator of exotic vendettas, the reforming politician. But in these early amateur years he was also preparing himself for a professional role: that of the scholar. And, although he was acutely aware of a kind of contradiction between the gregariousness of the man of action and the scholar's asceticism, he was, as we have seen, always convinced that "ideals which are constantly at odds with each other . . . [may] yet . . . have . . . something in common in the hearts of men."[1] And so his ideas about scholarship, during the brief period when he practiced this art, were tinged with the polemical fervor of the reformer, even as his forays into the world of action always had something about them that was speculative.

I   *The American Scholar*

During his early years at Columbia, Spingarn wrote frequent notices and reviews (mostly for *The Nation*) of the work of such men as George Santayana, Croce, George Saintsbury, L. E. Opdyke, and Arturo Farinelli. He wrote the article on Elizabethan prose published in the *Encyclopedia Americana* in 1903. Not primarily for the specialist, these pieces show their author's ability to write accurately, informatively, and entertainingly about specialized subjects. Spingarn was also engaged in these years in perfecting his mastery of the detailed instrumental skills of the specialist in such articles as "The Sources of Jonson's 'Discoveries.' "[2] The mastery was quickly achieved, for in 1908 and 1909 he issued the three volumes of his *Critical Essays of the Seventeenth Century,* a model of the best kind of editorial scholarship. And in 1911 official recognition of his scholarly respectability was accorded with the publication of Volume VII of the *Cambridge History of English Literature,* which contained a chapter by Spingarn on "Jacobean and Caroline Criticism," the only contribution by an American. But it is interesting to note that 1911 was also the year of the first independent printing of Spingarn's call to revolt in *The New Criticism* and the year of his departure from the academy.

These events led Spingarn into new worlds which are described in other chapters of this essay. But there is a paradox in "The New Criticism" that has a certain general relevance and a particular one also to the concern of this chapter, Spingarn's scholarly career. The urgent polemical tone of "The New Criticism" is that of the zealous reformer; but the argument is largely theoretical, and there is little sense in that essay and in the critical essays which were to follow of the concrete data of American literature and criticism which presumably made reform such an urgent problem.

Part of the explanation of this deficiency may be that Spingarn was trained in historical scholarship and was suspicious, as he said in the sixth of his New School lectures, of those professors of contemporary literature who acceded to the demands of critical fashion and made quick judgments of contemporary authors and works not yet distanced by historical and scholarly perspectives. But Spingarn's reluctance to deal with contemporary data in "The New Criticism" was also, paradoxically, a function of the reformer's zeal as much as a result of the historian's professional caution. The two sides of the paradox are not necessarily contradictory: for Spingarn's determination to avoid partisan political entanglements of the moment may be seen as serving his reformer's conviction that America's greatest practical need of the moment was to develop a capacity for the speculative life of theory.

A similar paradox can be seen in the attitudes toward scholarship Spingarn developed before his entry into the critical wars, and some examination of it may be helpful in understanding his later criticism. First of all, there was his prodigious learning and his control, as Lewis Einstein put it in his unpublished reminiscence, of "all scholarly apparatus." One of Spingarn's students, Robert M. Gay, who became himself a prominent

figure in academic life, recalled in a letter to Spingarn's widow
(November 6, 1942) that "his erudition was almost appalling."
Lewis Mumford asserted flatly that Spingarn was *the* brilliant
young man of the university,"[3] and even a colleague like John
Erskine, whose "Scotch memory" prevented him from forget-
ting personal animosities, acknowledged Spingarn's preeminent
scholarly abilities.[4] Marjorie Nicolson credited him with pio-
neering a new methodology in literary scholarship.[5]

Perhaps Miss Nicolson had in mind the *Critical Essays of the
Seventeenth Century*. Certainly Spingarn's "Introduction" to
the *Essays* was a remarkable combination of literary and intellectual history and a sturdy bulwark against scholarly parochialism. But it was more than an exercise in methodology: it was
also an example of his conception of "comparative literature,"
which, as we shall see, he thought of as offering a special opportunity for "synthetic" scholarship. Gay's letter suggests that,
existing alongside the confident professionalism of the scholar,
was another impulse of a different sort. He wondered if perhaps
Spingarn was not a "poet . . . trained to be a scholar": "He impressed me as sad even then and I think his course at the University bored him. . . . He really did have a rare combination of
scholarship and creative genius that never found adequate
expression."[6]

Perhaps "synthetic" scholarship was Spingarn's way of trying
to satisfy the creative urge. And perhaps his rigorous training in
conventional scholarly discipline gave a factual solidity to his
scholarly productions that his more active youthful adventures
lacked. The balance between speculation and fact in the scholarly work that he actually did seems to confirm Einstein's judgment that he "was made of the stuff of a great scholar." But
Spingarn was highly sensitive to the academic environment in
which he was operating, and his reformer's zeal prompted him
to theorize *about* scholarship and to emphasize the need to
transcend fact and learning in a creative act superior to local
scholarly disputes.

Even when he spoke, in the "Preface" to the *Critical Essays,*
about the need for "scrupulous accuracy," he insisted also on
the importance of "higher . . . speculations." And he made clear
that his "own interests as a scholar happen to be in the syntheses of literary history, rather than in the textual or philological

studies which are its servants." He spoke apologetically, in a
letter to Croce (December 8, 1902), about the first issue of the
Journal of Comparative Literature because "the articles . . . are
too much devoted to sources." In another letter to Croce (December 2, 1904) he lamented that English scholars often
neglected Continental literature and scholarship, but he admitted
that "they are saved by their ignorance from the vice of mere
'Quellen Forschung.' " And he answered (March 3, 1917) a
request by G. B. Donlin, the editor of the "reformed" *Dial,* for a
review of the *Cambridge History* by saying: "I am afraid that
reviewing the Cambridge History of English Literature would
hardly amuse me just now. Perhaps, as a contributor to one of
its volumes myself, I could hardly say what I think of it with
decency, and a man who lives in glass houses must not throw
stones, for there is nothing deader in the whole set than that
old chapter of mine."

This judgment on the *Cambridge History* was made in 1917,
when Spingarn, six years removed from the academic grove and
dismayed by the vision of Europe in flames, was especially likely to be impatient with "Jacobean and Caroline Criticism." And
yet such a judgment is a logical outgrowth of attitudes he was
developing in his early days at Columbia. His dissertation had
been an attempt at broad synthetic scholarship and so was his
"Origins of Modern Criticism" (1904). And in 1908 he had
praised the art of Francesco De Sanctis' synthetic approach to
literary history and criticism and had sharply criticized Arturo
Farinelli's scholarship for its lack of "critical intuition." Farinelli's talent was "essentially bibliographical," he wrote; consequently, it could offer "no new and large syntheses of literary
history."[7] Such "syntheses" were Spingarn's real aim from the
beginning of his graduate study; they were one part of what he
meant by "comparative literature." As early as 1900—ten years
before the radicalism of "The New Criticism" burst on the ears
of his surprised audience at Columbia—he had defined a radical
program for scholarship in his Paris address to the Congress of
Comparative History. And he had pinpointed in that address a
major motive of the later one: it was his sense of the special
needs and possibilities of American culture.

In "A Note on French Scholarship" in the 1931 edition of
Creative Criticism, Spingarn told how he had become impatient

during the congress with the massed erudition of "a succession
of learned monographs" and how he had cast aside the paper he
had prepared in favor of a more or less extemporaneous plea for
a more imaginative approach, "with special reference to the immediate needs of the United States." In the published version of
the speech, Spingarn described the history of American scholarship from the days of Ticknor to his own time as a process of
Germanization which gradually crushed the Emersonian ideal of
scholarship as a creative activity. The result was that "our scholars have become mere machines, tabulating facts, counting
syllables; and great scholars, like Child and Ticknor, belong to
the past only."[8]

Behind Spingarn's attack lay his special sense of the peculiar
needs of pragmatic, parochial America—needs which he also
hoped might be America's special opportunity. Unable to com-
pete with the European scholar "in the minute knowledge of his
own literature," American scholars could lead the way "in the
broad treatment of great literatures and of great and international movements"—lead the way, that is, in the study of "comparative literature." Thus would literary study be served and
thus would American horizons be broadened. Although Spingarn cautioned against sentimental Romanticism in literary
study, he concluded his Paris address by asserting that in
Emerson's "American Scholar" "the men of today may well
find both a stimulus and an antidote"—for the "Emersonian
ideal" could make scholarship a genuinely "creative activity."

II   Comparative Literature

The program for American scholarship described so emotionally in Spingarn's Paris address was to be carried out in the practice of the Department of Comparative Literature at Columbia.
As one means of implementing the program, the department
sponsored a *Journal of Comparative Literature,* which published
four issues in 1903. Woodberry wrote an introductory "Editorial" in the first issue in which he tried out his own rhetoric by
describing the new journal as a scholarly manifestation of the
world-wide drift to unity, the end of which was "one intellectual state . . . above the sphere of politics and with no more institutional machinery than tribunals of jurists and congresses of

gentlemen." Literary scholars, peculiarly suited to citizenship in such a state, must supplement their studies of national literatures with international comparisons, for "literary history has become in each nation a chapter of the history of thought, of the development of the human spirit, in all nations." The student of comparative literature, said Woodberry, must accept the accumulations of facts gathered from whatever sources. But he must always ask a question: "What shall be done with this mass of detail, to what does it lead, for what will it serve?" Woodberry answered as follows: "Though in this intellectual age the principle of relativity reigns supreme, the search for the absolute is still the burden of man's fate; the philosophic, poetic, creative mind cannot do other than follow on the old quest, however placidly the empiric, historical, receptive mind reposes in the relative. . . ." Thus, "the study of [literary] themes should reveal temperamentally, as form does structurally, the nature of the soul. . . . To disclose the necessary forms, the vital moods of the beautiful soul, is the far goal of our effort," for there only can we discover "those spiritual unities in which human destiny is accomplished."

Although this editorial, so Woodberryan in its language, may have been a little more mystical—or a little more sentimental—than Spingarn would have liked, it was not essentially different from his own view. Like Woodberry, Spingarn thought of scholars as cultural ambassadors whose work "cannot fail to cement" bonds of "affectionate sympathy" between nations.[9] And, like Woodberry, Spingarn insisted that literary scholars must take a broader and perhaps more "poetic" view of their field than most of his colleagues could encompass. He had, of course, demonstrated in his own work his understanding that literature was a part of intellectual or "spiritual" history. And he repeated this idea frequently in his definitions of the study of "comparative" literature. In a letter (December 8, 1902) in answer to Croce's objection that the adjective was "pleonastic," Spingarn hinted that the "intellectual" and the "poetic" were also, in some sense, moral: "Matthew Arnold, following Goethe and so many other predecessors, says that the 'criticism which alone can much help us for the future is a criticism which regards Europe as being, for intellectual and spiritual purposes, one great confederation, bound to a joint action and working to a common result.' . . . Therefore, to indicate clearly our point of view, we may justly employ the more explicit designation of 'comparative literature,' which (however it may be interpreted) always implies what Quinet calls 'l'unité des lettres et la fraternité des peuples modernes.' "

In the article on comparative literature that Spingarn contributed in 1913 to the *Cyclopedia of Education,* he repeated the quotation from Arnold and predicted that "ultimately the very existence of . . . separate departments [of literature] is likely to be threatened." For, though some scholars "may limit themselves to some special phase of this wide subject, the best of them acknowledge the larger and truer allegiance, when they use the term 'comparative literature' as a banner and a battlecry." As the sweep of the rhetoric grows, hints of "the far goal" of the program begin to appear: the discovery of "a connecting link of spiritual or artistic unity in all the literatures of the world." Historically, the first explorers in the field were, said Spingarn, the German Romantics of "the days of Herder; . . . [and] with Goethe's idea of a *Weltliteratur* comparative literature was really born." Spingarn's citation of these historical antecedents of his program confirms his earlier hints that the student of comparative literature must add to his broadened methodology something like "Emerson's ideals of scholarship."

Spingarn's interest in the "larger syntheses of literary history" arose from his conviction that only by "interpretation" does history, or life, become real. Only through interpretation, through a structuring act of the mind, is the mind defended against the flux of raw facts, which in their ultimate purity must always remain unknowable.

But Spingarn was not content to state the problem as a general problem of epistemology; he pressed beyond, and his argument grew more elusive as it approached its climax. His idea of literature as a single organic manifestation of the spirit and his attack on "philological" scholarship were perhaps anticipations of T. S. Eliot's famous speculations on "Tradition and the Individual Talent" (which Spingarn included in his own anthology of American criticism) and Allen Tate's remarks on "Miss Emily and the Bibliographer." But the fervency of Spingarn's rhetoric seemed to carry him into the transcendental realm: the study of literature must go beyond "linguistic or philological detail" to

"interpret" the "facts" of literary history as "spiritual" signs of
what Woodberry called the "search for the absolute." Like
Woodberry, Spingarn offered little real help in describing how
the transmutation of the "empiric" record is to be managed.
And, in his citation of Arnoldian slogans, he never quite admitted such criteria of value as moral truth at the same time that he
suggested their relevance. The end of all literary study would
seem to be spiritual insight; but, unless the adjective receives
more adequate definition than Spingarn was willing or able to
give it, this end remains for Spingarn's readers—as for Emerson's
—close to the relativism it is supposed to deny. Like all Romantics, Spingarn could not see literature as statement; he had to
see it as vision.

The conclusion that, early and late, Spingarn was trying to
glimpse a half-seen scholarly ideal that hovered beyond and
above methodology is confirmed by his "Scholarship and Criticism in the United States" (1922). And in that essay one of the
motives behind the urgency of his rhetoric seems clear: he was
responding with the fervor of the moralist to the condition of
American culture as he saw it. As much as Emerson in the nineteenth century or Irving Babbitt or Van Wyck Brooks in the
twentieth, Spingarn was deeply involved in the American tradition of examining the American psyche, prescribing for its ills,
and defining its mission. What American scholars needed above
all to learn, in 1922, he said, was the "discipline and illumination
that come from the intellectual mastery of a definite problem in
the spiritual (as opposed to the practical) life of man."[10]

III   *Creative Scholarship and New History*

"Scholarship and Criticism" also settled any doubts about
Spingarn's connection with the Columbia group that fathered
the "new history." The radical "revisionism" of some of the new
historians in matter and method (as in Charles Beard's economic
reinterpretations of early American history); their interest in
the history of ideas (as in James Harvey Robinson's work in
European intellectual history); the issue of academic freedom
which colored the departure of Beard and Robinson, as well as
Spingarn, from Columbia; the influence Croce had on all of
them; and perhaps even the invitation to Spingarn in 1931 to

lecture at the New School for Social Research (which Beard and Robinson helped to found)—these are the clues which might be said to suggest a kinship between the "new history" and the "new criticism."

But, except for Croce's influence, the connections seem merely fortuitous; and, in any event, the new historians were hardly a "school," except in their willingness to explore a variety of approaches. Croce's influence was largely to persuade them to develop an "objective relativism" in which "Knowledge can be 'objective' only *for* some determinate context."[11] Spingarn, on the other hand, found in Croce a thoroughgoing idealism that Beard, for example, interested as he was in aspects of economic determinism, was unlikely to accept; and Spingarn's idea of the primacy of spirit in all life was certainly more radical than anything Robinson allowed for in the "history of ideas."

Chester MacArthur Destler has pointed out that Crocean idealism was often merged in the minds of the new historians with Marxian or Freudian materialism.[12] But for Spingarn materialism was the archenemy, and Croce's "great mission," to borrow the words of his translator, Douglas Ainslie, was "nothing less than the leading back of thought to belief in spirit, deserted by so many for crude empiricism and positivism."[13] Spingarn had written despairingly (December 23, 1907) to Croce: "The name of Pragmatism is on the lips of all men here, even in shop and street. W. James is making his fellow pragmatists in Europe famous here, and it grieves me to see the names of such as Papini familiar to American thinkers who know little of your work." Fifteen years later, in his "new manifesto" to the "younger generation," Spingarn diagnosed the "disease" which had infected *"les jeunes"* as "part of a long period of suffering through which the world has been going for a century or more, and of which the world-war is a mere incident, though it may serve the unseeing as a climax and a symbol. The name of this world epidemic is Materialism."[14]

In "Scholarship and Criticism" (1922) Spingarn listed "the materialism of a national life directed solely toward practical ends" as the first cause of mediocrity in American scholarship. And he explained that the historians had been corrupted along with all the rest: "our historians seem to have a special aptitude for compiling summaries of historical periods, and some of these have an ordered reasonableness and impersonal efficiency not unlike that of the financial accounting system of our large trusts or the budgets of our large universities. To me most of them seem feats of historical engineering rather than of historical scholarship. . . ." When Spingarn reprinted "Scholarship and Criticism" in 1931 as "The American Scholar," he expanded his attack on the " 'new history,' " especially deriding "its childish subservience to the empirical sciences and the shallow and extrinsic character of its thought." Both "old" and "new" historians, he said, "are still immersed in the search for external causes, and fail to realize that the idea of causality in history belongs to the past and not to the future."

For Spingarn, the "truly philosophic conception of . . . history" he called for in "Scholarship and Criticism" would, as he explained in "The American Scholar," emphasize that the "facts" of history are generated through the development of the human spirit and that the "determining factors" of the real history which underlies the "facts" are "the great generating forces, religious and ethical, which move men to transform circumstances into a new life." The primacy of the human spirit did not imply subjectivism; for the spirit is literally the maker of life, and it cannot be self-deceiving. As we shall see in a later chapter, Spingarn sometimes had difficulty explaining this point, but he always insisted that no "causes" or conditions could be conceived as external to spiritual reality. Thus did the "new criticism" answer the "new history."

Spingarn's rhetoric made it difficult for practicing historians to join the battle, and they seem to have ignored the charges he made against them. Spingarn was, after all, not debating historical or scholarly method in any very concrete way. His central concern was really a very general concern for the quality of American life. And central to that concern was his anxiety for traditional cultural values in a young society enamored of novelty and change: the university, he said in "Scholarship and Criticism,"

is at one and the same time our greatest practical achievement and our greatest spiritual failure. . . . When we find that in such a place education does not educate, we cry for help to the only gods we know, the restless gods of Administration and Organisation; but scholarship cannot be organized or administered into existence, even by Americans.

. . . The scholar goes through all the proper motions,—collects facts, organises research, delivers lectures, writes articles and sometimes books,— but under this outer seeming there is no inner reality. Under all the great works of culture there broods the quivering soul of tradition, a burden sometimes disturbing and heavy to bear, but more often helping the soul to soar on wings not of its own making. We think hungrily that the freshness of outlook of a young people should be more than compensation; but the freshness is not there. . . . All is shell, mask, and a deep inner emptiness.

The role of scholarship, as Spingarn conceived it, was to be the chief support of the traditional modes of spiritual perception "against all the materialists under whatever name," against "scientists . . . , sociologists . . . , or practical men who have no use for the 'higher life,' " against "all who would reduce life to a problem of practical activity and physical satisfaction, all who would reduce intellect and imagination to mere instruments of practical usefulness."

William Albert Nitze attempted to answer Spingarn's "Scholarship and Criticism" at the Modern Language Association meeting in 1923: "America has no monopoly on the unscholarly scholar—he flourishes in other climes as well as ours," he said. Scholarship "is a meticulous undertaking. It cannot be conjured into being merely by good-will or what is called inspiration or brilliance. . . . Eloquence . . . is not the same thing as scholarship." Nitze then went on to agree, however, that "there is sober fact in Professor Spingarn's statement that the American University of today is 'timid and anaemic because it lacks that quixotic fire which inheres in every act of faith.' " The difficulty, said Nitze, *was* cultural: "We are forced to toil along without the zest that springs from companionship and a ready, personal exchange of ideas."[15] Stuart Sherman, four years later, was to state the problem more bluntly: "in America, for one reason and another, it is hard to find any man who is even civilly interested in abstract ideas."[16] Sherman's statement of the problem, or even Van Wyck Brooks' formula about the gap between "high-brow" and "low-brow,"[17] was much like Spingarn's complaint; and Nitze's statement that "the scholar needs the refreshment of direct action" represents a discovery Spingarn made at least as early as 1908, the year he ran for the United States Congress.

As far as Spingarn was concerned, the central issue behind these debates was a general "spiritual starvation" in the United

States. The disease was manifest: "you may see the signs of its restlessness gnawing on the faces of far too many American women beyond the first flush of youth; you may see some shadow of its hopeless craving on the faces of far too many American men." The fervency of Spingarn's plea for reform was undoubtedly increased by his patriotism; it was not scholarship or art that he cared for, nor even some generalized spirit of mankind, but the spirit of America:

We are all cocksure but bewildered children in a world we cannot understand. We are all newcomers—newcomers on a new continent, on the fringes of which some have lived longer than others, but the whole of which has been encompassed by none of us for more than two or three generations; newcomers in a world of steam and electricity, wireless and aeroplane, machinery and industry, which none of us has yet been able to subdue to a mould that satisfies our deepest cravings; newcomers in our culture, which still seems like a borrowed garment instead of flesh of our flesh and bone of our bone. What is the good of all the instruments that our hands have moulded if we have neither the will nor the imagination to wield them for the uses of the soul? Not in this fashion shall we justify our old dream of an America that is the hope of the world. . . . Here are more hearts empty and unfulfilled and more restless minds than the world has ever before gathered together; why not lead them out of their corrals, and find a fitting pasture for their brains and souls?[18]

IV *Controversy and Withdrawal*

Spingarn himself referred to his "lament" on "The American Scholar" as a "lyrical *cri du coeur.*" It echoes in discord against the optimism of Emerson's earlier definition of "The American Scholar," and the discord is all the more marked for being based on Emerson's scale of values. But it is well to recall that Spingarn's piece originally appeared in Howard Stearns' "famous inquest over American culture, sardonically entitled *Civilization in the United States"* (to borrow Alfred Kazin's description).[19] This "Inquiry by Thirty Americans," published in 1922, was certainly a calculated piece of shock tactics, at the other extreme from Nitze's professorial periods in his address to the Modern Language Association. The "most moving and pathetic fact in the social life of America today," wrote Stearns in the "Preface," "is emotional and aesthetic starvation." The mournful conclusion Stearns had arrived at in another article of the year before was that such "Puritans" as Stuart Sherman were forcing the "younger generation [to] make our plans for leaving the country of our birth and early affections. We do not want to cut ourselves off from our national life, but we are inexorably being forced to do it—many of us shall probably starve when we go to some alien country, but at least we shall be able, spiritually, to breathe."[20] Sherman's answer to Stearns' "fatuous and hackneyed Menckenisms and Dreiserisms" was as follows: "When Mr. Stearns runs on in this lugubrious vein, . . . I no longer feel that he is an Intellectual; I feel only that he is very young, which, after all, is not quite the same thing."[21]

This kind of wrangling points up Spingarn's dilemma. Insofar as he allowed himself to be drawn into the polemical squabbles of the cultural journalists, debating ill-defined problems of American intellectual life, he was ignored by working professional scholars. Or, if the scholars did listen, Spingarn's refusal to discuss individual authors or contemporary literary works, lest such discussion corrupt the purity of his theory, guaranteed the kind of academic rarification that characterized Nitze's article in the *Publications of the Modern Language Association.* The academic side of the dilemma can be sensed in the controversy that followed the publication in the *Romanic Review* in 1926 of Spingarn's quite specific criticisms of Maurice Magendie's *La politesse mondaine et les théories de l'honnêteté en France au xviie siècle, de 1600 à 1660.*

Spingarn began his review by disassociating himself from the kind of argument carried on by Stearns and Sherman. Although he could not entirely eliminate the edge from his voice, he strove to explain that his complaint about Magendie's failure in scholarly "imagination" must not be taken as part of an "indiscriminate war on erudition in general, such as is fashionable today among journalists but is out of place on the lips of a scholar." Though he criticized Magendie for having "poured out all his note-books on the printed page," he tried to explain the fault as a defect of method: Magendie's approach had been parochial rather than "comparative"; he had not read widely *enough,* especially in the relevant non-French sources; and thus he had not the perspective necessary to make an imaginative synthesis of his welter of notes and to do scholarly justice to his chosen subject.

Spingarn's criticisms seem today unexceptionable, but in

1926 he was known as a Crocean theoretician; and Daniel Mornet immediately answered that he had confused the history of literature, which must build carefully from smaller national units to larger ones, with the philosophy of literature, which may be satisfied with "une étude simplement 'parallèle'" aimed at proving "simultanéités."[22] Bernard Faÿ's defense of Spingarn also saw the issue in a large "philosophic" frame: "Des études littéraires dignes de ce nom devraient chercher avant tout le 'Beauté'..., et non se vouer à la poursuite du scientifiquement vrai, de l'authentique ou du réussi socialement." Faÿ insisted that Mornet's effort to recapture the truth about the past was a futile effort doomed to failure, for what is called "fact" is itself an arbitrary abstraction from the complex reality of life. The aim of literary studies should be instead the appreciation, even the creation, of Beauty.[23]

Quite predictably, Mornet, in his next article, reiterated his original argument and rejected esthetic evaluation as any part of the proper job of the cultural historian.[24] At this point, Paul Van Tieghem joined the fray and sought to end the dispute between "nationalists" and "internationalists" with the argument that national studies are legitimate if they take into account relevant international influences! But, like the other disputants, he felt that larger issues were in question. Therefore, he asserted that certain "manifestations parallèles, et indépendants," certain "simultanéités" may be even more interesting than sequences of causes and effects because they are "plus spontanées."[25] Finally, Philippe Van Tieghem, seizing on his brother's distinction, argued that esthetic judgment is the ultimate aim of literary history; truth, the ultimate aim of social history. But truth, he concluded, may be more than "fact," and esthetic judgment may yield new *truths*: "on arrive à ce paradoxe que des objets qui doivent former par le beau, on tire des leçons de vérité et d'instruction."[26]

When Spingarn reprinted the review which had started the furor in *Creative Criticism* in 1931, he himself said: "Much of the controversy seems to me wide of the mark, for my review does not touch the question of literary history or criticism as such. It is concerned solely with a phase of the history of culture, and with obvious defects of scholarship in dealing with that phase; the history of imaginative literature presents a quite different problem from the history of social ideas." But Spingarn never carefully distinguished between social and literary history; he seemed to make *all* scholarship part of a creative activity. As we shall see, he thought of the history of imaginative literature as an art; and in the discussion of art, ideas like those of Faÿ and the Van Tieghems *were* relevant. Such discussions were theoretical, and Spingarn often lamented his countrymen's inability to understand the life of theory. His efforts to educate them sometimes led him to adopt their tactics of argument; but the alternative to such a debate as that carried on in the *Romanic Review* was hardly educative. His dilemma was to make theory relevant to practice, and the effort had to be made in a country where the two seemed mutually exclusive.

Spingarn did not attack the scholars again after 1926. Apparently he was becoming more and more sensitive to the fruitlessness of arguing his case in America by adopting what he thought of as the American tactics of noise. His growing despair over the alienation of the creative *or* the scholarly mind from its cultural environment probably accounts for his withdrawal from public controversy. His friend, Geroid Tanqueray Robinson, who was in Moscow in 1926 working on his doctoral dissertation, wrote Spingarn (August 8, 1926) that "it is a hopeless business trying to put order and aim into life" because "the raw truth . . . is simply chaos." Spingarn replied in a letter of August 21: "Other men, actors, journalists, literary critics, novelists, popular writers of all sorts, bask in the blaze of publicity, which I suppose is the only heaven that Americans long for now. To be a scholar—ah, there's the rub—the years of silence, the struggles with facts and problems, the long wait, and the audience fit, but few."

This statement from a man who had challenged the whole international fraternity of scholars in his first year on the faculty at Columbia, from one whose critical polemics had opened with an attack on the professors in "The New Criticism," presents a contrast too sharp to be overlooked. In his letter to Robinson, Spingarn made it explicit:

I have had my fling at scholars and professors at the time when the fling seemed to be needed, but now I almost think that what America needs most of all is the men who have the courage and the brains to tackle this so un-American phase of life. I have cried out for the creative artist and now I am beginning to feel as if "creative art" were a curse—a hunger that is seizing those who can never satisfy it, and who were meant for other tasks not a bit humbler, but different. For the thinker can be as creative as the poet and the quiet scholar as creative as either of them. But he must respect his task as much as they respect theirs before he can achieve that power which their respect gives *them*.

The secret lay, after all, not in the external environment, but, as Emerson had said, in the integrity of the individual soul. Spingarn concluded: "to read old Burton's chapter on the 'scholar's melancholy' is to realize that *his* troubles were not born on American soil. . . . maturity means holding fast . . . , and if you have the courage now to hold fast to the scholar's fate, and make it your own fate regardless of the noise of the world, you will be, I know 'in te ipso totus, teres atque rotundus'—a great scholar and a happy man."

The tone of this private communication to a friend is different, of course, from the tone of Spingarn's public utterances; and the difference perhaps points up the difficulties in which Spingarn's public rhetoric had involved him. The experience of those difficulties probably accounts, in turn, for the change of mood and the self-accusations in the letter to Robinson. The problem of bringing together what is due to one's self and what is owed to one's social environment was, as we have seen, a central problem in Spingarn's theoretical consideration of manners, even as it had been a practical problem in his political activities. Perhaps the fusion of practice and theory which Emerson had called for was not quite possible. Perhaps an alternation between the two, a constant passage between two moments of the spirit, was all that could be hoped for. But whether fusion or alternation, the spirit had to be in each moment integral if it was to rise superior to the mere noise of experience, which was neither practice nor theory. Spingarn felt that spiritual integration was the central problem: for Robinson, for himself, and for twentieth-century America.

CHAPTER 3

Soldier of Reform

CERTAINLY Spingarn's early actions had not been marked by the virtues he urged on Robinson: patience, silence, and concentration. Rather had he been, in the years at Columbia and for ten years or so after he left, restless, vocal, and versatile. But early and late the virtue of courage and a jealous pride in individual integrity had ruled his thought and action. In his letter to Robinson he defined the particular kind of courage which he valued both in the battles of his youth and in the silence of his maturity: the courage to stand alone and to support loneliness.

In 1911 Spingarn needed all his pride and all his courage. For on March 6 of that year—just as he had entered on a new phase of his career with the publication of his lecture on "The New Criticism"—Spingarn was peremptorily fired from Columbia. The action was not, of course, without antecedents, both immediate and remote. The story begins, perhaps, with Nicholas Murray Butler's accession to the presidency of Columbia University in 1902.

I *"The Restless Gods of Administration"*

Nicholas the Miraculous, as he came to be called, set to work immediately to transform a school of a few hundred students into a university of twenty-five thousand. There were many things to be done: a football stadium to be built, new classrooms to be constructed, money to be raised, new curricula to be planned. Butler did these things.[1] He did them with his own great energy and with the aid of what Spingarn called the "restless gods of Administration and Organization."[2] To Spingarn, these gods of efficiency were horrible manifestations of the pragmatic "materialism" gripping American society, all the more horrible for their presence within the very citadel of the spirit.

It is not surprising that Butler should have crossed swords with individual members of the Columbia faculty ill-suited to corporate efficiency—with Edward MacDowell, for example, head of the music department and admittedly a "difficult" person. MacDowell left Columbia in 1904, and in the same year George Edward Woodberry resigned. Woodberry had had earlier experience with the power of university administrations. He had been dismissed from the English faculty of the University of Nebraska in 1882 because of his refusal to modify his "radical" ideas so as to conform to the "acceptable" codes of the "orthodox."[3] The whole episode had been spectacular enough. Apparently Woodberry was determined that his departure from Columbia would be different. On January 14, 1904, in advance of the official announcement, he wrote Spingarn of his impending resignation (in more than one sense of the term), and he wrote also of his fears concerning Spingarn's position. Conceding that his own position had become "impossible," but insisting that "There is no difficulty between me and the President, no difference even trivial," he urged his protégé to "make such arrangements at the University as may seem wise": "I advise you—and advise you strongly—not to comment on the affair . . . ; do not undertake to defend me," for that would be to risk drawing "on yourself the many enmities at Columbia that seek me as their object. . . . Your line . . . is to be one of silent and regretful acquiescence."[4] Twenty-two years before Spingarn recommended silence and patience to Geroid Tanqueray Robinson, Woodberry had urged upon Spingarn the same course.

The next chapter began with the firing of Harry Thurston Peck in 1910. Peck was a man of encyclopedic learning, a Classical philologist of wide reputation, the founder (in 1895) and editor (until 1902) of *The Bookman,* and the author of *Twenty Years of the Republic* (1906), a history of the United States from Cleveland to McKinley. He had taught Latin, Semitic languages, and literature at Columbia for twenty-eight years. But in 1910 he had the misfortune to be sued for breach of promise; and the plaintiff, who subsequently failed to bring the suit to trial, published his letters, an action which Peck considered blackmail. Whether Peck was guilty of breach of promise or his accuser of blackmail was not settled. But Peck was fired.[5]

Spingarn made no public comment on the justice or injustice
of Peck's dismissal at the time. He offered instead a one-sentence
resolution at a stated meeting of the Faculty of Philosophy held
December 9, 1910: *"Resolved,* that the Faculty of Philosophy
place on record its sense of the academic services of Harry
Thurston Peck, who was connected with the University for
twenty-two years, and was a member of this Faculty from the
date of its organization."[6] In a letter to Butler, Spingarn
defended his advocacy of "this slight act of generous pity" and
insisted that the resolution referred "only to the academic services of Professor Peck" and could, under no circumstances, be
construed as reflecting "on any action taken by others."

According to Spingarn's account in *A Question of Academic
Freedom,* he was permitted to make no explanations at the faculty meeting because his resolution was placed on the table. And
his efforts to have it removed from the table were, he says, met
by a warning from Butler that "If you don't drop this matter,
you will get into trouble." His own "exact answer" was: "I am
not in the habit of altering my conduct because of the prospect
of trouble, Mr. President." Ten days after this exchange Spingarn heard from Butler that the Committee of the Trustees on
Education had decided to recommend his dismissal. In the next
few weeks various statements were made concerning the reasons
for the recommendation (administrative convenience, financial
problems, etc.) and the likelihood of its being carried out. But
Butler wrote Spingarn on March 7, 1911, that the trustees themselves had voted the preceding day to relieve him "from further
academic service from and after March 6, 1911."

II *Departmental Politics*

It is difficult to believe that the Peck resolution was more
than a small part of the reason behind Spingarn's dismissal.
There is little doubt that personal friction had for some time
played a large role in Columbia politics. Woodberry said as
much in his letter to Spingarn about his own resignation. Upton
Sinclair recalled how, in Brander Matthews' class, Matthews used
to "sneer at Woodberry's 'idealism,' and at his methods of teaching."[7] Probably Spingarn's intense loyalty to Woodberry was

largely responsible for his personal antipathy toward Matthews, an antipathy which another colleague, John Erskine, could not forgive.[8] And Ashley Thorndike, the head of the English Department, was apparently not gifted as a peacemaker.

Spingarn himself was a proud man—"a man impetuous and intense," said Lewis Mumford, "slim, erect, austere with dark brown eyes that would ignite under the first spark of thought," "proud as Dante," and "capable of advancing resolutely in the face of the enemy, without faltering because no one followed."[9] He was not well liked by many of his colleagues, and he was apparently a forbidding figure to some of his students. Mrs. Spingarn's remark that her husband, "in maturity, had no close friends except possibly his brother, Arthur,"[10] confirms the suspicion that personally as well as professionally he was aloof and perhaps contentious. These traits seem external signs of Spingarn's belief that any final determination of duty was ultimately a matter of spiritual conviction not commensurable with the rationalizations that might be its proper preparation. We shall see in Part II of this book an incipient nominalism in Spingarn's "theory of the universe"; but in his actions, too, there is some justification for the assertion by W. E. B. Du Bois, later a co-worker of Spingarn's in the National Association for the Advancement of Colored People, that he was a "natural anarchist of the spirit."[11]

Spingarn's loyalty to Woodberry apparently prevented him from making "arrangements at the University." In 1910 the Department of Comparative Literature was amalgamated with the English Department over Spingarn's protests.[12] Relations between Spingarn and some of his colleagues apparently worsened, and Butler was drawn into the dispute by Thorndike in November, 1910. Spingarn answered Butler's summary of Thorndike's complaints about his uncooperativeness by denying that he had "ever refused to any of my colleagues . . . the benefit of such counsel and scholarship as it is in my power to offer them." But he added:

I confess that my heart sickens at the very thought of administrative tasks for which I have neither capacity nor inclination, and I do not propose to have the leisure for productive scholarship interfered with by any additional burdens of this kind; . . . certainly every manly and high-minded scholar . . . would sympathize with my refusal to perform such tasks whenever they conflict with my knowledge of my capacity or my devotion to my own scholarly ideals.[13]

Various meetings were arranged, and various assurances and reassurances were exchanged; and on January 9, 1911, a modus vivendi was apparently worked out between Thorndike and Spingarn. But the Peck incident had happened by then, and on January 16 Butler wrote his letter reporting the action of the Trustees' Committee on Education, which recommended Spingarn's dismissal. Butler made no mention of the Peck affair. The reasons advanced for the committee's action included Thorndike's complaints about Spingarn's lack of cooperation; Spingarn's "comments thereon"; the "subsequent conversations" between Butler, Thorndike, and Spingarn; and budgetary considerations that made it "inexpedient . . . to maintain a second Professorship of Comparative Literature." According to Spingarn, Butler assured him orally that the recommendation was only "an administrative move," that he would urge the Committee to reconsider, and that Spingarn would not be fired.

On January 30, however, Spingarn registered a written protest with Butler, asserting that satisfactory arrangements had been made between him and the English Department at a meeting on January 9, and disputing the legal right of the university to terminate his contract, which was drawn for three years from July 1, 1909. But, most important of all, Spingarn insisted that larger moral considerations were involved: considerations of honor and honesty, of service and loyalty, and of academic freedom. "After five or ten years of apprenticeship as assistant, tutor, and instructor, the professor has a right to feel that the University is under specific obligations to him which cannot be evaded by the mere plea of financial stringency, unless we are to assume that all obligations of service are on the professor and none whatever on the University." Spingarn suggested that the Peck incident had also played a part in determining the committee's action, and he concluded: "I reassert my loyalty to my alma mater; but if security of tenure in the professorship, if fidelity to contract or a sense of obligation to the academic profession, if freedom of speech and conduct do not exist at Columbia, it is right that the academic world should know it."

Butler replied immediately, denying the relevance of the Peck affair and charging that Spingarn's account of the events of the preceding months had been "inaccurate" and "misleading." Although he felt that Spingarn's letter had made "a most unfavorable impression, both in tone and in content," he announced that the committee had not made a final decision. Spingarn responded by asserting that "every statement of fact in my letter of January 30 was made with careful and deliberate accuracy." He then repeated the substance of his earlier letter. After Butler's brief acknowledgment of this repeated protest, there was silence for nearly a month. Then on March 6, 1911, the trustees fired Spingarn as of that date.

III   *The Larger Issues*

Spingarn and his brother Arthur, who was a lawyer, began to prepare a suit against the university for breach of contract; but they dropped their action when the university sent a check for the unexpired term of the contract. The legal letter of the law, though important, was not, to Spingarn, the whole of the issue. Practical matters were reflections of the spirit, and institutional arrangements were important as they encouraged or inhibited the development of the spirit. Public conduct should be the objectification of private virtue.

In the "Introduction" to *A Question of Academic Freedom* Spingarn sketched the administrative organization of Columbia, which, "unlike the old universities of Europe, is governed by a self-perpetuating Board of Trustees, consisting of financiers, lawyers, divines, and other men, not one of whom is a scholar by profession or familiar with the more intimate atmosphere of academic life." The board, said Spingarn, had very broad powers over finances, appointments, and educational policy; but no faculty member had access to the board except through the president of the university. Nor was that the worst. In practice everything relating "to the educational policy of the university and the status of the teaching staff"—that is, "all that concerns the university as an institution of learning"—was referred to the Committee of the Trustees on Education, whose recommendations were often "accepted without independent investigation and often even without discussion by the board as a whole"; thus, this committee, whose meetings "are seldom attended by more than three or four" of its seven members, had become "in a sense the ultimate power" at Columbia: "the destinies of Columbia," said Spingarn, "are settled at . . . secret conclaves between the President and three or four of his friends."

Characteristically, Spingarn found the greatest evils in what the "materialism" of such a system did to the spiritual capacities of those subject to it:

the President is surrounded by sycophants, since sycophancy is a condition of official favor; . . . intellectual freedom and personal courage dwindle, explaining, if not justifying, the jibe of European scholars that there are three sexes in America, men, women and professors; . . . permission to give utterance to mild theories of parlor socialism is mistaken by American Universities for superb freedom of action. . . . so far from being above the commercialism of its industrial environment, [the University] actually employs methods that would be spurned in the humblest of business undertakings. . . . The University should be the cradle and the home, not only of Reason, but of honor. . . . [But President Butler] has made mechanical efficiency and administrative routine the goal of the University's endeavor. The nobler ends of academic life will never be served so long as this spokesman of materialism remains in power.

Spingarn's rhetoric sounds extreme, but there is some evidence to suggest that the situation at Columbia was extreme. Bayard Boyesen, a disaffected English instructor, wrote Upton Sinclair of the "utter cowardice" engendered at Columbia by the ruthless methods of the administration, though in his own case the threat of legal action seems to have caused the charges preferred against him to be written off as a "misunderstanding."[14] In 1917 Leon Fraser incurred official displeasure by criticizing the Plattsburgh Officer's Training Program. In the same year Professor J. McKeen Cattel, who had held the chair of psychology since 1891, and who had feuded with Butler over hiring a professor in his division who had given money to the university, was fired because of a letter on university stationery sent to the Congress in support of a measure prohibiting the sending of conscripts to fight in Europe against their will. When Cattel brought suit for libel and threatened to sue for his pension, the trustees settled by paying $45,000. Also in 1917 Henry Wadsworth Dana was dismissed from the English Department, apparently for making antiwar speeches before the People's Forum; and a week later Charles Beard resigned as a result of administrative interference in teaching and in matters of faculty appointments. In 1919 James Harvey Robinson followed Beard.[15] Cattel and Beard echoed Spingarn's complaints and his metaphors in charging that Columbia was run by Butler and a few reactionary trustees as if it were a department store or a factory in which administrative convenience and managerial efficiency stifled all freedom of thought and creative effort and denied to professors any voice concerning the terms of their employment or any hearing before their peers.[16]

Spingarn, who had led the way, became, thus, a member of a distinguished company. He boasted of belonging to a club for "Professors Who Were Fired or Resigned Under Pressure from Columbia University," and he celebrated regularly the anniversaries of "the proud day I was fired out of Columbia."[17] He might also have boasted of being the first to make public protest against conditions at Columbia. According to Lewis Mumford, his "sturdy campaign" for reform from within the academic community itself "eventually paved the way for the notable revision of the whole system . . . now being worked out in the City Colleges of New York."[18]

The decade preceding Spingarn's dismissal from Columbia in 1911 was the decade of the muckrakers: Lincoln Steffens' *The Shame of the Cities* and Ida Tarbell's *History of the Standard Oil Company* were both published in 1904; Upton Sinclair's *The Jungle* appeared in 1906; and *McClure's, Collier's, Cosmopolitan,* and other magazines and newspapers during these years carried a continuous series of exposés on corruption in various aspects of the national life until the surfeit of such pieces caused a falling-off about 1908. Spingarn was fully aware that the academic world was as vulnerable as other parts of the establishment to this kind of attack, and he was even willing to admit the importance of documentary journalism in publicizing the need for academic reform. But there was also a personal dimension in his response to the Columbia experience. He tried to give public utterance to these private feelings in verse. In "Héloïse (A Modern Scholar to a Medieval Nun)," he wrote:

> O passionate Héloïse,
> I too have lived under the ban,
> With seven hundred professors,
> And not a single man.[19]

In these lines, as in much of Spingarn's verse, we sense his recurring dilemma: his uncertain search for a form adequate to bridge the gap between his passionate personal commitment to his "ideals" and the sordid world of "facts," between inner feeling and public expression. In his verse, the result of the dilemma is often embarrassingly personal and embarrassingly flat.

IV   *The Personal Problem*

Spingarn himself sensed the need for assimilating his personal passion to a larger frame; and in a letter of May 7, 1911, he wrote defensively to Woodberry about the problem:

Your letters came in the thick of the fight [with Butler], and though they counselled peace they served me for armor . . . as I went forth to renewed combat. . . . to speak truth I needed not so much solace as a restraining hand. For I have felt like a crusader fighting wrongs, and those wrongs not my own but the world's (at least the academic world's), and not the slightest bit of personal rancor or chagrin has entered into the matter at all. . . .

Yet even while writing in this vein, Spingarn could not suppress his weariness with the effort to find a public formula for his private feelings. Anticipating the mood of his letter to Geroid Robinson, he admitted to Woodberry that the blare of publicity provoked in him a contrary response. Opposed to his sense of duty was a longing for the silence of a more private life: "if I were to follow my own inclination," he wrote, "I should retire to Troutbeck (the home of my dreams) and forget the sordid Columbia world." He had, in fact, just returned to the city from his country house when he wrote this letter; and he concluded: "I spent most of last week at Troutbeck, where the narcissi I planted last fall are making the green grass golden everywhere, and all these academic squabbles seemed foolish and trifling things at best."

Spingarn's ability to indulge opposite moods may have been some reassurance to Woodberry. For Woodberry knew that "the first square experience of injustice, especially from the hands of a group of men so high in public power and position as the Trustees of Columbia, is one to give a moral shock, whose lingering effects may last for years in one's thought of the world." He knew that "Such a blow tends to corrode even the healthiest

mind, and to embitter the sunniest disposition." He was, therefore, "very glad to see that you are already a man, with a wider
outlook on the whole of our social life, and other activities orig-
inating in your own personality, with a life of which the University is only a province that has been wrested from you."[20]

But, while in the act of congratulating Spingarn on his maturity of spirit, and while hopefully predicting for him new suc-
cesses, Woodberry could not banish his fear that Spingarn might
become disillusioned and bitter. Woodberry's description of the
way to silence is worth quoting at length, for it seems at once
persuasive and prophetic. He began by describing

the brutal reality of power, the mechanical move of it, its lack of conscience, its essential servility, its freedom from moral as well as legal re-
straint, in one word—tyranny, which in one form or another seems to be
the master of the world. It is as native to the good as to the bad, to the respectable as to the vicious, and in the good and respectable it seems to me
to reach its maximum of evil. . . . I daresay your thought would not com-
panion mine to the ultimate of my guesses. But something of the hollowness of our state—the moral hollowness, I mean, of the system of control
that wealth has developed in the community—you must realize; and more
easily perhaps the moral hollowness of what goes under the name of character in the respectable circles. It is as well to put aside from the start any
expectation of justice as of happiness; if either comes, it is good fortune;
but neither is rationally to be sought as an end in itself by any one who
looks to make a career in society. And with justice, all our childhood theories of merit and reward, of any causal effect between virtue and prosper-
ity, go by the board. Every act of hope is to me the leading a forlorn hope
—we look for nothing in return, nothing to be gained—we act, and die,
and leave it there.[21]

For Woodberry, the only escape from futility lay in an individual integrity which enabled men to commit themselves to acts of
hope, even while recognizing that they might be "forlorn." Hope
could, perhaps, be made into faith. But faith was a fragile thing;
and, lest it die of inanition, the individual must provide it with
new experience to feed upon. For this reason Woodberry
rejoiced that Spingarn was out of Columbia and free to "enter
the larger career."

But there was also a regretful nostalgia in Woodberry's voice;
and it tended to make his brave protestations of hope suspect.
He had misgivings about Spingarn's casting off from his academic haven. His misgivings centered around the question of individ-

uality, around the necessity for a unified individual program—without which all action was soon the "leading of a forlorn hope." There was paradox, too, in Woodberry's fear: he had preached the nobleness of individual freedom; now he was worried that too much freedom might dissipate energy. He feared that Spingarn would react against the things he could do best:

> your personality must be integral, concentrating, repeating, intensifying, and not discursive, scattered—not a thing of "short swallow-flights" and little attempts. And at the same time, and tho' it seems contradictory, I urge you to do what you can find always, to do what you *want* to, especially, and to lead your own life ever, even if it led you to a hermitage. And I do hope (for I am getting prolix) that you will take your present fate easily, and not brood over it, or let it obsess you in any egoistic form. Forget it—and Columbia, and go on to other things, things of the great world that know nothing of Columbia, as if Columbia were but the obscure hamlet where you were born. Oh, the power of oblivion in hope is a great power, and this is a good time for you to exercise it, possess it, and use it. Forget, and when your sleep is over, you shall have morning air and a new world.
>
> Your affectionate old maestro—it's a score of years!   G.E.W.[22]

Spingarn's reaction to his dismissal from Columbia was, like most of his reactions, not simple. It was compounded partly of the things Woodberry hoped for and partly of the things he feared, partly of the things Spingarn "longed" for and partly of the things he compelled himself to do. Hopes and fears, longings and compulsions; disillusion, desire, and duty—to fuse these diverse elements into a coherent whole, to weld them into a platform that would support action, was Spingarn's problem. The competing claims of these personal feelings, intensified by the competing claims of the larger, noisier world he now entered, may help to account for the uneasy balance in Spingarn's critical essays between journalistic polemics and theoretical argument, though certainly the complexity of his feelings predated his dismissal from Columbia.

The year of Spingarn's firing was also, as we have noted, the year of the publication of *The New Criticism,* which he had originally delivered as a lecture in 1910. This essay has been invariably described ever since as a plea for pure art, independent of "life"; and it is certainly easy to quote from it to support that view. But Spingarn's emphasis on "spirit" in that essay, when seen as a part of his own private and public concerns, is an emphasis dictated in large measure by his understanding of, and response to, actual contemporary American life. Irving Babbitt, with *Literature and the American College* in 1908, and Van Wyck Brooks, with *The Wine of the Puritans* in the same year, had already in their different ways mounted an attack on the complacency of such critics as Hamilton Wright Mabie and Thomas Bailey Aldrich, who wrote of literature as if it were a collection of Victorian parlor platitudes with no relation to the realities of twentieth-century American life.

As Spingarn's campaign for academic reform was part of a larger reform movement which included the muckrakers, so the view of art put forward in *The New Criticism* was part of the early beginnings in the first decade of the twentieth century of a critical movement which sought to establish *connections* between American life and literature, to wrench literature and the life of the mind into some meaningful relationship with the national experience, whether through the neo-Humanism of Babbit or the Socialism of Brooks, or Spingarn's own war against mindless materialism. Spingarn shared the passionate concern of these socio-literary reformers—for that is surely what they were —that art, pure or impure, old-fashioned or new-fangled, traditional or experimental, be seen as an important and integral part of the life of America, past, present, and future. The problem was not an abstract problem for Spingarn but, as Woodberry suggested, a private one, too. The problem had always been for Spingarn, and was to remain, as Woodberry wrote him, and as Spingarn himself wrote to Robinson, a problem of integration.

CHAPTER *4*

Veteran

SPINGARN'S longing for Troutbeck was not a momentary feeling brought on by the Columbia crisis. He had rented and then purchased this homestead and two hundred acres of land in Amenia, New York, several years earlier; and, soon after taking title, he had added another one hundred and sixty-seven acres. From his earliest acquaintance with the place, he had shown a keen interest in its history: in Myron B. Benton, its former owner and an amateur poet; in Benton's friend, John Burroughs; and in the other literary and historic associations that hovered over Troutbeck.[1] He had spent much of his free time there and had also expended time and money in making physical improvements in the house, gardens, and grounds. It is not surprising, therefore, that, banished from Columbia, Spingarn should want to retreat to Troutbeck. And certainly his feeling was something that his mentor, Woodberry, could understand. The intensely personal, yet patriotic, localism of Woodberry's attachment to his own family home in Beverly, Massachusetts, seems the perfect model for Spingarn's devotion to a "single spot of American earth" at Troutbeck.[2]

I *"Tory Squire"*

W. E. B. Du Bois, who first went to Troutbeck for the Amenia Conference on Negro affairs, described the country surrounding it as "a long southerly extension of my own Berkshire Hills. There was the same, slow, rocky uplift of land, the nestle of lake and the steady murmur of brooks and brown rivers. Afar off were blue and mysterious mountains, and there was a road that rose and dipped and wound and wandered and went on and on past farm and town to the great hard world beyond." The village of Amenia was "small, important, complete." And

[58]

Troutbeck itself, with its "great trees bending over the running brook," gave Du Bois "a sense of utter friendship and intimate memory, though in truth I had never seen it before. . . . one could trudge from the more formal home and lawn, by lane and fence and rise and fall of land, until one came to the lake. The lake, dark and still, lay in the palm of a great calm hand. The shores rose slowly on either side and had a certain sense of loneliness and calm beauty."[3]

But Spingarn's retreat to Troutbeck was not simply an escape; it was the first maneuver in a new campaign. If the academic province had been wrested from him, there were, as Woodberry said, always new worlds to conquer. Spingarn's old interest in the *civitas* was not dead, nor were his interests in politics and social betterment. In 1912, and again in 1916, he was a delegate to the Progressive party's national convention in Chicago. But, like Woodberry, Spingarn also had an intense interest in local affairs. In 1911 he bought the *Amenia Times*, which had been established in 1852 under the editorship and general management of Joel Benton, a Troutbeck poet, essayist, and uncle to Myron Benton. According to Spingarn's notes, his purchase of this paper was "part of a general programme of community improvement." He changed the name to the *Harlem Valley Times* and raised its circulation to a high of about eleven hundred weekly—chiefly among the residents of Amenia and Dover, New York, and Sharon, Connecticut.

Charles E. Benton, anticipating perhaps the playful epithet of "Tory squire" that Stuart Sherman applied to Spingarn,[4] wrote, in his historical sketch of Troutbeck, that Spingarn "had no thought of playing the role of retired gentleman, but . . . entered wholeheartedly into the life" of the community around him.[5] Oswald Garrison Villard agreed that at Troutbeck Spingarn "lived the life of a country gentleman in the best sense, a leader in the community, always actuated by public spirit, ever eager to serve others."[6] He brought "new ideals into this country life," said Benton, citing as proof the Amenia Field Day, an experiment in "co-operative recreation" (contests, pageants, picnics, prizes), "managed by the whole community and free for all." Spingarn's sponsorship of the event from 1910 to 1915 suggests his peculiar desire to combine *noblesse oblige* with folk democracy.

II *The Amenia Conference and the NAACP*

Troutbeck was also the scene of another, larger social project —the Amenia Conference. Spingarn had become interested in the National Association for the Advancement of Colored People. It is probable that Woodberry's passionate and compassionate interest in the plight of the American Negro and the American Indian[7] helped prepare Spingarn for assuming the role of active champion. Du Bois says that Spingarn "joined . . . eagerly, ready for a new fight, a new thrill and new allegiances."[8] He worked hard but unsuccessfully to get the Progressive party to include a plank in its 1912 platform condemning racial discrimination;[9] in 1913, he was made chairman of the directors of the NAACP; in 1914, he founded the Spingarn Medal,[10] still awarded annually to a Negro in recognition of outstanding accomplishment; and, in 1916, sensing that racial relations in the United States were entering a new phase (Booker T. Washington had died in 1915), and realizing especially that, in spite of differences, workers in the field "were already . . . standing together to an extent unparalleled since Reconstruction," Spingarn "proposed to call in August a conference of persons interested in the race problem at his beautiful home Troutbeck, in the peace and quiet of Amenia, where once John Burroughs dreamed and wrote. Here colored and white men of all shades of opinion might sit down, and rest and talk, and find agreement so far as possible with regard to the Negro problem."[11] Du Bois emphasized that the Amenia Conference "was to be 'under the auspices of the NAACP,' but wholly independent of it"; and the invitations, issued by Spingarn personally, made clear that "the guests . . . would not be bound by any program of the NAACP. . . ."[12]

The success of the conference was mainly symbolic. But its success was also real, a proof of Spingarn's lifelong conviction that the world of symbols is integral with the world of action in the total life of the "spirit." Even Du Bois, who clashed with Spingarn over the internal politics of the NAACP,[13] and who was later to urge a kind of separatism sharply opposed to Spingarn's hopes for spiritual integration of the races, paid tribute to Spingarn's feeling for *zeitgeist*: "The old order was going and a new race situation was to be developed." Of this change, "the Amenia Conference was a symbol. .... It was a 'Close ranks' before the great struggle that issued in the new world." Though no concrete programs were adopted, a new unity of purpose emerged, which, according to Du Bois, made the Amenia Conference a "landmark" in the history of the emancipation of the American Negro.[14]

Spingarn's dedication to the work of the NAACP was, of course, a protest against injustice, and he worked hard in the cause, indefatigably traveling from place to place to organize new local chapters, tirelessly arbitrating disputes in the national organization, helping to plan policy, and even contributing emergency financial aid.[15] But, most of all, his dedication was an act of hope—perhaps a "forlorn hope," to recall Woodberry's phrase—hope for a sympathetic spiritual integration of diverse racial experiences as a prerequisite for the solution of social and economic problems. Race, he said in his article on Woodberry in the *Dictionary of American Biography,* was "not so much an ethnic entity as a spiritual quality of mind made up of imaginative memories and experiences." Accordingly, he did not seek the absorption of the Negro spirit into middle-class American society. He rejected the uniformitarian idea of the melting-pot theory and argued for a cultural pluralism based on mutual respect. Such a course would enable the Negro to think of himself as truly American and thus forestall the dangerous alienation of his spirit which, Spingarn feared, would result from any direct confrontation on exclusively economic or political grounds.[16]

Given such an emphasis in the practical world of social reform, it is perhaps not so surprising that, in the development of the critical polemic on art that Spingarn had begun with his lecture on "The New Criticism," he avoided discussion of particular authors, all the more so because in these years before World War I the literature of social protest seemed—in the work of Theodore Dreiser, Winston Churchill, Ernest Poole, and Upton Sinclair—to blur the line between art and propaganda. He complained of the difficulties of discussing protest literature in "The Negro in Art" *(The Crisis,* April, 1926); and, as we shall see in Chapter 6, he had always been anxious to disentangle the criticism of art from an exclusive concern with "the conditions of actual and contemporary life."[17] His emphasis on the need for the leaven of the informing and organizing spirit of the art-

ist's vision was in part a response to what he found missing in
American life and literature, and he did not wish to be dis-
tracted from this need by side issues.

III   *War and the Rhetoric of Patriotism*

The critical essays Spingarn wrote during the prewar years
were, of course, not his only tie to earlier intellectual interests.
As we have seen, he continued to contribute articles to the
scholarly journals and to write verse. He even made brief
appearances in the classroom.[18] But his activity in behalf of the
Progressive party and particularly his work with the National
Association for the Advancement of Colored People suggest
that he was searching in these years to solve the problem of a
career in the world of action rather than in the study. The
search culminated in his response to the outbreak of World War
I. Confronted with what seemed to him a challenge to civilization itself, he began to devour books on military tactics; and in
August, 1915, he reported to a semiofficial training camp at
Plattsburgh, New York, where he immediately immersed himself, as he put it in a series of unpublished autobiographical
notes, in a "new experience." Though a revulsion from the vio-
lent world of action might come after the war, Spingarn threw
himself for the moment into the new experience with a passion
which he recognized as both "my danger and my delight."
Characteristically, however, Spingarn's passion was different
from that of his fellow trainees, with whom he felt "strangely at
odds": "Their complete acceptance of the conventional propaganda of the newspapers, the unanimity with which they wanted
to go to war immediately, chilled me. . . . I knew that my country drew me to its heart with so intense a passion that the conventional rhetorical patriotism made me ill." This judgment of
his feelings, recorded in notes some years later, seems confirmed
by a letter he wrote G. B. Donlin (March 3, 1917) just before
the entry of the United States into the war. He was, he said,
"overwhelmed . . . by the national crisis" and could "think of
little but . . . military duty"; but his state was "not that of a fire-
eater the least in the world, but of a man shaken out of his easy
illusions by the tragic fate of humanity." Spingarn had been too
well schooled in Woodberry's conception of patriotism to feel

any contradiction between loyalty to country and service to humanity. One was the means of defining the other.[19]

Perhaps Spingarn was a victim of what he himself (in his un-published notes for an introduction to "The Birth and Death of a Gentleman") had called a kind of "martial mysticism"—a com-mon ingredient in "all human conduct that has not been thor-oughly rationalized." Certainly, his own actions seem hardly rational. Despite a physical collapse as a result of the rigorous regime at Plattsburgh and a long, slow convalescence, he insisted in May, 1916, on attending another camp, this one at Fort Ogelthorpe, Georgia. Then he went to Fort Terry, New York; and in the winter of 1916-17 he drilled at Governor's Island and at various New York City armories. He seemed determined to test his own physical endurance, perhaps as a way of testing also his "ideals," of discovering that life which escapes definition, and of keeping his "faith" from crumbling under the cold scrutiny of the defining intellect.

While preparing himself for direct participation in the war he knew was coming, Spingarn also carried on a continuing fight for a training camp for Negro officers.[20] Late in April, 1917, just after the United States' entry into the war, he extracted a promise from the Secretary of War that such a camp would be opened. Then, at forty-five years of age and in ill-health, he de-termined to enlist. Miraculously, he passed the physical require-ments and was assigned to Madison Barracks, New York. He reported for duty May 4, 1917; and on August 15 he was com-missioned as a major in the infantry—one of only two of his group to receive that rank.

After assignment to Camp Dix, New Jersey, where he helped organize the Seventy-eighth Division as a commander of the Third Battalion of the Three hundred and eleventh Infantry, he suffered another physical collapse; this time an emergency oper-ation was required to save his life. After two months' sick leave, he returned to his battalion, collapsed again, was granted addi-tional sick leave, and then was ordered to report to Camp Dix Base Hospital. Finally, he was transferred to the Military Intel-ligence Department in Washington, D. C., with the recommen-dation that he never be used for field duty and never be permitted to go overseas. He was made director of propaganda in the civilian section of the Intelligence Department.

One of Spingarn's responsibilities in his new job was to combat "Negro Subversion." He determined to attack the problem by winning the Negro's loyalty for the army rather than by disciplining him to subservience. He wanted to begin by commissioning Negro officers in military intelligence, even though he was well aware of the opposition such a plan was bound to encounter. He sought first of all, says Du Bois, to enlist the active support of Negro students at Negro universities and then of Negroes in general through a campaign of publicity "aided wholeheartedly by the *Crisis,"* official organ of the National Association for the Advancement of Colored People, of which Du Bois was editor. Spingarn wanted the Negro population to join the national military effort, and he wanted the nation to treat the Negro as a full-fledged citizen. He pressed his views on the Secretary of War, Newton D. Baker, and "urged that President Wilson break his long silence and say a clear word against lynching. Especially," says Du Bois, "did he want me associated with him in his unit of the Intelligence Department, to be used for my first-hand knowledge of the American Negro and my ability to express their needs and plan a consistent program."

There were difficulties, Du Bois says, with the NAACP over how much editorial control Du Bois should retain on the *Crisis,* and a fear that his voice would be muted by his official participation in the war machine. But, of course, the greatest resistance came from the non-Negro groups who were "aghast" at the prospect that W. E. B. Du Bois, a Negro "radical," was being proposed as head of a special bureau within the War Department. And so this part of Spingarn's plan failed, though Du Bois has stated flatly that "Had it not been for Joel Spingarn . . . no Negro officers would have been trained or appointed," and further that through Spingarn's "advice and influence" he himself "became, during the World War, nearer to feeling myself a real and full American than ever before or since."[21]

Spingarn had been aware from the beginning of the possibility of failure in his battle for the Negro, but the vigor of his advocacy was apparently increased by this awareness: if he became *persona non grata*, he might even be sent to the front, which was what he hoped for. He was indeed ordered to Europe, and he did get to the front. Although he minimized his experience in France in his autobiographical notes as "of little consequence," it is apparent that he was proud of his service in the Saizerais, Marbanche, and St. Mihiel sectors, and of his part in the Battle of the Moselle on November 10-11, 1918. "I smelt gun-powder," he wrote. "I had a taste of both defensive and offensive warfare. I talked with German soldiers on the other side of No Man's Land within an hour or two after the Armistice. I was the first American officer in several German towns. It was not a very rich military experience, but it was a larger one than that which won Roosevelt the Presidency of the United States."

Spingarn's military experience was intense and exhausting to body and soul. In his autobiographical notes he described his exhaustion, and he specifically recalled his bitterness at "a literary critic who had stayed quietly at home during the war," and who had had the temerity to "impugn my patriotism and my Americanism at the very height of one of my physical crises, because in some of my earlier essays I had ventured to utter theories of art and beauty which he did not approve. . . . [This] was the bitterest pill, not because it was just or unjust, but because the feelings it aroused in me proved to me that the nadir of my strength had been reached."

The critic was undoubtedly Stuart Sherman, who had attacked Spingarn's "alien-minded" critical theories in an article in *The Bookman* for October, 1920,[22] and who had twice repeated the charge: in "The National Genius," in the *Atlantic Monthly* for January, 1921, and in "Literature and the Government of Men" (published along with a revised version of the *Atlantic* article in Sherman's book on *The Genius of America* in 1923). Spingarn protested in early 1921 in a personal letter to Sherman containing a description of his record and a "summary" by a "friend," and he wrote a public protest to the *Nation,* August 8, 1923. When Sherman's "The National Genius" was reprinted in 1923 in *The Genius of America,* Sherman added that "Mr. Spingarn . . . , as a man, is concerned with truth, morals, and democracy, and has a personal record of civil and military service." But Sherman stood by his original language when referring to Spingarn's critical theories: the theories were still foreign to "Anglo-Saxonia," they were still the elaborations of a "quick Semitic intelligence" working in "a super-subtle Italian fashion," they still "separated beauty from her traditional associates in American letters," and they were still rejected by "the American schoolboy" as "false to the history of beauty in this country."

Perhaps Spingarn, exhausted as he was, was hypersensitive to Sherman's tasteless attack. But the complexity of the feelings recorded in his autobiographical fragments suggests an inner orientation which was not the result of a single insult:

Perhaps I should be grateful [for gratuitous advice, and] in the hope of a new wisdom, should forget the stay-at-home hero's impertinence in lecturing the soldier on patriotism. But I had no need of this assistance: from earliest youth I had recognized the meaning of love of country, not as a theory (for the fashionable abstractions of nationalism left me cold) but as a concrete reality that could be met only in the equally concrete realm of duty. I left to others their own way of singing the noble hymn of patriotism and the ignoble hymn of hate. . . . I felt that each man must find his own place of duty, and that rightly or wrongly, *my* hymn of patriotism must be service in camps, on drill grounds, and on battle-fields. For this, despite the reaction against war which is in all our hearts, I have no regrets, begrudging only the intervening hand of fate that made me render less service than I had dreamt it within my power to render.

Spingarn may, as he said, have preserved this fragment because the feelings expressed in it are evidence that the "nadir" of his strength had been reached. But it reveals more than bitterness and the polemical bent of his rhetoric: it indicates also how such feelings as pride, anger, and despair could mingle in Spingarn's personality; it shows his "mysticism" and his sensitivity to criticism; it exhibits his concern for duty, honor, and patriotism. But most of all, the passage evinces clearly Spingarn's contempt for free abstractions: he was convinced that no opinion was reliable unless it was rooted in concrete experience; and no experience was meaningful for him unless it was, somehow, a function of theory. As he wrote to Mumford: "There is this to be said for the military life, that it makes you realize as nothing else does how much your country means to you, and to love anything with your whole soul is an experience worth while."[23]

There is no doubt that World War I was, for Spingarn, an experience of the utmost spiritual importance. One side of his nature recoiled from its exhausting confusion, and he wrote Croce (April 6, 1918) of his longing to "embrace the muses" again and of his determination "to return to books and the intellectual life" (November 30, 1918). But return he could not; the scholarly temper of the prewar years belonged to a ghostly past, a simplified life that was now very far away.[24] Aware of the new complications the war had brought into the national life, Spingarn seems not, however, to have become, as O. G. Villard suggested, "completely disillusioned by the war to end war, by the results of his own sacrifice."[25] He never made such easy identifications between the course of events at large and his own role. To the end, he remained proud of his soldierly response to duty; his sacrifices had been spiritual acts of faith and thus they remained untouched by "results" in Villard's sense.

In 1919, Spingarn joined in a new publishing venture with Alfred Harcourt and Donald Brace, both of whom had just left Henry Holt and Company. The new firm, Harcourt, Brace and Company, was to be responsive to modern, postwar trends, both American and European. Spingarn was to contribute, besides some cash, his scholarly skills and his "wide continental connections."[26] He was made general editor of the European Library which, according to the company's fall announcements of 1920, was "to keep Americans in touch with the intellectual and spiritual ferment . . . of Europe," especially with those aspects of European thought that represented "a new outlook" and challenged "American standards of taste or morals."

During the four years of its life (1920-24), the European Library fulfilled these purposes by bringing out works by Pierre Hamp, Jacob Wasserman, Heinrich Mann, Walter Rathenau, Ramón del Valle Inclán, Giovanni Gentile, Rémy de Gourmont, Babette Deutsch and Abrahm Yarmolinsky, Benedetto Croce, C. F. Ramuz, and Giovanni Papini. Harcourt, Brace also published work by some of these authors outside the European Library; and Spingarn was surely important in persuading the new company to publish Francesco de Sanctis' *History of Italian Literature*, Vilfredo Pareto's *The Mind and Society*, Karl Vossler's *Mediaeval Culture*, several of Herman Keyserling's books, Harold Stearns' *Civilization in the United States*, and, of course, Spingarn's own *Criticism in America*. As he recorded in his notes, Spingarn also "recommended" Knut Hamsun's *Growth of the Soil*, Hendrik Van Loon's *Story of Mankind*, John Dos Passos' *Three Soldiers*, Ludwig Lewisohn's *Upstream*, and "brought to the attention of H. B. & Co." the work of Sigrid Undset.

Spingarn himself was in these postwar years intellectually adventurous, and his editorial work at Harcourt, Brace seemed to promise the opportunity to combine his intellectual interests with his sense of public responsibility and with his patriotic concern for the cultural life of the nation. The forum would be larger than academia, the issues broader than those of literary criticism, and yet the whole enterprise would in no way interfere with Spingarn's continuing his special interests in the realm of esthetics, or in the history of the gentleman, or in the politics of the National Association for the Advancement of Colored People. But in 1924 Spingarn, overtaken by the same illness which had so plagued him in the army, was forced to go on inactive status at Harcourt, Brace. He never returned to full duty.

IV   *Withdrawal and Prophecy*

In a sense, 1924 marks a change from active to inactive duty in Spingarn's career as a whole; but the change perhaps began before that date and was not completed until some years later. It was in 1924 that he brought out his anthology of *Criticism in America,* a kind of summing-up of the critical renaissance in America. He himself had virtually stopped writing on criticism in 1922, and the two important essays he produced in that year —"Scholarship and Criticism" and "The Younger Generation"— had brought him to a position of pessimism and conservatism. When he did break his silence briefly in 1931 in the New School Lectures, he began by confessing that he was "appalled by the prospect of lecturing again on Criticism" and added that he "should much rather talk about philosophy and politics and religion." For criticism certainly could not, Spingarn thought, help the poet directly; and the possibility that it might help indirectly by educating his audience seemed in 1931 less and less likely. The problems confronting the human spirit in America were very large cultural problems, and they were no more amenable to literary solutions than to economic panaceas. Spingarn himself turned in his later years to the study of comparative religion.

The studies of his later years were perhaps, as Spingarn said in a letter to Croce on September 20, 1921, a reaction against "the years wasted in politics, war, and the world of action"; but his "return . . . to the intellectual life" was made "with a sigh of relief": it was not a return to the academy so much as a retreat to privacy. For Spingarn published no results of his postwar studies except the review of Magendie's *La Politesse Mondaine* (1926) and a bibliographical note for Karl Vossler's *Mediaeval Culture* (1929).

In 1924 Spingarn's poetic activity also seems to have come to a close with the publication of a slim volume of his *Poems,* and two years later he wrote in his letter to Geroid Robinson that he felt "as if 'creative art' were a curse—a hunger that is seizing those who can never satisfy it." Certainly Spingarn's own verse is not satisfying as poetry, though it provides a touching summary of many of the causes to which he gave the energy of his life. In one of his earliest public poetic performances, the Columbia Phi Beta Kappa poem of 1901 entitled "The New Hesperides," Spingarn announced his idealistic faith in the imaginative and spiritual mission of America; and in the even earlier "The Alkahest" he saw a kind of cultural pluralism as one of the great possibilities favoring a new imaginative life in America.[27] But in 1924 a "Footnote" to the *Poems* tells us that "The New Hesperides" was reprinted "chiefly as a reminder of those far-off forgotten days when young poets still dreamt of the quest of the perfect land," and in a late poem, "Caverns," Spingarn's sharp awareness of the restlessness and loneliness bred by the American environment answered his earlier optimism, though even here it is still clear that man's spirit is the maker of life—of misery as well as of joy. In another late poem, "Art (A Nightmare)," Spingarn entertained the possibility that art is a curse and Beauty a deceiving sorceress and tyrant: "We shall not enter Eden till she die."

The idea of suffering replaced in these postwar poems the adventurous voyage as the means to the promised land. Spingarn's boldest statement of the virtual deification of man through individual suffering is in "Resurrection," one of six poems in *Poetry and Religion,* privately printed in 1924 as the first of the *Troutbeck Leaflets.* But as his own sense of the inevitability of suffering—his own and the world's—increased, Spingarn's poetic muse, like his scholarly one, seems to have fallen silent.

We may imagine that Spingarn's silence was a function of inner convictions that grew more intense rather than less; and thus the difficulty of responsible expression became greater and the danger of betraying the convictions by the inadequacy of a public language more pressing. The intensity of his patriotism during World War I was, as we have seen, matched by his revulsion at the slogans and abstractions available for its description. More and more, it seems, Spingarn was sensitive to the grossness of abstraction; and, like the poet or critic of his esthetic theory, he seemed entangled more and more in the problem of trying to express the inexpressible.

About 1930 Spingarn made a few tentative gestures toward public expression. He issued (privately) his *Enchiridion* in 1929. In 1929 he was invited to the summer conference at the Bread Loaf School of English, and in the following year he actually made his "first speech to a college audience since the World War"[28] when he addressed a class in literary criticism at the University of Arizona, where his son, Stephen, was enrolled. In 1931 he reissued *Creative Criticism,* revised and enlarged; but there was really nothing new in the new edition: of the four substantial essays added to material from the edition of 1917, the latest dated from the spring of 1923, and the latest note in the Appendix was from January, 1925. Also in 1931, Spingarn delivered his lectures on *Literature and the New Era* at the New School; and, according to a letter to William Aspenwall Bradley a year later (March 11, 1932), he hoped to make a book of them. But he never did. Instead, his silence deepened.

Spingarn seems almost to have felt that all public language had been corrupted—but also that more and more men had come to rely on manifestos. "You liberals think," he said to Lewis Mumford as early as 1928, "that your liberal and pacifist world, with its peace treaties and disarmament conferences and material improvements will last forever. I read history differently. You pacifists are preparing the way for bloodier wars. I predict that you will live to see the restoration of caste, and even slavery."[29] Spingarn "did not believe that voting or revolution in industry was going to bring the millennium,"[30] for he regarded the political and economic programs of his day as only efforts to tinker with man's environment and finally as admissions that man was simply a function of his environment, an economic or political statistic or a mouthpiece for institutional interests.

In a time that emphasized collectivisim and worshiped operational efficiency, Spingarn remained the unregenerate "anarchist of the spirit"; he insisted that "moral and religious forces are the only generative forces in history" and that a truly religious force begins in an idea, not in a program. In "the great religious crisis of the nineteenth century," Spingarn said, "Men had lost God"; in the twentieth century they were seeking Him again, but in the wrong places: they were seeking Him in various theories or programs which pretended to be based on "external material facts," and not on ideas. And so there were created "idols," not ideals; and we have "reached an age of insoluble problems, . . . problems for which the solution in the mind of each person is a determinate thing which admits of no other solution. And so you have one solution absolutely fighting a life and death struggle against another solution."[31] Ideas were confused with facts, and the dialectical gave way to the doctrinaire. Spirit had succumbed to matter.

Spingarn's concern over the policy of the National Association for the Advancement of Colored People in the 1930's illustrates the problem. He apparently tried, for example, to curb W. E. B. Du Bois' power and influence in the Association because, as Du Bois put it, he "was afraid that I was turning radical and dogmatic and even communistic."[32] It was the dogmatism Spingarn feared, and his fear of Marxism was the same fear. To imagine that any program was sanctioned simply by the facts rather than by our judgment of their relevance, and to imagine that our judgment was simply a matter of fact, rather than an imaginative synthesis, was to be a dogmatist; the Marxian emphasis on economic materialism encouraged just such doctrinaire argument. "Whatever your economic program is," said Spingarn in his first lecture at the New School in 1931, "the question always arises: who shall carry out . . . that program?" Hence, "all our problems are rather political than economic and even in Russia, not an economic, but a great political experiment is being carried on, of which the economic is merely one of the many materials."

Politics rather than economics, spirit rather than fact, imagination rather than dogmatism—these were the distinctions on which Spingarn based his opposition to Du Bois. Addressing the National Association for the Advancement of Colored People on "Racial Equality" in 1932, Spingarn said:

I know that there are purblind doctrinaires who believe that economic emancipation solves all the problems of humanity. . . . The economic problem is today . . . immediate and pressing; faced by the agony of millions of men, only the heartless fool can deny that the economic problem is vital; but how easily solved compared with the questions I am raising. . . . The plea for [complete] racial equality for the Negro . . . [means] equal and unrestricted admission to the duties and discipline of American life.

It means "an American 'religion' of the spirit that will destroy the sense of . . . race difference." "There are today all sorts of new movements to cure our national ills, movements called the new this and the new that; but what we need most of all," said Spingarn, "is the New Humility." If we do not find our new religion of equality, he warned, all our plans and programs cannot stop the alienation of the colored races from an American loyalty, nor counteract "the centrifugal forces that are endangering our country."[33]

However accurate Spingarn's warnings may have been, the time was not likely to be responsive to religious exhortation and moral preachment. To many of the Marxist persuasion who attended the second Amenia Conference, held at Troutbeck in 1933, the irrelevance of their host's message was an amusing anachronism; and they troubled little to disguise their feelings. The conference accomplished very little, and we may surmise that Spingarn's pessimism increased.[34] His "philosophy had small effect upon my generation," wrote Lewis Mumford; and so his sense of frustration increased, and his "contempt" for those who would not listen hastened what Mumford termed his "spiritual withdrawal."[35]

Thus Spingarn did not "come back" as Mumford had thought he might in 1931, and "his abstention from literary effort, during the last dozen years of his life, created at least among those who knew him, a stir of uneasiness."[36] But that was all. Spingarn occupied himself in his study with books on comparative religion and in his garden with raising clematis. This second occupation accounted for most of his "publications" in these last years; numerous articles in various horticultural journals, "Clematis in America" in Ernest Markham's *Clematis* (1935), and "Clematis" in Norman Taylor's *Garden Dictionary* (1936). Mumford thought it ironic that at the end "this soldier and thinker was known throughout the world as the chief authority on—clematis!" But Robert M. Gay thought "his love of that family of beautiful plants [was] only one more characteristic touch."[37] Perhaps both were right.

In the fall of 1938 Spingarn accepted an invitation to teach at Atlanta University; but, before he could go, he fell ill. It was his last illness. He died July 26, 1939, just two months before the outbreak of World War II.

Spingarn had early derived from family tradition a conviction that the strong-spirited individual could dominate external circumstances, and his youthful literary tastes encouraged him to think of the literary imagination as a spiritual act of domination or control anterior to, and superior to, intellectual analysis. His mentor Woodberry, who "had actually . . . talked with Emerson," had represented for Spingarn a continuation of "New England idealism" which helped prepare him for Croce's esthetic. Spingarn had carried his idealism into the practice of life, into the world of action, with the Romantic zeal of Emerson's American scholar brought up to date and bent on "illuminating," as Spingarn said of Woodberry, "the meeting-point of art and life."[38] There imaginative vision defined moral obligation, and the performance of duty was in turn held to an esthetic standard.

It must have been hard for Woodberry, believing that the spirit of man was the maker of life, to confront the world of Nicholas Murray Butler. And certainly it was hard for Spingarn, believing that "moral and religious forces are the only generative forces in history,"[39] to confront the brutal post-depression world of the 1930's in which the ideal of an inner, spiritual grace—moral and esthetic—seemed irretrievably lost in the shrill competition of irreconcilable abstractions aspiring to the status of final solutions. Woodberry's attenuated idealism of the early years of the century had led him by 1920 to a decade of quiet that seems wistful and nostalgic. But Spingarn's vigorous polemics of the pre- and post-World War I years brought him in the decade of the 1930's to a deepening silence that seems, even now, increasingly prophetic.

CHAPTER *5*

A Conception of the Universe

SPINGARN'S youthful escapades and the importance he later attached to these adventures—both physical and intellectual—are indications perhaps of romantic exuberance. Though his view of the world may have darkened in his later years, his pessimism seems only the obverse side of his earlier enthusiasm; for the prophet of doom is himself a common enough Romantic figure. The reconciliation of opposites is not, of course, unexpected in a student of Croce, as Croce was surely the leading neo-Hegelian of the time. Nor is it surprising to find that a disciple of Woodberry should discover synthesis in "the heart of man."

But the list of actual paradoxes Spingarn synthesized in the living of his life is impressive. The militant patriotism that carried him into the army did not prevent him from thinking of the Great War as both an international crusade and a personal duty. His strident attacks on parochialism in scholarship did not contradict the fervent localism of his attachment to "a single spot of American earth" at Troutbeck. The humanitarian zeal which fired his work for the National Association for the Advancement of Colored People and the democratic zest with which he entered the political arena were not inconsistent with his aristocratic conception of manners and his final lonely retirement into semiobscurity. The proud "radicalism" of Spingarn's challenge to President Butler and the trustees of Columbia University was not betrayed by his humble advice to Geroid Robinson.

I ˙ *The Unity of the Spiritual Life*

These advances and retreats were the responses of his romantic "heart" to the shifting tactical situations with which he was confronted. And the romantic heart knows neither contradictions nor inconsistencies; it knows only the unity of its own "ideality," and it defends itself against the attacks of "mechanism" and "materialism" whether these are launched by conservatives or radicals. For, as Spingarn himself put it, "the distinction between radicals and conservatives is as old-fashioned as that between monarchists and republicans, nominalists and realists, Platonists and Aristotelians, Jacobins and Girondists. Beyond mere sects, beyond political divisions, there is a larger field of combat. There is only one real division to-day that has any reality, and that is the difference between an old-fashioned materialism and a new idealism."[1] It is of the utmost importance to understand that Spingarn's idealism is an assertion of the primacy of spirit, which is the only reality, and that the divisions of spiritual activity are, as we shall see, speculative constructs for the sake of describing that ever changing activity. Such discriminations are part of the enabling act of the spirit, and they do not deny the original unity of the spirit, which is their ground.

These basic assumptions are important in understanding Spingarn's relationship to Croce. Sometimes he quarreled with aspects of Crocean theory, as in his reviews of the *Estetica* and Croce's book on *Vico,* or, as we shall see, in his remarks on religion in the New School lectures. Sometimes he seemed to misinterpret the theory, as we shall see in his controversy with A. B. Walkley. Invariably, his disagreements and misinterpretations seem to have sprung from his occasional momentary suspicions that Croce could be taken as isolating art from the whole life of the spirit;[2] and, conversely, his generous admissions of the "inadequacy" of his own interpretations of Croce (in "The Growth of a Literary Myth," in the Foreword to the "Tsang-Lang Discourses on Poetry," in "The Rich Storehouse of Croce's Thought," in his note to the 1931 reprint of "The Ancient Spirit and Professor Babbitt," and in the New School lectures) give clear evidence that his Crocean advocacy was based on his conviction that the main thrust of Croce's doctrine was to *unite* art with the whole spiritual life.[3]

The idealistic basis of Spingarn's thought and the indissolubility of the whole life of the spirit which it entailed were not, however, apparent to the readers of "The New Criticism."

Spingarn began that essay by pointing out that most criticism "tends to get away from the work of art and to substitute something [else] in its place": history, biography, morality, politics, erudition, or the rules and models of various dogmatic schools. Because he feared that in his own time criticism exaggerated the usefulness of external, "scientific" tests for art, he gave a sympathetic hearing to an imaginary apologist for Impressionistic subjectivity. Though Spingarn admitted that Impressionist criticism shifted attention to the feelings and sensations of the critic, and easily lost itself in passive enjoyment, he also praised its emphasis on "the free play of the appreciative mind." Though he agreed that judgment was as necessary as enjoyment, learning as important as responsiveness, he concentrated his most withering fire on the censors and the pedants. He insisted that art could not be measured by the standards of morality or by rhetorical rules or by its environment or historical causes. For "we know that art . . . is complete in itself," and that when the artist "has expressed his thought in its completeness, . . . there is no equivalent for his expression except itself." The critic, therefore, can only ask what the artist has proposed to himself to do and how far he has fulfilled his aim.

Such conclusions as these seemed to most of Spingarn's readers to leave both artist and critic in a state of helpless indeterminacy or isolation in which anything or everything or nothing was possible. But Spingarn did not wish to make art autotelic; he wanted to emphasize its inextricable integration with all of life. Paradoxically his conviction that art is indissolubly linked with the whole life of the spirit was precisely what accounted for his extreme reluctance to develop a system of objective weights and measures for the practicing critic. And his failure to make clear the idealistic basis of his philosophy of spirit accounts for the difficulty experienced by those committed to such systems in agreeing on what his critical position was. Judged by the multiple standards of the sectaries, his critical theory, like his life, seems a series of contradictions.

Harry Hartwick thought Spingarn an advocate of literary nationalism; but Stuart Sherman thought him un-American; and Ludwig Lewisohn charged that he was a New York Jew "pleading *pro-domo* within the framework of America . . . seeking to conquer America for his children." Gorham Munson saw Spingarn as "a leisured gentleman" who offered "literally nothing for the mind to work on," and the pseudonymous Mr. Blum saw his theory only as a "journalistic paraphrase" of Croce. Bernard Smith, James Farrell, and Stuart Sherman (during what George DeMille termed Sherman's Rotarian phase) called Spingarn's ideas antidemocratic; but Irving Babbitt saw them as too democratic. Babbitt, Harry Hartwick, Randolph Bourne, and even Woodberry feared that his theories encouraged irresponsible license; but Horace Kallen feared his dogmatism and called him a supporter of "aesthetic and moral imperialism," and no "less eager a missionary than that puritanical mossback from the academic Main Street, Mr. Irving Babbitt."[4]

This glossary of epithets may provide some inkling of the fury of the critical battles of the pre- and post-World War I era. And such name-calling made it difficult for Spingarn to develop the "philosophic" theory of literature he yearned after—the "ideal" theory that could reconcile opposites. His contentious nature and his sensitivity to personal attack lured him again and again, in his early years, into minor skirmishes; and, later, his growing ill-health and the pressure of other interests prevented him from regrouping his scattered ideas into a grand strategy. Spingarn, himself, was not unaware of his predicament; in 1922, in "Scholarship and Criticism," he wrote somewhat plaintively:

[American] critics are constantly carrying on a guerilla warfare of their own in favour of some vague literary shibboleth or sociological abstraction, and discovering anew the virtues or vices of individuality, modernity, Puritanism, the romantic spirit of the Middle Ages, the traditions of the pioneer, and so on ad infinitum. This holds true of every school of American criticism, "conservative" or "radical"; for all of them a disconnected body of literary theories takes the place of a real philosophy of art.[5]

Despite repeated involvement in these tactical skirmishes, Spingarn had from the beginning an interest in grand strategy. His preoccupation with theory is evident in his doctoral dissertation. And, in 1903, in his review of George Saintsbury's *History of Criticism,* he complained of Saintsbury's lack of education in esthetic thinking. The complaint is the same in his review, in 1913, of Irving Babbitt's *Masters of Modern French Criticism.* Even in the midst of the polemics of his address in 1910 on "The New Criticism," Spingarn was careful to note that he was only trying to clear the ground of the "dead lumber" and "weeds" of criticism in order to make room for more systematic philosophic structures. He had always believed what he wrote in 1922: that the literary critic "cannot criticize . . . without some understanding of what all literature attempts"; and that "Back of any philosophy of art there must be a philosophy of life. . . ."[6] So really to define what criticism is, he said in 1931, "the critic had to give you his conception of the universe."[7] Only in that conception could contradictions be reconciled.

For Spingarn's conception of the universe, for the best clues to the synthetic principles underlying the diversity of his critical utterances, it is necessary to turn to his later writings, and especially to the unpublished New School lectures. The principles these lectures discover are, for the most part, implicit in his earlier work, and they bind that work together with his later work into a changing but unified whole.

II   *Theory and Practice*

Spingarn's "conception of the universe" began with the idea that man was the "maker of life."[8] And, although his most explicit formulations of the idea were Crocean, the concept itself was rooted in Spingarn's own character and had animated his whole life. Following the language of Croce, Spingarn began the New School lectures (I, 8) by making a "distinction between theory and practice." For Spingarn, "theory includes . . . poetry and the arts, philosophy, and if you will religion. And practice includes all the activities of practical life, the activities of the business man, of the manual worker, of the statesman, of the soldier, of the professions, all the activities of practical life."

The cardinal point of Spingarn's distinction is that practical activity can hardly be said to exist, and certainly cannot be known, except as structured by theory, by the vision of the poet, the philosopher, or the theologian. And the clear implication is that such visions are multiple, not single; continually creative, not static. Practical contradictions, thus, may be synthesized by theoretical vision. As Emerson had said, consistency is a hobgoblin only for those unaware of the resources of the creative imagination.

The distinction between theory and practice is not, for the

Romantic idealist, a distinction between mind and matter. Spingarn was a "monist," not a "dualist"; he insisted that practice is as much a product of the human spirit as is theory. For practice is conducted according to categories imposed on experience by "theory"; and theory is generated in practice. Reality is not known until it has been structured by language or thought or by a "ritual" of action—organized by an a priori synthesis, as Croce would say. "Even the materialist," said Spingarn in his revised version of the "New Manifesto," "posits no concrete and individual kind of matter, but the idea of matter, an idea of the mind."

Thus the distinction between theory and practice, and the distinctions within either category are "conceptual" rather than "actual"; for, as Spingarn said in both versions of his "manifesto," "all true idealism rests on the assumption that inner and outer reality are indissolubly intertwined in the realm of the spirit," whereas the crude "religion" of materialism rests on "the blind, unreasoning faith of the scientist in an inexorable external Nature."[9] Thus, Spingarn insisted in his New School lectures (I, 9) that "We are not making practical or empirical or psychological distinctions of any kind whatever . . . ; we are making philosophical distinctions, if you will, speculative distinctions. . . . they are distinctions, but distinctions of a unity."

Spingarn insisted on this point from 1922 on, for by that time he was painfully aware of the charge that he had artificially segregated art from other human activities and had made it a phenomenon *in vacuo*. It is true that Spingarn's earliest critical writings had emphasized the "theoretical" nature of art, but his whole life had emphasized the "spiritual" side of practice. He had not intended to deny the practical relevance of the old scholarship or the new history; instead, he had wished to attack the despiritualization which the mechanical administrative techniques of men like Butler at Columbia had foisted on American universities, and which the empirical methods of "objective relativism" had imposed on history. His opposition to the Marxian emphasis on economic materialism which he thought threatened the National Association for the Advancement of Colored People in 1932 is surely of a piece with his own "practical" political adventures in 1908.

It is understandable that Spingarn's contemporaries should

not have used his life (although they sometimes *misused* it) as a gloss on his critical writings. And Spingarn *had* emphasized the difference between art and practice in the early writings. But it is now apparent that his life does provide a suitable comment on his esthetic theory, and it is evident that his early reluctance to emphasize the intimate *connection* between art and practice derived from his fear that, in the circumstances, practice would be taken to mean something non-spiritual; the result, he feared, would be a reduction of art to the level of behavioristic science.

This fear was still with him in the New School lectures (II, 30-31), where he condemned I. A. Richards, because "Mr. Richards says that . . . anything which has certain psychological values has an artistic element. . . . In other words all is brought together in a vague concept of one concept of values and with that one concept we are lost in confusion." It is not that Mr. Richards is a monist, but that he is the wrong kind of monist. It is not that he connects art and life, but that his "vague concept" of "psychological values" misrepresents life.

Spingarn's early "separation" of art from life was, therefore, a tactical maneuver to avoid the identification of art with behavioristic psychology or sociology. In 1922 he had written, in "The Younger Generation," that "It is this philosophy of materialism which has made us believe that the whole of life can be summed up in some single side of life—the economic side, the physical side, the psychological side." But early and late Spingarn was committed to the interdependence of theory and practice, art and life, within the spiritual realm, which was the only "real" area of experience. Distinctions between the parts of a spiritual unity were, he argued, necessary in order to avoid "confusion"; but they were "speculative" distinctions created by the "self-generating science of philosophy"; they were "not concrete realities." The great error of Butler, Marx, Richards, and others was to mistake one aspect of a spiritual unity for the whole and, furthermore, to forget that that aspect had no independent existence at all outside a conceiving spirit or, more accurately, outside spiritual activity.[10]

As we have seen, Spingarn encountered difficulties in trying to act out during his life a practical definition of the meeting of theory and practice. And to define, speculatively, the exact locus of their meeting is surely the most difficult problem confronting the Hegelian philosopher—whether reformed (like Spingarn and Croce) or unregenerate. But Spingarn's assertion that theory and practice are synthesized in the "heart of man" is perhaps somewhat more satisfactory than Richards' belief that they are absorbed in psychology; for Spingarn was more careful than Richards to recognize the part played by "theory" in creating the categories of thought. Aware, however, of the danger of vagueness in his own definition of spirit, Spingarn strove mightily to stave off the threat of tautology on the one hand and nominalism on the other by emphasizing and re-emphasizing his "speculative" distinctions. The New School lectures are an extended record of this labor; they are a labor of definition. The definitions they contain were implicit in Spingarn's life, in his early writings, and, of course, in Croce.

The first lecture is largely concerned with the distinction between theory and practice described above. The history of Western thought, said Spingarn, had been the history of an oscillation between the two; and "the history of the modern world" has been "a history of a struggle between theory and practice, with practice becoming "more and more the ideal of European man until in the nineteenth century it became overwhelmingly the more important." The consequences of this struggle, as Spingarn saw them, remind us of the early Van Wyck Brooks' formula for the history of American thought and culture. Brooks, a lifelong friend of Spingarn, wrote in 1915: "Human nature itself in America exists on two irreconcilable planes, the plane of stark theory and the plane of stark business."[11] Spingarn, sixteen years later, put it this way in the first New School lecture: the "tragedy of the man of letters since the nineteenth century" has been, in part, that he has been "faced with a world entirely devoted to the practical [and] has revolted . . . against the practical and has despised it"; thus, "the real disease of literature since the middle of the nineteenth century, if not, indeed, since the Renaissance," has been "the split between theory and practice." The two movements, he said in his second lecture, which represented the extremes best in 1931 were "the New Humanism, which overemphasized theory, and . . . Marxianism [*sic*] which . . . overemphasizes practice."

Perhaps Brooks and Spingarn were talking about something similar to T. S. Eliot's dissociation of sensibility. At any rate,

Spingarn's historical metaphor made clear that he did not believe that the theoretical activities of the poet, the philosopher, and the priest could prosper without an understanding of "the conduct of our daily life—the work of the statesman, the business man, the professional man, the manual worker, and those passions and emotions which are the warp and woof of practical life."[12] For without practice, there is nothing for theory to organize, and it becomes empty. Conversely, practice without theory becomes anarchic and meaningless, a mere suffering of life instead of a mastering of life. Mind and matter are both functions of spiritual activity. Depending on the dominant error of the time, theory or practice would need to be emphasized. Spingarn's historical metaphor explained his own emphasis.

III   *Philosophy and Religion*

The distinctions Spingarn made *within* the category of theory —distinctions between philosophy, art, and religion—are sometimes difficult to follow. Philosophy, he said in his second lecture at the New School, is "eternally to be distinguished from the methods of empirical science"; for "philosophy never begins with the generalization from sciences but is always an independent and self-created science." Philosophy does not generalize from empirical evidence because, in one sense, philosophy, whether elaborated in action or in study, makes an anterior determination of what the evidence shall be. In his first lecture, he said:

[Philosophy] aims to find a permanent something in the flux of things. In other words it restates or attempts to find, let us say, the eternal. Now in so far as it is an eternal in the flux of things, it must seem conservative. But in so far as it is in the flux of things and restates the eternal in ways that are new or have been misapprehended, it must be novel and explosive. And so every philosophy that is worth its salt is both conservative and radical, both conservative and revolutionary.

But what is then left for the other theoretical modes? Presumably nothing within the theoretical realm. Spingarn's difficulty is especially clear with respect to religion. Croce had denied that religion was a separate category; it was, he said, "philosophy in process of becoming, philosophy more or less imperfect, but philosophy."[13] At least that was the status of religious myth according to Croce for those who *believed* it; for those who used it as "metaphor," religious myth was art.

For Spingarn, however, religion had a perfectly legitimate "use" in the world; but his descriptions of it were confusing. Like philosophy, religion sought the eternal in the flux; but, unlike philosophy, which was "speculative," religion was "believed." A philosophy became a "faith" when it lots its dynamic, dialectic character; when it stopped criticizing itself; when it "goes out and wins millions like any religion." Philosophy became a "faith" when "it finds a convert, and that convert takes it over whole." Such had been the career of Marxism, which Spingarn took to be an ideal philosophy gone wrong, one which had gone into the business of manufacturing opiates (powerfully stimulating ones), one which had begun "coining . . . myths, superb myths, so superb that they are fascinating the imagination of men everywhere."

Such statements suggested that religion was half politics and half art (an idea Croce had advanced), half practice and half theory. But Spingarn rejected such an interpretation: "religion may be a permanent category which belongs side by side with art and philosophy as one of the permanent divisions of theory of the human mind."[14] Again we ask a question: What are the differences among these three modes? This question returned to plague Spingarn (and Croce, too) in the definition of art.

IV   *Art as Expression*

Spingarn's basic assumption about art was the Crocean assumption that "art is one of the eternal categories of the human spirit," as he put it in the New School lectures in 1931. But Spingarn, even in his early "Origins of Modern Criticism" (1904), had indicated that the constitutive element in the definition of the esthetic, as that definition had developed historically, was to be found not so much in the physical art work as in the creative "spirit." The first glimpses of such a definition in "modern" times, he said, were to be found in the questions about artistic taste proposed by Italians like Benedetto Varchi and Torquato Tasso, though Varchi's tentative interest in taste assumed an "individual basis [for] the pleasure or displeasure poetry gives," and Tasso's efforts to generalize about the universal grounds for individual taste emphasized the structure of poetry rather than that of the mind.

The questions they asked, however, after being buried under "the rationalism of the classic spirit," were resurrected in the eighteenth-century concepts of taste and the *je ne sais quoi,* and were answered by the Romantic movement in the "concept of the creative imagination." The gradual displacement of "external rules . . . , as a basis for critical judgment, by internal or psychological tests," and the attempt of the critic "to be at one with the creative mind," "alone make the history of this period [the eighteenth century] vital."

In his introduction to *Critical Essays of the Seventeenth Century* (1908), Spingarn repeated the arguments of his "Origins of Modern Criticism." At the very outset he set the terms of his argument by noting that Bacon had connected art "with a particular division of the mind," whereas Jonson had tended to emphasize "the external and objective side of literary art." Spingarn's own sympathies emerge in his summary of the more or less systematic tendency of criticism in the seventeenth century "to connect poetry with the mental functions which create it. This development of criticism was naturally sympathetic to the new school [of taste], which, by insistence on taste, sentiment, the heart, and similar concepts, connected poetry more intimately with the inner processes necessary to enjoy and appreciate as well as create it." Again in his essay on "Jacobean and Caroline Criticism" (1911) in the *Cambridge History of English Literature,* Spingarn reiterated his belief that the answer to the question, "What is art?" lay in "the relation between the creative mind and the work of art." That is, art was imaginative creation or theoretic vision. But the question of its difference from other kinds of theoretic vision is still not answered.

Spingarn's early statements about the theoretic nature of art recall his Romantic allegiance. Coleridge had said that "What is poetry? is so nearly the same question with, what is a poet? that the answer to one is involved in the solution of the other."[15] But, unlike some of Coleridge's twentieth-century interpreters, Spingarn was convinced that any investigation of the psychology of art should be an investigation of the spiritual realm of theory and not of the nervous system. In "The Younger Generation" he lumped "Freudian instinctivism, and a still cruder behaviorism" with "Bergsonian intuitionalism," sociological religion, "Confucianism," and "the dry bones of political liberalism or radicalism" as the products of "the philosophy of materialism."[16]

Spingarn's allusions to Romantic esthetic theory usually provide only a negative definition of the poetic faculty. Thus his agreement, in the *History of Literary Criticism in the Renaissance,* that poetry's function "is, as Coleridge says, to give definite and immediate pleasure" (56), becomes a way of denying (the emphasis is on the word *immediate*) that poetry is instrumental with respect to narrowly utilitarian or didactic interests. But, even before he had read Croce,[17] Spingarn was sure that the hedonistic accompaniment of the esthetic activity was symptomatic rather than constitutive. And he explicitly divorced himself from the hedonistic Impressionism of such critics as Lewis Gates when he wrote, in his "Criticism in the United States" (1924), that the recognition of the hedonistic accompaniment was a step forward in the history of criticism, but that "the idea of pleasure no lunger sums up for us the whole spiritual world of art."[18] He might have quoted Coleridge: "the Apollo Belvedere is not beautiful because it pleases, but it pleases us because it is beautiful."[19]

Because Spingarn did *not* believe that the spiritual activity of art had anything to do directly with the artist's nervous system or with pleasure psychology, he rejected "emotionalism" in literature. But, because he had seemingly separated art from the rational faculties, critics like Irving Babbitt were quick to accuse him of "making . . . the imagination the irresponsible accomplice of the unchained emotions."[20] In answer to such charges, Spingarn protested in "The Growth of a Literary Myth"(1923) that

My sin would be great indeed if I were in any way responsible for the fact that Croce, a master of logical distinctions, has been regarded by some Americans as the advocate of "emotional debauch" in aesthetic theory or critical practice—Croce, who in Italy has come to be regarded more and more as the leader of a classical reaction intended to transcend romanticism without losing sight of its permanent values, and who has been called by the more morbidly romantic of his countrymen "intellectualistic," "moralistic," and even "prosaic."[21]

In his New School lectures (II, 8), Spingarn, still grouping philosophy and art together, called "this idea of giving out your emotions raw without going into the serener sphere of theory" an aspect of "the Romantic spirit" which was to be condemned as an "artistic defect." He condemned it for the same reason he had condemned the "confessional element" in poetry and the "stream of consciousness" in novels:[22] all three habits made art a reproduction of life rather than a theoretical criticism of it.

Throughout his book on Renaissance criticism, Spingarn praised "imagination" (identified with Romanticism), "poetic sensibility," and "inspiration" as the "true qualities that go to make up a great poet," because they *deny* false emphases on "reason" (identified with neo-Classicism), didacticism, "logic," the "merely empirical formulas of rhetorical theory," and the merely dramaturgic formulas of such men as Castelvetro.[23] But neither in his dissertation nor in his New School lectures did he make very clear the distinctive characteristics of the esthetic mode except in the most general way. Both early and late Spingarn knew that "literature is not religion, is not philosophy, is not history, is not politics"; that "out of that material it has got to make something else which we call poetry or literature or art."[24] But one question remained: "what is the quality of mind that makes up poetry, what is imagination?"

In "The New Criticism" Spingarn explained that imagination is a Romantic concept, and he offered as a synonym *expression*. What was of enormous value to Spingarn in the idea of expression was that it called attention to the interdependence of form and content, to the part played by spirit in creating the subject of its own discourse; and it rejected the notion that the artist was an imitator or reporter of a world pre-existing outside his own spiritual perception of it. Yet, in summarizing the idea of expression as it had developed in the nineteenth century, he wrote: "for all these critics and theorists, literature is an expression of something, of experience or emotion, of the external or internal, of the man himself or something outside the man; yet it is always conceived of as an art of expression."[25] The trouble with such an explanation of "expression" is that it implies again the old distinction between the sign and the thing signified which the new concept was meant to annul.

"The New Criticism" was conceived and executed as a bit of calculated shock tactics. Spingarn was reacting against the polite world of American literary gentility; but the rougher Populist protest of local colorists like Hamlin Garland, with its borrowings from the French environmentalist critic, Hippolyte Taine, seemed to Spingarn to provide no basis for criticism. Nor did the essential triviality of Vance Thompson or James Huneker, whose efforts to bring the cosmopolitanism of Europe to America were as thin as the native strains of the local colorists. The academic Impressionism of Lewis Gates seemed irrelevant as well, as did the intellectual opportunism of Brander Matthews,[26] Spingarn's colleague at Columbia. "The New Criticism" is a destructive attack on a whole list of critical formulas, whether moralistic, sociological, or rhetorical; and yet Spingarn, for all the fervor of his rhetoric, refused to call the names of contemporary authors and critics (however largely he might invoke the large lessons of history), lest partisan debate sully the nearly inviolable purity of the idea of esthetic expression. For example, when Sinclair Lewis refused the Pulitzer Prize for *Arrowsmith* in 1926, Spingarn made no comment, though Harcourt, Brace was Lewis' publisher. Spingarn's aloofness from contemporary literary politics was paradoxically a function of his reformer's zeal, a tactical decision to avoid partisan entanglements that would betray the clarity of theory at the very moment when he thought America's greatest practical need was a greater capacity for the speculative life of theory.

Conversely, however, Spingarn's urgent sense of the practical situation and his negative emphasis on what needed to be destroyed blurred the theory he wished to propose. Though he confessed his allegiance to Croce in "The New Criticism," he did not attempt a systematic exposition of the Crocean esthetic; nor did he do justice to its key term, *expression.* Lacking an explanation of the Crocean sense of expression, and remembering his description of what expression had meant to certain Romantics, Spingarn's audience was almost sure to ask, "What does art express?" To have this question answered by the assertion that "art has performed its function when it has expressed itself" was to have confusion worse confounded.[27]

The confusion persisted through the years, though glimpses of Spingarn's better meanings are now possible. Sometimes he would say that poets "express themselves," or "the secret of a unique personality," or a "state of mind."[28] But increasingly he came to suggest that artistic expression was an a priori synthesis of experience and not a momentary whim or eccentricity. He said that poetry expressed "the essence of unmixed reality," or a "vision of the life of man," or "the whole reality which . . . imagination has to encompass," or "a new life in which the imagination can breathe and move," or "the whole content of human life (in its inner as well as its outer manifestations)." [29] Spingarn had begun in 1899 with the idea that poetry was concerned with "the permanent and universal"; and he ended in 1931 with the same idea: "poetry may give you a sense of the eternal. . . . Utter one line of poetry, . . . and if you submit to the music of the line, for that moment you have a sense that you are in contact with the whole universe." [30]

Spingarn admitted in the New School lectures (VI, 11-12) that, although "a true philosophy of the imagination first came into being" in "this much condemned Romantic period" (III, 17), many Romantics had erred in thinking of art as an expression of something more or less independent of the artist's mind —and almost all modern critics had continued the error. Spingarn's own formulation of the idea of expression in 1931 is unequivocal in correcting the error: art "is in itself a category of the mind." [31] His listeners must then have understood that he meant that literature created its own subject through form. But even in 1931 it was not clear how art was different from the other forms of creative or speculative activity such as philosophy and religion.

V   *Croce and Intuition*

Whether Spingarn's confusion on this point can be cleared up by referring to Croce's writings is doubtful. Croce's distinctions are certainly sharper than Spingarn's, but they are not distinctions easily maintained. In the well-known opening passage of his *Aesthetic* Croce wrote: "Knowledge has two forms: it is either intuitive [esthetic] knowledge or logical [philosophic] knowledge; knowledge obtained through the *imagination* or knowledge obtained through the *intellect*; knowledge of the *individual* or of the *universal*; of *individual* things or of the *relations* between them: it is, in fact, either of *images* or of *concepts.*" [32]

Croce made clear that he did not mean that the artist intuits something already existing and knowable outside of the intuitive act any more than Spingarn meant that the artist "expresses" society, ideas, emotions, or experience. Crocean intuition is a formal act. The materials of such intuition—"impressions, sensations, feelings, impulses, emotions, or whatever else one may term what still falls short of the spirit"—are only "postulated for the convenience of exposition."[33] As Croce wrote in *The Breviary of Aesthetic*: "a thought is not a thought for us, unless it be possible to formulate it in words; a musical fancy only when it becomes concrete in sounds; a pictorial image only when it is coloured. . . . Thought, musical fancy, pictorial image, did not indeed exist without expression, they did not exist at all previous to the formation of this expressive state of the spirit."[34] Or, as Croce had said in the *Aesthetic*, "The aesthetic fact therefore is form, and nothing but form." Consequently, *"there is no passage* from the qualities of the content to those of the form," because before the content is formed, "it has no determinable qualities."[35] To determine is, of course, to form.

The problem remains, however, to differentiate the formal activity of art from philosophy. And in the Crocean answer we may discover one source of Spingarn's persistant refusal to undertake the job of the practicing critic. For Croce, art is concerned with the imaginative intuition of the individual image; philosophy, with the intellectual elaboration of the concept: "Intuitions are: this river, this lake, this brook, this rain, this glass of water; the concept is: water, not this or that appearance and particular example of water, but water in general, in whatever time or place it be realized; the material of infinite intuitions, but of one constant concept."

Because "Concepts are not possible without intuitions," philosophy may have an esthetic aspect; but, as intuitions are always prior to concepts, art has not a philosophic aspect: "To speak is not to think logically; but to *think* logically is also to *speak.*" "There is poetry without prose, but not prose without poetry."[36]

These definitions of the relation between intuition and concept, which lay behind Spingarn's insistence that each work of art is complete in itself, seem to be a Crocean version of the old distinction between haecceity and quiddity, raising all the old problems without particularly solving them. It is difficult to understand how "this tree" can be intuited without a simultaneous conceptualization of "trees."[37] Should not there be but one formal activity instead of two? And, if there are two, will not the radically discrete character of individual intuitions make inapplicable to art the categories of discursive thought, and thus enormously complicate the task of the critic? Croce's effort to distinguish art from philosophy *asserts* the existence of a separate realm of human experience called "aesthetic,"[38] but defines that realm in such a way as to make it virtually impossible to find one's way there. Though Spingarn never attempted a technical explanation of Croce's distinctions, his own belief in the autonomy of the esthetic realm and his exaggerated fear of "abstractions" in the criticism of individual literary works were confirmed by Croce's insistence that art is independent of conceptual analysis.

VI   *Esthetic Communication: A Dilemma for the Critic*

The problems of how separate art is from other human experience and of how silent or articulate the critic may be are thrown into sharp relief when we consider the process of artistic communication. In the *Aesthetic* Croce explained that in the "complete process of aesthetic production," "the capital point, the only one that is properly speaking aesthetic and truly real," is the formal determination of an internal vision, and that the "translation of the aesthetic fact into physical phenomena" for the purposes of communication is not, strictly speaking, necessary. Croce, who was intent on emphasizing the central role of the spirit in artistic production, did not intend to deny that internal vision included sounds, tones, colors, etc.—only that these qualities need be "physical."[39] To the charge that external beauty precedes internal vision, he replied: the artist "never in reality makes a stroke with his brush without having previously seen it with his imagination; and if he has not yet seen it, he will make the stroke, not in order to externalize his expression (which does not yet exist), but as a kind of experiment and in order to have a point of departure for further meditation and internal concentration." Thus, the manipulation of the artistic medium becomes "a means that may be called *pedagogic*"[40] for discovering or courting the internal vision. Nevertheless, the point in Croce's scheme most often attacked is the "translation of the aesthetic fact into physical phenomena," because it is at this point that the problem of communication seems most acute. R. A. Scott-James, for example, could not see "how any other than the artist . . . is able to gain a beautiful intuition by regarding the physically beautiful object," for Croce "has insisted that art is intuition, and intuition is individuality, and individuality is never repeated." Scott-James also paraphrased the objection of A. E. Powell (Mrs. E. R. Dodds): "the artist's intuition is elaborated out of his own experience; but the appreciator is required to elaborate just the same intuition out of something quite different—namely, the physical work of art." Even F. F. Carritt, good Crocean though he was, thought that Croce's idealism made the belief "in the existence of other minds with whom we might communicate . . . a leap in the dark as indefensible as to believe in external objects." Horace Kallen joined Carritt in accusing Croce of solipsism.[41]

Spingarn never met the problem of communication on the level where the issue of solipsism was likely to present itself. But his *Creative Criticism* bore the subtitle, *Essays on the Unity of Genius and Taste.* And it is precisely this "unity" that forms the basis of Croce's escape from solipsism[42] and of his insistence that an appreciator can reproduce the artist's vision as a result of confronting its physical embodiment: "the objection to the conceivability of the aesthetic reproduction is founded upon a reality conceived in its turn as a shock of atoms, or as abstractedly monadistic, composed of monads without communication among themselves and harmonised only from without. But that is not reality: reality is spiritual unity, and in spiritual unity nothing is lost, everything is an eternal possession."

For Croce, "the doctrine that individuality is irreproducible and the universal alone reproducible is certainly a doctrine of 'sound' philosophy, but of sound scholastic philosophy, which separated universal and individual, making the latter an accident of the former (dust carried along by time), and did not know that the true universal is the universal individuated, and that the only true *effable* is the so-called ineffable, the concrete and individual."[43] By postulating a sort of universal "spiritual energy" in which all individuals share—as Spingarn said, a temperament "individual yet representative of our common human nature"[44] —and by postulating a "reality" which is a function of this spiritual activity, Croce was able to hold that an appreciator of a work of art could move from the physical art work back to the internal esthetic synthesis experienced by the artist.

Croce's idealistic explanation of communication seems as acceptable as a mechanistic or dualistic explanation; but it does not really solve the problem created by the separation of intuitive vision (art) from conceptual vision (philosophy). Although we may grant that "*there is no passage* from the physical fact to the aesthetic"[45] without internal creative synthesis, it seems unnecessarily perverse to insist that the internally synthesized experience is immune from conceptual categories, even less amenable to definition than a non-esthetic experience, so inviolable, in fact, as to be critically indiscussable, and thus, in effect, unverifiable.

Spingarn's involvement in this central critical dilemma is clear in one of his earliest essays—his reply in 1912, to John Galsworthy's strictures on "The New Criticism."[46] Galsworthy had doubted the identity of the creative and the critical acts, though he admitted some kinship. His point was the same as Croce's critics raised: the artist works from experience, whereas the critic works from the art object. Spingarn's reply was like Croce's: both artist and critic share a common imagination, and it is this internal faculty, not the external limitations of material, that is important in the production and reproduction of esthetic synthesis. If, as Galsworthy had said, the artist works "intuitively" from his whole "experience" in the "creative" act, so, said Spingarn, must the critic intuitively invoke experience in the interpretive act, including his experience with the physical art object. As for Galsworthy's assertion that the artist is of "brusquer stuff" than the critic, and his citation of Leonardo and Walter Pater as examples of the difference, Spingarn answered: "It needs little argument to prove that the 'universal man' of the Renaissance is made of . . . brusquer stuff than the Victorian don."

To identify artist and critic as closely as Spingarn did recalls the Romantic esthetic of Emerson, who taught that each reader must be himself a poet, and it raises in another form the problem that bothered Galsworthy: what distinctively critical procedures are available as a means to the re-enactment of the artist's vision, if the primary faculty of the critic is an expressive imagination which itself is unanalyzable? Some answer to the first part of the question can be essayed in another chapter, but here it may be appropriate to note Croce's frank admission that the idea of art as intuition "obtains its force and meaning from all that it implicitly denies and from which it distinguishes art."[47] Spingarn's "New Criticism" is likewise a labor of negative definition which emphasizes the inapplicability of conceptual categories in the criticism of art: art is not a set of rhetorical categories, nor is it moral instruction, nor is it, as art, historical or sociological effect. The definition of Crocean "expression" must be negative because expression is, as E. F. Carritt has said, "a primary spiritual activity" that "can no more be explained than can thinking itself"; art is "a simple ultimate fact behind which we cannot go."[48]

Or as D. G. James' neo-Coleridgean definition of the Romantic imagination has it, "we should recognize the arts as the expression of the unique activity of the imagination, instead of setting out to reduce the imagination to something other than it is. And when we say that the imagination is 'unique' we do not mean that it is something merely 'aesthetic,' but that it is an irreducible factor present in all experience whatsoever, yet operative in the arts with a high degree of power and concreteness."[49]

An important consequence of such an insistence on the imagination's fundamental role in our "conception of the universe" is that it denies by definition any possibility that art is the servant of special interests. In the Crocean view, art is anterior to special interests, which are the result of conceptual systems. Art discovers the world which we later may wish to systematize and so use. If there is a difficulty in understanding such a distinction —even as there is an analogous problem in Spingarn's tendency to blur the distinctions between art, religion, and philosophy— we may nevertheless find also an advantage. Though the idea that the art of expression will create its own adequate form may lead the critic to conclude that "the poem expresses simply whatever it expresses,"[50] we may also see in the suspicion of "external" criteria a healthy recognition that experience is never adequately described by abstractions. As Spingarn had said: "Life, by definition, escapes defining."[51]

Spingarn saw quite clearly in the pre- and post-World War I era the central dilemma which later critics like R. P. Blackmur learned from living through the period of the 1930's, during which Marxist critics often seemed to want to reduce literature to sociological polemic and formalist critics tended to want to reduce it to rhetorical formula. The question of Spingarn's possible influence on later "new critics" like Blackmur must be addressed in a later chapter. But certainly Blackmur understood the critical problem that lay at the center of Spingarn's theory. "It is the sensibility, in the end," Blackmur wrote, "that absorbs, and manifests like light, the notion of order."

Blackmur knew how hard it is for the critic to find authority in his own sensibility, "in the very tone of experience itself"; and he knew how strong is the temptation "to resort to constructions of the mind outside the data of experience." The discipline of the sensibility is an arduous and elusive discipline. "Other considerations are desperate to cry out. The mind makes invasion; the sensibility is violated by ideas, and all is lost, at just the wrong times, for the sake of principles, formulas and terminologies." Blackmur was more willing than Spingarn to let critics begin with principles, formulas, and terminologies; but the final act of criticism for Blackmur must be an act of the "convicted imagination."[52] Or, as Spingarn had put it two decades earlier, it must be a "leaping over and beyond" "convictions."[53] Blackmur's "sensibility," like Spingarn's expressive intuition, is the common possession of artist, reader, and critic. This common possession, for Blackmur as well as for Spingarn, makes "the critical act . . . what is called a 'creative' act."[54]

The dilemma, of course, remains. Spingarn's efforts to solve it by admitting, hesitatingly and haltingly, that intellectual constructs and scholarly research might be a means of courting intuitive insight—and thus a means of redeeming the critic from the dark silence into which the identification of the critical and the creative had threatened to throw him—are described in another chapter. Here we may note that this identification is, for

Spingarn, a way of emphasizing the radically idealistic basis of his esthetic, and indeed of his "conception of the universe." The idealism is the basis of Spingarn's famous double-barreled question for the critic, which he first asked in "The New Criticism" in 1910: "What has the poet tried to do, and how has he fulfilled his intention? What is he striving to express and how has he expressed it? What vital and essential spirit animates his work, what central impression does it leave on the receptive mind, and how can I best express this impression? Is his work true to the laws of its own being rather than to laws formulated by others?"

The "vital and essential spirit" is what the critic must deal with, and it has come into being, its "own being," as an act of creation, almost literally *ex nihilo*. The "how" of the poet's creation, or the origin of his "intention," exists only in our clumsy, verbal formulations of the critic's task; perhaps there is really only "one supreme question: Has [the poet] or has he not created a work of art?" Spingarn strove to make his meaning clearer in the 1917 printing of "The New Criticism" by inserting a *caveat* about the meaning of "intention" in his original questions: "The poet's aim must be judged . . . by the art of the poem itself, and not by the vague ambitions which [the poet] imagines to be his . . . intentions before or after the creative act is achieved." And he returned to the point in "The Growth of a Literary Myth" (1923) where he explained that judging "artistic excellence" by the poet's intention in the narrow sense of the phrase was only another version of the cardinal critical sin of judging by "external and mechanical standards." For to Spingarn the poem's intention—not the poet's—was what really counted.[55]

Whatever may be the special difficulties of the Crocean view of the uniqueness of esthetic intuition or Spingarn's merger of genius and taste, Spingarn's idealistic "conception of the universe" had the general advantage of emphasizing that "external and mechanical standards," though perhaps useful as pedagogic devices, are not a substitute for the action of the creative spirit, which is itself, ever and always, the maker of life. Such an emphasis and whatever dilemmas it brought in its train Spingarn thought healthy antidotes in an age of "materialism" for the

tendencies of critics bent on discovering final solutions through
the application of doctrinaire formulas. If Spingarn's distinctions within the life of "theory" between art, philosophy, and
religion seem awkward, perhaps the best reply is that such distinctions *are* "speculative." If "philosophy rightly conceived 'is
not harsh and crabbed, as dull fools suppose, but musical as is
Apollo's lute,' " then surely poetry may sometimes bow to
Athena.[56]

The important point for Spingarn was that all theory is a
kind of "vision," the kind Emerson had in mind when he wrote
in his *Journal* (January 20, 1833), "It is all in the anointed eye."
And, if reliance on the animating "essential spirit" behind and
in the vision seem an invitation to irresponsibility and whim, we
may recall Emerson's reply in "Self-Reliance" to the charge that
"rejection of popular standards is a rejection of all standards,
and mere antinomianism": "If anyone imagines," he said, "that
this law [of "self-reliance"] is lax, let him keep its commandments one day." In *Nature,* Emerson had argued that words
"cannot cover the dimensions of what is in truth. They break,
chop, and impoverish it." The consequence is, as he explained
in "The Over-Soul," that the users of words must "speak from
within the veil, where the word is one with what it tells of." For
the end of speech is "that thought may be ejaculated as Logos,
or Word." Spingarn, who was fond of quoting Emerson, directed
his negatives at "the lie of One Idea." For Spingarn, easy doctrine was certain error. And for Spingarn, as for Emerson,
"artistic vision" was one of the synonyms for "truth." "You
cannot be satisfied," Spingarn said, "with anything but truth—
that whole truth which is life—even in the service of art and
beauty."[57]

CHAPTER 6

Art, Life, Politics, and Morals

SPINGARN'S general view of "theory" as a structuring act of the spirit is the necessary prerequisite for understanding his ideas about the relationships between art and life, art and "politics," and art and morals. But the way in which he dealt with these specific problems in an attempt to counter the attacks of other critics helps also to clarify his general view. It suggests, too, the particular difficulties confronting the Romantic idealist during the 1920's.

I Critical Debate in the 1920's

The charges brought against Spingarn's view of art are various in the particular terms of their statement but similar in their general reference. Both the variety and the similarity are suggestive of the dominant critical temper of the 1920's: most American critics of the time were strong in their advocacy of particular sociological or moral precepts; and most of them were, perhaps as a consequence of their own sectarianism, suspicious of anyone who condemned, as Spingarn did, all "special interests." The warring sects seemed to agree that this worst of all heresies was irresponsibility incarnate, though the terms of their anathemas varied according to their own doctrine.

Thus Bernard Smith charged that Spingarn preached "the artist's irresponsibility" because his criterion was an aristocratic "taste," which is always "the final standard of the most cultivated, most disenchanted of the rootless, cosmopolitan upper classes." And Stuart Sherman, after his defection from neo-Humanism, thought Spingarn an antidemocratic and irresponsible bohemian because he had neglected to "cultivate acquaintance with our eminent 'builders of civilization.' " Irving Babbitt reversed the line of the Marxists and the Rotarians and insisted that Spingarn was *too* democratic because he preached all the vices of "unchained temperament." Ludwig Lewisohn, whose Freudian bias might have made him sympathetic to the expression of "unchained temperament," thought Spingarn had simply opposed "an empty aestheticisim . . . to an empty moralism."[1]

In the notoriously inexact lexicon of the American critical jargon of the time, there is a sense in which "aristocratic," "rootless," "bohemian," "irresponsible," and "aesthetic" can mean the same thing. If the partisanship of the critics of the 1920's is kept in mind, it will appear that their complaints against Spingarn mean, as H. L. Mencken said in summary, that, in relation at least to their own ardent creeds, he seemed to want to make beauty "an apparition *in vacuo.*"[2] Mencken was, for the most part, a friendly witness. Yet he, and others—like Van Wyck Brooks, John Chamberlain, Robert Spiller, and even Woodberry,[3] whose personal friendship with Spingarn or whose removal from the time or temper of the guerilla warfare made them gentler in their judgments—agreed that Spingarn had more or less divorced literature from life.

Part of the difficulty was, as already noted, that Spingarn refused to discuss the data of contemporary American literature while still eagerly adopting the most polemical of tones. John Chamberlain suspected that Spingarn's vulnerability was, thus, a function of his rhetoric rather than of his thought. And "Cornelius Blum" opined that "there is something nice about Mr. Spingarn reading to the critics of America from the Aesthetic of Croce—like a man reading the sermon on the mount to a director's meeting." This judgment is unfair; yet Mencken's left-handed compliment in 1919, that *Creative Criticism* was "at least magnificently unprofessorial," is less a contradiction of Blum's error than a confirmation that Spingarn's rhetoric sometimes ran away with his thought.[4]

The charge that Spingarn had encouraged the irresponsible divorce of literature from life seems rooted, therefore, either in the partisan commitments of his opponents or in his own tactical and stylistic ineptitude. He himself seemed aware of these two problems. The whole burden, for example, of his article on "Grocer-Shop Criticism and Real Criticism" (1914) is that he does *not* wish to do away with "standards," but that he *does* wish to avoid reliance on merely conventional weights and measures. And, in 1931 in the sixth of the New School lectures, he complained that "Professor Babbitt" "thinks that the codes and manners of our own day are the permanent categories by which a poet shall be judged," and that John Dewey erred in thinking that "art . . . must be the expression of the accidental details of actuality at the moment." Spingarn's attackers were not more concerned than he that literature be connected with life; they were, he said, only concerned that he did not connect it with their kind of life.[5]

Spingarn was also aware that the formulation he had given his own views had not been adequate. He frequently complained of the low level of discussion forced on American critics by the journalistic habits of the time. In a letter to his daughter Hope (January 21, 1927), he complained that "the trouble with publishing a book" was that "you can never escape from it again." And so the "half-truths" and "immaturity" of *Creative Criticism* would pursue him: "At least until I publish something better and more convincing." But Spingarn never did his "something better and more convincing," though he wrote to his friend Frederick W. Skiff (February 6, 1929) that he had "outgrown" many of the ideas expressed in *Creative Criticism*; and he wrote to William Aspenwall Bradley (March 11, 1932) that he was "hoping to make a book out of my New School Lectures."

In those lectures he seemed hypersensitive to the dangers of partisan debate—as if he had been there before. He insisted over and over again that, "In this room, even in America, which is the great workshop in the world devoted to practice, we are going to live in the serene world of theory, of contemplation. Those who bring their angry passions, their practice, with them are not wanted." Once he rebuked a questioner who had called attention to a certain "timely" idea by saying: "We are thinkers here and therefore we should revolt against any popular fashion and hold it out to the eternal test."[6]

If we cut through Spingarn's incautious rhetoric and if we discount the narrow partisanship of his opponents, we will find, I think, that he is not guilty as charged. He did not think of literature as a phenomenon *in vacuo,* nor was he guilty of the minor specifications of the charge, that "content" was unimportant and that criticism was not evaluative. What he did intend to emphasize was that the content of art and the criteria of criticism should *not* be limited by local convention. Art was theoretical; theory was not irrelevant to practice; but it was not the slave of practical exigencies.

II   *Spingarn versus Babbitt*

Irving Babbitt was, perhaps, the sharpest controversialist Spingarn had to contend with. An examination, therefore, of Babbitt's handling of the charge of anarchic irresponsibility may provide the best example of the kind of critical tactics with which Spingarn was constantly confronted. Typical was Babbitt's attack on Spingarn in "Genius and Taste," published in the *Nation* of February 7, 1918. He began by labeling Spingarn a "primitivist" and charged that his doctrine encouraged the artist "to let himself go both imaginatively and emotionally." Having thus equated imagination and emotion, Babbitt next equated taste with "literary conscience" and then with "conscience in general," which had come, he said, in the days since the early eighteenth century, "to be regarded as itself an expansive emotion." Thus Spingarn's doctrine encouraged "an indeterminate vagabondage of imagination and emotion," and his advocacy (in "Creative Connoisseurship") of art's "divine madness" (as an antidote to stale cliché) prompted Babbitt to his sarcastic conclusion: "Mr. Spingarn promises us that if we follow his prescription, we shall not only have genius—which will turn out to be identical with taste—but that we shall also go mad."

Babbitt's whole deductive method, with its pulpit rhetoric and its hasty appeal to history and general philosophic principles, suggests that he was interested in art mainly in respect to its moral and cultural effects. It was, for him, a sociological phenomenon. Thus he easily equated Spingarn's plea for freedom in the arts with an advocacy of license in life. The result was that Spingarn's theories became "high treason to civilization," although in the next breath Babbitt admitted that they were hard for anyone "even moderately versed in literary history to read . . . without yawning."

It was precisely Babbitt's method of argument that Spingarn

criticized in his review in 1913 of Babbitt's *Masters of Modern French Criticism.* Babbitt is identified by Spingarn with French "academic" criticism as represented by Brunetière and with "the wailing cry for lost traditions. . . . Both are moralists, controversialists, pamphleteers, rather than literary critics; both exhibit the same suspicion of the imagination on its purely creative side." Babbitt has no idea of art as a part of the realm of "theory"; he has no unified idea of art at all; and hence his book is not about art or criticism: "He is a defender of tradition, an historian of ideas and tendencies, a moralist of considerable power, a populariser of general ideas; anything and everything . . . except a critic or a student of criticism. . . . His utterances are controlled . . . by . . . his personal bias in respect to the practical needs of the culture today."[7]

Babbitt replied to Spingarn's review by reminding him that "the literary critic is confronted today with the same fundamental problem as the philosopher." He related the "critical impressionists" to philosophic impressionists and relativists like William James and Henri Bergson, "who revel in the infinite otherwiseness of things, the warm immediacy of individual impulse, and dismiss everything that makes for unity as cold, inert, merely conceptual." Presumably Spingarn was of this tribe, but Babbitt proceeded to the refutation, not of Spingarn, but of James and Bergson. For their work encouraged living "in a universe with the lid off," whereas Babbitt's work was "a protest against the romantic tendency to withdraw into the tower of ivory."[8]

Spingarn's reply to Babbitt's reply ignored the question of whether Babbitt was not trying to treat life as something apart from art, and ignored also the question of whether Spingarn ever advocated living "in a universe with the lid off" or in an ivory tower—or perhaps in a tower with the lid off. Instead, it doggedly returned to the original objection: Babbitt had no real literary theory, and he "is not concerned . . . with the way in which criticism interprets creation, but . . . is wholly obsessed with the problems of modern culture on their practical side."[9]

As Spingarn pointed out in "American Criticism Today" (1920), Babbitt's interests, like those of most contemporary American critics, were not literary: "literature or criticism as an

art seems scarcely to exist for him; he lives in a world . . . in
which poems and novels serve merely as documents in the history of culture."[10] Babbitt could not conceive of art as a theoretical act, which might condition practice and be conditioned by
it, but which was not bound by the actualities of practice or by
the compromises which practice demands.

After announcing this fundamental objection to Babbitt's
work, Spingarn, as often happened, found himself drawn by his
rhetoric into making statements in "The Ancient Spirit and Professor Babbitt" (1914) which were, from the Crocean point of
view, rather doubtful doctrine. In answer to Babbitt's charge
that his theory of expression led to anarchy, he wrote: "Disciplined art and undisciplined art are both art; or perhaps we
should rather say that disciplined minds as well as undisciplined
ones may express themselves in art. . . . bad English is English as
much as good English; the art of a child is art as much as that of
Michelangelo." Perhaps Spingarn meant that some expressions
are simple and some complex, but the totality of his rhetoric
made this interpretation difficult. Even the sympathetic reader
was likely to object that undisciplined minds cannot subdue
their impressions to form and therefore cannot express them.
The idea of undisciplined expression seems a contradiction
in terms.

Spingarn denied that the idea of art as expression "must
necessarily indicate a preference for the undisciplined form,"
and he allowed that "It may be important to distinguish between the art of the child and that of Michelangelo . . . and [to]
encourage the latter at the expense of the former." But also he
insisted that "the writer on esthetics should at least understand
what they have in common as well as what they differ in." Nevertheless, Spingarn's negative approach and polemical manner
made Babbitt's response understandable, if not excusable.
Wrenching Spingarn's comparison of the art of the child to
Michelangelo's art from its context, Babbitt triumphantly asserted that it proved Spingarn's preference for childish art and his
rejection of "the higher or human spontaneity."[11]

To the careful reader, it is now apparent, however, that
Spingarn's approval (in "Creative Connoisseurship," 1913) of
the "madness" of the Cubist painters was basically an approval

of the principle of experiment in art and not an approval of individual experiments which had failed through formlessness or lack of discipline to rise to the level of "expression." It was in this almost Jamesian sense that he insisted that "madness and courage are the very life of all art." Furthermore, Spingarn was talking about art in a particular time and place. Life in the United States was one-sided, he said; society had taken its cue from industrial regimentation. America had forgotten theory and sought only the practical. Thus, "All the greater is our American need of art's tonic loveliness, and all the more difficult is it for us to recapture the inherent madness without which she cannot speak or breathe." In the realm of "practical advice" or moral exhortation, Spingarn and Babbitt flatly disagreed. "To let one's self go," said Spingarn, "—that is what art is always aiming at, and [what] American art at this moment needs most of all." Spingarn admitted that some of the artists at the Armory Show "may have forgotten that the imagination is governed by an inner logic of its own, and not by unreasonable caprice." But in 1913 he thought that "even caprice is better than the lifeless logic of the schools."[12]

In "The Growth of a Literary Myth" (1923) Spingarn seemed to understand the dilemma his polemics had created; for, beneath the belligerence and sarcasm of his rhetoric, he sounded a faint note of apology: "if the less intelligent of my critics have assumed that by expression, or self-expression, I have meant the very things I specifically excluded from it, whim, eccentricity, the habits and manners of the poets, practical personality, I shall on my part charitably assume that this has been due to the ambiguity of the term, 'self-expression,' which, so far as I remember, Croce himself never employs."[13] The "real self" was a "speculative" ideal. In its experimental freedom it must seek out its own discipline. And so, as Spingarn explained in the sixth New School lecture, there are "two duties for the artist— one the duty to let himself go, and the other the duty to master self-control. And of course the second duty is artistically impotent without the first. How can one artistically control himself if one cannot first artistically let oneself go?"

But Spingarn never really described the kind of control the artist should submit to. He rejected the *external* control of

social, political, philosophic, or rhetorical dogma; and his polemical manner prevented him from explaining how any or all of
these controls could be generated internally in the act of "expression." He admitted in his "Notes on the New Humanism"
(1931) that there had been "perhaps a justifiable touch of exaggeration" in some of his strictures on Babbitt's work, but only
in the New School lectures (where he sounded the note of apology again) did he make clear that the expressive act was a
formal act: "what Babbitt calls expression versus form is exactly
the same as Croce's impression versus expression or form,
except for this—that the Crocean conception conceives of art as
uniting these two moments, form resolving the material into
itself. Professor Babbitt, himself, admits . . . that expression and
form must stand not as clashing antinomy, but as reconciled
opposites." Thus Babbitt contradicts himself when he "conceives
of form as a circumscribing and limiting law, something from
the outside," because such a view leads *away* from the intimate
connection of literature and life, which are integral, toward an
opposition between literature and formula.[14]

The obverse side of the charge of anarchy was that Spingarn's
theory made art too exclusive. Babbitt himself sometimes talked
this way. And the younger neo-Humanists, whether liberal (like
Stuart Sherman) or conservative (like Robert Shafer), agreed
that Spingarn encouraged "escapism" and "exclusivism"—
though, like Babbitt, they also sometimes thought of him as an
anarchist or "libertarian." But, for the most part, it was the
"progressive" critics who developed the idea that Spingarn
wanted art to be precious. Ludwig Lewisohn, whose friendship
with Spingarn should have taught him better, and whose Romantic vocabulary sometimes sounded like Spingarn's own, framed
the charge in Freudian terms. Bernard Smith, James Farrell, and
V. F. Calverton used a Marxian vocabulary.[15] But in a sense
they were all playing variations on Babbitt's theme: Spingarn
was relieving art from any responsibility to life; and especially
was he removing it from the realm where their special versions
of life were relevant to its judgment.

When Spingarn wrote, in a passage in "Criticism in the United

States" (1924) to which Robert Shafer took exception, that the poet creates "a world of fantasy" which "must not be confused with reality nor subjected to the moods and tests of actual life,"[16] he was attempting to differentiate beauty from raw experience. Beauty was a creation of the real, not a reflection of the actual. Art's reference was "synthetic" and "theoretical," not technical. Or, stated another way, art was a realization of the world, not an imitation of it. In the very passage which Shafer cited, Spingarn was contrasting the poet's "world of fantasy" with the pedant's sterile imitation of the manner of the business man.

The terms of this contrast remind us again that Spingarn, in talking about art, never had the actual American scene far from his mind. Art was the antidote for American practicality, and artists were to challenge those "restless Gods of Administration" who threatened even the scholars in their classrooms and libraries—and threatened, in the doctrine of artistic Realism ("essentially a middle class . . . conception"),[17] American artists themselves. If Babbitt's war against Naturalism was a moral rather than a literary crusade, Spingarn's fervor in behalf of the Crocean esthetic seems also rooted in his sense of what his countrymen needed at that moment in their history to know: they needed to differentiate *art* from *fact*. But Spingarn also insisted that they must not divorce art from life. And so, admitting that he himself was a "preacher" with "a message" for the men of his day, he cited Goethe as one who had known that poetic success was partly based on "practical experience."[18]

Spingarn might have cited his own life as an example of the effort to wed manners and manliness in an artistic elaboration which yet remained grounded in "actual" life. Art as the useless plaything of the esthete Spingarn condemned unequivocally in "Criticism in the United States" (1924) and in "Mr. Spingarn's Position" (1925), but he had always an antipathy to the precious,[19] and he had insisted in 1910 in "The New Criticism" that "art has no origin except from man's life"; or, as he explained in "Criticism in the United States": "Life, teeming life, with all its ardors and agonies, is the only limit within which the poet's vision can be cabined and confined."

III   *Literature and Politics*

Spingarn's special view of "politics" provides perhaps the best vocabulary for describing his idea of the relation between literature and life. In 1921, not long after he had come home from his great adventure in the army, and while he still burned with patriotic fervor, he wrote in praise of Goethe's "constant denial of the compatibility of poetry and partisanship."[20] Yet Goethe and Spingarn had both deliberately sought political experience. The point was that "politics is a spiritual act" in the realm of "practice" in the same way that poetry is a "spiritual act" in the realm of theory.[21] In "Politics and the Poet" (1942), Spingarn emphasized that the politician must transform brute "fact" into "spiritual reality": "Now the politician doesn't feel that sense that all is rotten in politics. He feels that the evil and good in the world are the very material with which he has to deal. He feels like the poet." As befits a student of the Italian Renaissance, Spingarn believed that the politician accepts the "corruption" of compromised actuality in order to transform it into spiritual reality. Political action is, therefore, a rehearsal in the world of practice of the role of the poet in the realm of theory.

The politician, said Spingarn, must of course be aware of the vision of poets and philosophers; but, conversely, the world of practice is important to the poet. Participation in that world through devotion to "the daily task" will involve any man in "creating the world and changing it," and give him a sense of the "larger whole, . . . of the *civitas* which grows out of your own labor."[22] Such participation is not the way of partisan politics, which is divisive,[23] but that of patriotism; it is a way which had almost fallen from sight as a result of the intellectual and political crises of the nineteenth century. But it is a way we ignore at profound cost: "a lack of love of country is a symptom of a lack of love of everything else, because . . . a . . . noble love of country symbolizes all human activity. . . . Love of country is the symbol of a connection with a whole; and a real connection with the whole will, conversely, follow it."[24]

Spingarn's emphasis on patriotism was not a plea for nationalism[25] but a search for manhood. Deprived of the sense of *civitas,* poets "no longer celebrate heroes, when . . . the whole purpose of poetry, almost, is to celebrate heroes." Repelled by the antiheroes in the novels of Dreiser, rejecting the consciously apolitical heroes in the work of Hemingway, and impatient with the middle-class documentaries of Sinclair Lewis, Spingarn complained that the failure of the idea of heroism was a failure of the political sense. And the result of the twin failure was a loss of "that conception of manliness which is essential to every poet."[26] The political sense, said Spingarn, is absolutely necessary for the complete man. And the complete man must surely be the better poet.

The pattern of the Marxists' dispute with Spingarn about politics is strikingly like that of Babbitt's argument with him about anarchic irresponsibility. There is a similar loose "logic," for example, in V. F. Calverton's contention that the Soviet ban on Tolstoi and Turgenev proved that "prevailing material conditions" determine literature rather than the other way around.[27] And there is a similar "carelessness" in Calverton's quotation from Spingarn's "The New Criticism": "In the world where morals count we have failed to give them (the poets) the proper material out of which to rear a nobler edifice. In so far as this is inherent in the nature of our humanity, *it is not affected by the special conditions of any single society in space and time.*"[28]

Calverton's comment is that the poet "must get his ideas from his social environment, and to speak of his not being affected by his environment is sheer fatuity." But one idea that Spingarn was surely intent on expressing is that the poet, in all societies and in all times, is bound to build less than an ideal poem precisely because his environment prevents him from doing so. And Spingarn was denying the effects of *particular* time and place only "in so far as" the poet may be successful in eliminating them from his poem, only "in so far as" he may be successful in his struggle to reduce the margin of imperfection in the poem to that final "inherent" disproportion between human nature and the ideal.

Spingarn wished to emphasize that the work of art resulted from a fusion of external condition and internal imagination, even as he had insisted that content and form were ideally one, however many traces of "practice" might remain in actual works of art. He knew, of course, that the fusion was not always complete, as the unassimilated bits of Thomistic philosophy in *The Divine Comedy,* or Elizabethan Protestantism in *The Faerie Queene,* or partisan propaganda in the protest literature of his own time, or even the personal idiosyncrasies showing in the verse of a poet like Robert Frost proved.[29] And Spingarn knew also that, though the poet might, as poet, remain indifferent to the practical consequences of his work, he must always, as a whole man, be concerned with the world he lived in.

Calverton began his quotation with a half-sentence (though he capitalized its first word), and he ended with a half-sentence. The restoration of the two half-sentences he left out and of one other sentence at the beginning certainly shifts the emphasis from the place where Calverton put it:

The poet's only moral duty, as a poet, is to be true to his art, and to express his vision of reality as well as he can. If the ideas enunciated by poets are not those we admire most, we must blame not the poets but ourselves: in the world where morals count we have failed to give them the proper material out of which to rear a nobler edifice. In so far as this is inherent in the nature of our humanity, it is not affected by the special conditions of any single society in space and time: though art is a symbol of the eternal conflict between aspiration and reality, it must at the same time remain forever a symbol of mortal imperfection.

The last sentence (half of which Calverton italicized) does not even appear in the early printings of "The New Criticism." It was added in 1924 when Spingarn included the essay in his anthology of *Criticism in America,* probably because Stuart Sherman had cited this same passage in 1921 as proof that Spingarn believed the opposite of what Calverton accused him of: the artist expresses "not merely himself, but also the dominant thought and feeling of the men with whom he lives."[30]

IV *Literature and Morality*

Spingarn's ideas about the relation of literature and morals repeat the story of his adventures concerning literature and life, and literature and politics. Again his rhetoric is sometimes exaggerated: "We have done with all moral judgment of art as art.

. . . It is not the inherent function of poetry to further any moral or social cause, any more than it is the function of bridge-building to further the cause of Esperanto. . . ." Again he argues, however, the esthetic obligation of the poet to include all of life: the poet has a "moral duty, as a poet, to be true to his art," which means "to express his vision of reality as well as he can."[31] There also is for the careful reader a distinction between moralism and morality, analogous to Spingarn's distinction between partisanship and the sense of *civitas.* Moralism is "the narcotic of all aesthetic discussion," and the inhibitor of free experimentation.[32] It is the vice which, in the allegorical theories of some Italian critics of the Renaissance, had made poetry "a popularized form of theology."[33] But morality, like the sense of *civitas,* is a prerequisite for being a man; in this sense it is "the content of [the poet's] work." For "It is true that art is the product of human personality, and that personality has little meaning when divorced from moral personality. . . ."[34] "You have got to be a man to write a poem and as a man you have a moral personality."[35] And, finally, there is the insistence that the incorporation of morals in art, like the use of political material, transforms this material: "Out of morals or philosophy [the artist] has to make, not morals or philosophy, but poetry; for morals and philosophy are only a part . . . of the whole reality which his imagination has to encompass. . . . It is a vision of reality, and not reality, imagination and not thought or morals, that the artist gives us."[36] Spingarn's language is certainly subject to misinterpretation. But especially the last sentence implies that his distinction is between ideal "theory" and practical partisanship, perhaps even between what "ought" to be and what is.

Spingarn's critics usually addressed this whole problem out of a concern for the *consequences* of art. Stuart Sherman charged that Spingarn was an "alien-minded" critic, whose theories, "imported from beyond the borders of Anglo-Saxonia," and elaborated by "the quick Semitic intelligence," in a "super-subtle Italian fashion," were part of a revolt being conducted by writers "whose blood and breeding are as hostile to the English strain as a cat to water." Spingarn's distinctions were such as "Charles the Second would have understood," and they were designed to liberate us "from Puritanism and from Democracy."

But the liberation would only extend "the ordinary man's preoccupation with sex"—"serving sensual gratification and propagating the curiously related doctrine that God cares nothing for the Ten Commandments or for the pure in heart." Invoking the authority of what every "American schoolboy knows," Sherman concluded that the divorce of "beauty from her traditional associates in American letters . . . has left her open to seduction"; for "Beauty, whether we like it or not, has a heart full of service."[37]

Sherman may have been suffering (in 1921 and 1925) from the aftermath of the "war psychosis" which Ludwig Lewisohn diagnosed in *Expression in America* (1932) as the motive behind Sherman's earlier book, *On Contemporary Literature* (1917). It must have been difficult, though, for Spingarn to hear Sherman argue that literature encouraged patriotism and that the business of the poet was to slip "spiritual gold-pieces" into the hands of his "fellow countrymen."[38] Spingarn made no public protest against Sherman's charges;[39] and to read, for example, Ernest Boyd's counterblast, "Ku Klux Kriticism," in *The Nation* (June 20, 1923), or "Whose Flag Is It?" in the *New Republic* (December-February, 1920-21), is not really to be enlightened about Spingarn's attitude toward poetry and morality. Spingarn's attitude toward the question of the practical moral *consequences* of artistic expression was of course simple enough: "I do not deny," he said in "Mr. Spingarn's Position" (January 14, 1925), "that everything man does is subject to a moral judgment; I merely doubt the relevance of such a judgment at a given 'moment' of the spirit."[40]

On one level, Spingarn was, of course, right; there is nothing more to be said. But, on another level, the problem returns, as can be seen in Croce's statement that "An artistic image portrays an act morally praiseworthy or blameworthy; but this image, as image, is neither morally praiseworthy or blameworthy."[41] We may agree to the idea of esthetic "distance" and agree also that art does not move the will to practical action in determinate situations; but if, as Croce admitted, art "portrays" moral judgments, if it betrays a point of view (as certainly all *language* does), then we may wish to agree with Yvor Winters that "Poetry . . . should offer a means of enriching one's awareness of human experience and of so rendering greater the possibility of intelligence in the course of future action." Thus poetry is "a civilizing influence: it trains our power of judgment, and should . . . affect the quality of daily judgments and actions."[42] And the critic, therefore, may legitimately concern himself with the civilizing influence, or its absence, in the art he criticizes.

Croce occasionally allowed for such a view,[43] but his insistence on the intuitive moment as anterior to the moment of conceptualization and his emphasis on the radical individuality of artistic intuitions made such allowances infrequent. Perhaps these difficulties inhibited Spingarn's argument, but Spingarn was aware in "The American Critic" (1931) that "in the larger sense . . . a poem may be said to be moral in so far as it aims at unity and order." Or, as he put it in the sixth New School lecture, insofar as the formal activity of "the imagination . . . creates a kind of order out of chaos . . . [it] may be said to be moral in the sense in which any ordering . . . [of] the universe is a moral order."

Spingarn's failure to develop this sense of morality may derive in part from Croce's difficult distinction between image and concept or from Croce's limitation of morals to "practice," but it seems also to be a function of Spingarn's own determination to meet the sloganeers on their own ground by a flat denial of moralistic didacticism. Ironically, his decision only encouraged the formula makers. Even Ludwig Lewisohn charged him, as we have seen, with being "a New Yorker and a Jew" whose "tissue of international borrowings . . . thoroughly falsified the moral seriousness of his inheritance."[44]

V   *Literature and Philosophy*

Spingarn's approach to the problem of poetry and philosophy, poetry and truth, repeats the tale already thrice-told. In his effort to demolish what he thought of as naïve didacticism he could write: "Sense, sense, nothing but sense! as if poetry . . . were not always a kind of nonsense. . . . logic is not the arbitress of art." But he also admitted that poetry "gives a different kind of truth than philosophy but still a truth."[45] The poet intuits the spiritual background, the inward human necessity, out of which philosophy grows. But, conversely, unless his sensibility has assimilated philosophical material, he will be the poorer in experience, an incomplete man, and a lesser poet. In the second of his New School lectures Spingarn observed that "Perhaps the reason why Mr. Sinclair Lewis is not a greater writer than he is . . . is because his philosopher was only Mr. Mencken."

After laboring to confine poetry to the treatment of the individual image and philosophy to the treatment of the conceptual relations between images, Spingarn ended by seeming to merge the two: "The poet needs a philosopher behind him. . . . Here is this enormous world pouring into him all the impressions that it can give. . . . It is a chaos. How can you get order out of it? Why some philosopher can give it to you. He can have some contact with some philosopher that will give rest to his spirit."[46]

But poetry itself has been defined as a formal act, as a subduing of chaotic impressions to theoretic order. The old question returns. Why are there two theoretical moments? How are they different? Is not true philosophy "musical as is Apollo's lute"? Is it not, too, superior to logic-chopping? Is not literature a completion of philosophy, a condition toward which the most sophisticated and most subtle philosophy is always tending, and which such philosophy may in fact achieve through a full exploitation of the resources of the expressive medium? Except for Spingarn's temperamental commitment to Romantic theories of inspiration and his intellectual commitment to a Crocean vocabulary which makes poetry anterior to philosophy, Spingarn might well have answered affirmatively.

Perhaps such an answer would have received from the guerilla fighters of the time no more respectful hearing than was accorded any other voice of sanity in those years; it might, nevertheless, have clarified for Spingarn himself the final large problem of his esthetic—the problem of how the practicing critic is to get on with his job. His efforts to deal with this problem were handicapped by his unwillingness to admit openly the relevance of conceptual thought to esthetic expression. This problem and Spingarn's treatment of it are the subject of the next two chapters.

CHAPTER 7

Criticism of Criticism

SPINGARN did not deny that literary criticism was, at least in part, a judicial activity. But the party platforms of Babbitt—or of the Marxists, or of whomever—were not the simple answer to questions of esthetic value. The popular use of the word *criticism* in the 1920's had little more to do with genuine literary criticism than "a clothes-horse has to do with a real horse, or a geometrical circle with a literary circle, or a progressive euchre party with the Progressive Party, or a firing line with a line of verse."[1] The task of making discriminations of esthetic value was a complicated and delicate operation beset by subtle epistemological problems.

In "The New Criticism" Spingarn had hinted at the difficulties when he said that masculine and feminine forms of literary response always fall "short of their highest powers, unless mystically mated,—judgment erecting its edicts into arbitrary standards and conventions, enjoyment lost in the mazes of its sensuous indecision." In the sixth New School lecture he said: artistic judgment "is a combination of concrete fact and the universal category." It is "eternal and temporary. . . . Eternal because it is a statement of truth in terms of a universal category which is art. And relative because it is a relationship to a particular problem."

I Critical Judgment and Impressionistic Sympathy

Spingarn is emphasizing here the Crocean perspectives which had, as we have noted, contributed to the development of "objective relativism" in the new American historical studies of the 1920's; and, as we shall see, the Crocean idea of history formed an important part of Spingarn's program for literary criticism. But Spingarn's attempts to define the universal category of art, as already noted, brought their own special difficulties. The mystical marriage he called for was a mysterious ceremony. Of course, the union of principle and particular has always been difficult: it is an imaginative act; yet, to borrow Blackmur's language, the imagination, though free in one sense, must be "convicted" in any particular exercise of the faculty. Or, as Spingarn put it, "the relativity of taste does not in any sense affect its authority."[2] But, in emphasizing that the problem of judgment in literary criticism was an epistemological problem, Spingarn seemed to want to reduce the practicing literary critic to virtual silence.

However sound Spingarn's theoretical position was, it could hardly please the critics of the 1920's, who were nothing if not vocal. Even Woodberry thought the two questions, which Spingarn had attributed to Goethe, about the artist's "intention" and his success in fulfilling it barred the critic from "interpretation," and so Woodberry wanted to add a third question about "the wisdom of what is said." Randolph Bourne had early written that Spingarn's failure to ask this third question amounted to a renunciation of critical judgment. Bernard Smith and James Farrell made essentially the same charge, as did the neo-Humanists from Babbitt and More to Foerster, Sherman, Hartwick, and Shafer.[3] Babbitt concluded somewhat pompously that "Mr. Spingarn owes the public an explanation of how he came to reduce Goethe's three questions to two, with the result of transforming him from an Aristotelian humanist into a Crocean aesthete."[4]

Usually those who complained of Spingarn's neglect of a "third question" were understandably confused about his Crocean use of *expression*. They thought he recognized a difference between the thing expressed and the expression, that he wished to confine the critic to a discussion of the means of expression, and that he forbade discussion of "content." They did not recognize that, for Spingarn, the thing expressed was known only in the expression. But even those, like Robert Shafer, who understood him on this point, complained that this very identity of meaning and expression made critical judgment impossible: for, if each expression generates its own unique meaning, "every contribution to literature must be uncritically accepted just as it is."[5]

It is clear that Spingarn had intended nothing of this kind. From his point of view, his opponents were interested only in measuring art by practical formulas; and, in his own practical zeal to combat their errors, his negatives overwhelmed his insistence on standards, even in such pieces as "Grocer-Shop Criticism" (1914) and "The Younger Generation" (1922). To be told, however emphatically, that the critic must invoke standards that are "internal and vital," or that criticism must be "guided by knowledge and thought,"[6] is not necessarily to be enlightened on just how to proceed, especially if the category of art remains a category of the unique.

The tangle Spingarn got into through his sense of the tactical situation is illustrated by his quotation, or misquotation, of Goethe. The full text was of course given when he edited *Goethe's Literary Essays* in 1921. But he omitted Goethe's "third question" (Was the author's "plan reasonable and sensible . . . ?"[7]) in "The New Criticism," apparently because he feared it would suggest to his contemporaries an identification between the criticism of literature and the criticism of practical affairs. Even before Babbitt asked for his "explanation," Spingarn had referred to the disputed quotation as "one of Goethe's most casual utterances," and with mock humility he expressed chagrin that any misunderstanding should have arisen through "the mere accident of quotation." And, when he reprinted "The Growth of a Literary Myth" in 1931, he explained that his original use of Goethe had been motivated by the need to combat "the academic dry rot of that day." But, when he added that Goethe's questions referred, in any event, not to the practical effects of art, but to art's "universal side," we feel that even then Spingarn was being evasive about the job of the critic.[8]

The fault, however, was not all Spingarn's. The difficulties of being precise were compounded even by the misrepresentations of his friends. Ludwig Lewisohn had included one of Spingarn's essays in his *Modern Book of Criticism* (1919); and, amid many wild exaggerations in the Introduction, he had grouped Spingarn with the other "shivering young Davids" of criticism who, "slim and frail but with a glint of morning sunshine on their foreheads," were marching out to "face an army of Goliaths." As captain of this company of young Davids, Lewisohn addressed the enemy (in the person of Paul Elmer More) as follows: "I love beauty in all its forms and find life tragic and worthy of my sympathy in every manifestation. I need no hierarchical world for my dwelling-place, because I desire neither to judge nor to condemn."[9]

It is not surprising that Mr. More was not felled by Lewisohn's missile, nor is it surprising that he did not bother to distinguish exactly which one of the troops had fired it. When More asserted that Spingarn taught that "art is only expression and criticism only impression, and that no one need bother to hunt for standards of taste, which are not and never were"—he was probably directing his assertion at *all* the "shivering young Davids" indiscriminately, rather than at Mr. Spingarn particularly. Carelessness seems to have been the order of the day. James Farrell, for example, could quote from "The New Criticism" to prove that for Spingarn expressionism was a synonym for Impressionism, even though the passage he cited was an elaboration of the arguments of an hypothetical Impressionist for the purpose of refuting them![10]

Spingarn did find, however, in the responsive "sympathy" of the Impressionist and in his lack of prejudice a kind of first requisite for the practicing critic. The "anarchy of impressionism" *was* "a natural reaction against the mechanical theories and jejune text-books of the professors." But it was only "a temporary haven and not a home," for serious critics could never be satisfied with criticism "in which 'ideas' are struck out in random and irresponsible flashes like sparks from the anvil of a gnome."[11]

Beyond the Impressionist's sympathetic responsiveness, the critic needed "a rounded scholarship" and "a deeper brooding on the meaning of beauty."[12] Bernard Smith was alone among Spingarn's contemporaries in understanding that Spingarn was distinguished from the Impressionists by his desire to save "learning" from extinction.[13] The rest, from the genteel Woodberry to a Marxist like Granville Hicks,[14] suspected him of wanting to disregard scholarship. The confusion may have been caused in part, as Smith said, by Spingarn's "sneers at pedantry"; but it also derived from a failure to understand Spingarn's idea that scholarship itself was a "spiritual discipline." True literary scholarship led the critic to regard literature "as an art and not merely as a document in the history of a nation's culture"[15] because it clearly proved that art was always *more* than its external causes and unpredictable in its practical effects. Spingarn did not deny that art had causes (though he despaired of finding them, or found them only when art had not been completely achieved); nor did he deny that art had practical effects (though he thought that they should be referred to the moralist). But he did not think the literary critic should use his scholarship to tell the history of these causes and effects, except in so far as doing so would help define what had not risen to the level of true expression.[16] This part of the job was negative. For the rest he wanted the critic to use his scholarship to help the business of esthetic reproduction.

For Spingarn, criticism *was* an act of the "convicted imagination"; the critic must listen to the "evidence," but then he must pray for grace. Spingarn insisted most strongly that there was always an unexplained margin that could be accounted for only by "taste"; "To look for a poet's power outside of his work rather than in it, to assume that his relation to his environment is of any concern whatever to a lover or critic of poetry, is to confuse criticism and sociology." The language is extreme (as Spingarn acknowledged when he reprinted this essay, "The Seven Arts and the Seven Confusions," in 1931); but the intention is clear.

The same intention had prompted him to say in the New School lectures: "biography helps us only to explain what is not art, what is not thought in the thinker. . . . What is not his real thought, where he does not rise to theory, that is explained by his empirical personality. What does [rise to theory] is never explained. . . . we all feel that when we read a work of art we want to read it without the intrusion of the empirical personality of the artist."[17] Romantic critics in America, from Emerson to Stedman, had long insisted on the reality of genius and inspiration. Spingarn was adding his voice to theirs, but he made his plea at a time when most critics were embarrassed by such language and convinced that true answers were sociological or psychiatric, or, in the case of the neo-Humanists, moralistic.

II *Practical Criticism*

Spingarn's role as a cautionary theoretician interested in negative admonition may account in large measure for his failure to produce concrete examples of the art of criticism. The failure was noted as early as 1917 in a review of Spingarn's *Creative Criticism* in the *Times Literary Supplement*; and the next year Van Wyck Brooks pointed it out. So did Mencken in 1919.[18] Since that time almost every writer who has discussed Spingarn's ideas has commented on this failure. And many have suggested that the nature of his ideas, rather than the tactical exigencies of American critical debate, explain the failure.

Bernard Smith argued that Spingarn had not replaced the things he had cast out with a criterion of taste that "we can scrutinize"; instead, he has introduced a "creative" taste "too mystical to talk about": "We must be Shakespeare when we write of Shakespeare, Baudelaire when we write of Baudelaire, and Ezra Pound when we write of *him*." Smith concluded that "of course there never were such critics," and Henri Peyre agreed with him: "Such 'creative criticism,' " he said, "would loom so formidably that it would instantly kill the critical ambitions of nine-tenths of the present writers of reviews, essays and monographs." V. F. Calverton wrote that Spingarn's theory was simply "a delicate evasion of the main issues involved in the problem of criticism." Stuart Sherman agreed with the Marxists.[19]

Spingarn's theory denies the possibility of a formula for practical criticism because it denies the possibility of a formula for art. The critic may discover what the poet has done (or what he should have done), but he can prove his discovery only by rewriting the poem. Critics who aspire to such achievement have only the pedagogic devices of the studio and their own "taste" to guide them. The first, Spingarn did not choose to discuss in any detail; the second, he could describe only negatively. Maybe H. L. Mencken was right: "the transcendental, to some extent at least, must be done into common modes of thinking." In literary criticism "what are morality, trochaics, hexameters, movements, historical principles, psychological maxims, the dramatic unities—what are all these save common modes of thinking, short-cuts, rubber stamps, words of one syllable?" We would certainly not wish that Spingarn had taken over Mencken's whole vocabulary of one-syllable *words*, however "common" (or uncommon) it might be. And, if Mencken's trumpetings on behalf of Theodore Dreiser were an example of "the critical ambitions of nine-tenths of the present writers of reviews, essays and monographs," Spingarn simply was not interested. But some concession to the "empirical approach" would have helped. For, as Mencken said, "The really competent critic must be an empiricist. He must conduct his exploration with whatever means lie within the bounds of his personal limitation. He must produce his effect with whatever tools will work. If pills fail, he gets out his saw. If the saw won't cut, he seizes a club."[20] Spingarn had no scruples about using a club when he was criticizing criticism. But he would not permit the critic to use one when he was criticizing a work of art. Empiricism was at best a preliminary to the spiritual act. And the exact connections between practice and theory must always remain unpredictable.

In the New School lectures, Spingarn agreed that the poet "can't express his state of mind, his form, without using meters, modulations, rhythms, stanzas, free verse, whatnot." But—because these things, once incorporated in a poem, "disappear as a part of the unified state of mind" of the poet, and because, as abstractions, they become "what he shares with everybody, not . . . his own particular state of mind,"—they are not "the real concern of criticism," which is "the special and unique quality of a poet's work." Spingarn had concluded in "The New Criticism" that "what must always be inexplicable to mere reflection is just what gives power to poetry."[21]

Perhaps Spingarn shared in the recurrent yearning of the American in the wilderness for purity, the Romantic yearning of Poe for pure Beauty, Emerson's yearning for the Oversoul, Ahab's concern for naked confrontation, or Henry Adams' stubborn, persistent pursuit of ultimate solutions in pure abstraction. The work of the masters of the American novel—beginning with Hawthorne's "romances," and not excluding Mark Twain's archetypal fables, or Henry James' mannerly myths, or the work even of Fitzgerald and Hemingway, and certainly of Faulkner—

tends to seem allegorical when measured alongside the novels of Jane Austen, Dickens, Thackeray, Trollope, H. G. Wells, or E. M. Forster. Perhaps we may also suggest that Spingarn understood that side of the American psyche which feels, because of the relative absence of received traditional modes of accommodation, naked and defenseless in the face of brute fact.[22]

As we have seen in Spingarn's comments on American historians, he felt the dangers of being overwhelmed by unassimilated data seen close-up, raw and random. In "The New Criticism" everything is distanced in theory, however polemical the tone; and it is characteristic that in his later critical essays too Spingarn avoided discussing contemporary authors, only giving the barest mention to Sinclair Lewis, Robert Frost, and T. S. Eliot in his unpublished lectures at the New School for Social Research in 1931 (though he had included an essay by Eliot in his anthology of *Criticism in America* in 1924), and never undertaking to discuss Fitzgerald, Hemingway, Dreiser, or Pound. Even in addressing himself to the work of critics, he was most willing to engage Irving Babbitt, whose heavy theoretical bias provided an opportunity for the kind of argument Spingarn managed best.

Spingarn's scholarly training had taught him that facts demanded patient respect and that their ordering required discipline. But he had been early convinced of the need for creative insight, and the task of combining fact and theory—without vulgarizing the one or smothering the fire of the other—had posed a dilemma for him in his scholarly career like the one he faced in trying to elaborate a methodology for literary criticism. His experience as a scholar and his idea of a university had developed in him a growing conviction that the patient study of the great works of the past was a fitter exercise for the critical imagination than partisan dispute about current fashion. And yet he was engaged in urging the value of historical perspective as a pressing practical necessity for the present.

During the last of his New School lectures, one of his audience asked Spingarn to list "a few of the contemporary English and American poets who would be poets according to the standard you have set up." Spingarn's lengthy refusal to make such a list is mostly an attack on the habits of professors of contem-

porary literature, who make lists readily enough, but who have
not found out what art is by studying the great art of all time,
and who arrogate to themselves a right of final judgment that
ultimately must be borne by "the secular sense of humanity."
The present is apt to be entangled in practice and prejudice.
Americans, he said, above all need to know the distance of
the past.

But then Spingarn did offer a brief criticism of Robert Frost,
based on the distinction between the theoretical and the practical, between ideality and actuality, between the pure and the
impure:

> You hear him read his poems and you feel by an *immediate intuition of
> taste* that you have been lifted out of your . . . apprehension of the prac-
> tical. . . .
>   But the fact is that there are other things; that when Robert Frost reads
> to you, *something* tells you, your own taste, [that] there is some little
> quirk of eccentricity in him perhaps, as charming a poet as he is, maybe
> there is the practical coming out, some hobby of his, some little prejudice,
> and there you feel you are not lifted into that pure sense of theory which
> if you have any artistic taste you almost *immediately recognize.*

As an example of applied criticism, these remarks are only suggestive. Spingarn would not say more. He concluded quite
simply and, we may imagine, with a shrug: "I don't care to give
a catalogue. In each poet you will see you find something theoretical, something practical."[23] Spingarn had said in 1910 that
"art's pale shadow, thought" was inadequate to wrest final answers from "the silent sons of light." In 1931 he said that "contact with a poem or a great work of art is essentially a thrilling
experience, nothing that at the first impact can be reasoned
about or thought of, but something that in itself is a life and a
full life."[24] Spingarn had always been more interested in "life,"
the "full life,"—in the "life of the spirit"—than in the "little
questions" of practical criticism.

In *Literary Criticism in the Renaissance* Spingarn had admitted his preference for "theory" and "principles" over "the
methods and results of applied, or concrete, criticism," which
too often became "merely" discussion of "external form" and
thus "trivial and futile." But in this same book he praised "that
criticism which has its eyes directly on the poet's page."[25]

Admiration for such criticism is implied also throughout his
later work, and it is undoubtedly this attitude that made some
critics group Spingarn with the "aesthetic school." But it is
clear that he was not of that school, if by esthetic criticism is
meant formal rhetorical analysis—for that Spingarn considered
empirical busy work. Such work was more or less irrelevant to
theoretical synthesis in criticism in the same way that German
philological scholarship was irrelevant. It was perhaps compara-
ble to the fact-finding activities of the new historians: interesting, even useful in a preliminary way, but mainly an amusement
for the scholar's idle times and not a constitutive element in
his creative work.

The introduction to *Critical Essays of the Seventeenth Century* provides part of the answer to how Spingarn could reject
the "empirical" criticism of "externals" and yet demand that
the critic keep his "eyes directly on the poet's page." In that
Introduction he praised Thomas Rymer for having encouraged
critics in the use of "concrete illustration and comparison"
(lxiv-lxvi). Rymer was wrong, said Spingarn, in his concern for
"set themes" (and for his moralistic and intellectualistic carp-
ing); but he was right in citing "illustrations" of his views and in
his practice of "comparative criticism": "It is something to have
transferred the concrete beauties of poetry to the pages of criticism, something to have illustrated that criticism by comparison
which Saint-Evremond was urging as a substitute for criticism
by precept and rule, and to have anticipated that method of
judging by particulars, by examples and illustrations." In the
nominalistic world of art, precepts will discover similarities; but
particularities, the concrete examples which escape rules, may
discover art. If the critic is mostly silent, it may be in the end
the touchstones that will tell.

The critic may begin with the sympathy of the Impressionist;
he may add scholarship and learning; he may cite examples of
achieved art and make comparisons; but Spingarn's concern for
the ideal "spirit" of art made him reluctant to handle its body.
He refused to discuss the anatomy of the art work for fear of
betraying the organic principle of its life. The refusal led him
even to distort Crocean doctrine.

III   *The Artistic Medium and Technique*

It is true that Croce had said that "the beautiful has no physical existence," that the decision to communicate an intuition to others comes "under the utilitarian and ethical criterion,"[26] and that the success of communication is a technical or practical matter. But Croce's meaning was *not,* as many of his critics assumed, that the artist's medium has no importance at all in the process of creation or re-creation. He was only insisting that the physical existence of the completed art work gives rise to moral and utilitarian considerations concerning the *effects* of that work in the world of practice, and that these practical effects are not the concern of the artist as artist or of the esthetic critic.

Furthermore, Croce was insisting that, if an artist, having "fixed" his intuition internally, should will to externalize his work, he might do so badly. Such problems of externalization are matters of "technique" as Croce used that word. It is possible that the artist may be careless in producing with his chisel, brush, or pen the physical embodiment of an already "achieved" vision, and thus betray that vision. It is possible that indiscriminate communication of the artist's completed vision through a physical embodiment of that vision may be immoral from the practical point of view. But such lack of moral judgment and such technical failure are not identical with failure of intuition.[27]

Croce did *not* deny that the artist's medium is important *esthetically.* In fact, the medium is obviously *part* of the artist's completed intuition, whether the intuition is externalized or not. That intuition and its appreciation are mental or spiritual phenomena; but Croce certainly admitted that, during the act of creation and before expression has been achieved, many artists need to work with a physical medium as well as with an imagined one; they may need to experiment to discover their intuition, their expression; and the critic may wish to repeat the process.

Croce himself was interested in differentiating the whole process of intuition-expression from the idea of physical beauty in order to emphasize the central importance of the creative spirit, whether of artist or critic, over the physical details of the art object, which have no existence at all except insofar as they are interpreted by the mind. But pedagogic directives, whether about materials or techniques, "do some good," Croce admitted, "by aiding artists to discover themselves, that is, their own impressions and their own inspiration, and to acquire consciousness of the task which is, as it were, imposed upon them by the historical moment in which they live, and by their individual temperament." Such a directive "generates" nothing, but "merely recognizes and aids the expressions, which are already being formed. It believes itself to be the mother, where, at most, it is only the midwife."[28]

Croce's description of the process of creation helped prepare the way for a commonplace of modern criticism: that technical experimentation is a means of "discovering" subject matter and that the study of such experimentation is relevant to criticism insofar as it leads to an appreciation of achieved style. For, just as "the writer cannot know his subject until he knows it through form," so for the critic "technique [is] the means by which we describe the material itself." Cleanth Brooks acknowledged Croce's importance in establishing such a view by quoting from Louis Urban, whose *Language and Reality* is an effort to draw the consequences from, and give greater consistency to, Croce's identification of intuition and expression: "The artist does not first intuit his object and then find an appropriate medium. It is rather in and through his medium that he intuits his object."[29]

Spingarn insisted on Croce's point long before Urban and Brooks took it over. But sometimes Spingarn insisted so vehemently on the inextricable involvement of form with content, idea with medium, that he seemed, when he came to discuss criticism rather than art, to go beyond anything that Croce had intended in disabling the critic from practicing his craft. He rejected stylistic and rhetorical analysis because, as he said in "The New Criticism," this approach rested on "the assumption that style is separate from expression, . . . an external embellishment, instead of the poet's individual vision of reality, the music of his whole manner of being."

When Spingarn wrote that "The technique of poetry cannot be separated from its inner nature," he was, in one sense, only repeating the Romantic doctrine of organic form. But the doctrine, as he developed it, had consequences for the practicing critic: "only physical things can be measured, and . . . what can be so measured in a poet's verse, or in any other work of art, is without artistic value, and a matter of complete indifference to all true criticism." Therefore, "To deal with abstract classifications instead of artistic realities,—versification instead of poetry, grammar instead of language, technique instead of painting,—is to confuse form as concrete expression with form as an ornament or dead husk."[30] How to deal with form as "concrete expression" Spingarn does not say. Far from overemphasizing the cult of form, as Farrell, Henry Seidel Canby, Lewisohn, and Sherman charged,[31] he seemed to err in the other direction.

In Spingarn's essay on "Dramatic Criticism and the Theatre" (originally published in 1913) and in the debate with A. B. Walkley that followed, some glimmering of a way out of the dilemma posed by the absolute identification of form and content is discernible. In this essay, for example, Spingarn explained his view of the relationship "between inner impulse and outer influence" as follows:

A poet, let us say, finds that a brisk walk stimulates his writing, or that he can write more easily when he has smoked a cigarette. The walk or the cigarette has not produced the poetry. It opens the faucet, but who would be so foolish as to maintain that it produces or alters the water that gushes forth? Other poets find that they cannot write easily without the stimulus of imagined reward,—money, the plaudits of the crowd, the resplendent beauty of theatrical performance. . . . whatever the imaginary stimulus, there is only one real urge in the poet's soul, to express what is in him, to body forth his own vision of reality as well as he can.

This passage admits, but much more grudgingly than Croce's remarks about midwifery, the pedagogic value of external acts. In his New School lectures Spingarn went a bit further: he admitted that Longinus' comments about the imitation of models were "useful," the "first stage in education" (VI, 28), and he allowed some heuristic value also to the prescription of subject matter in the same spirit in which he had earlier welcomed the experiments of the artists exhibited in the Armory Show of 1913, or had conceded that "empirical observations" might have educative value for the novice in matters of manners.

The polemical fervor, however, with which Spingarn emphasized the "internal" as opposed to the "external" part of the esthetic process led him, in "Dramatic Criticism and the Theatre,"
almost to destroy the critical process. His statements are so extreme as to be explainable only on the grounds that he was less
interested in propagating Crocean doctrine than in stamping out
American heresy. These were the years of Brander Matthews'
ascendancy in the universities and George Jean Nathan's popu-
larity in the journals—a time of popular superficiality in scholarship and glib exhibitionism in criticism. These were the years
also in which the importance of theatrical success as a criterion
for measuring the value of a play seemed to threaten the de-
struction of serious drama. The subordination of the dramatist
to the theatrical "star" and to commercial and managerial
circumstance had begun in the nineteenth century. Spingarn was
revolting against the system as it operated in the twentieth.[32]

Spingarn had attacked critical overemphasis on the external
conditions of the theater, on "dramaturgic formulae," and on
the "psychology of the crowd" in both his *Literary Criticism in
the Renaissance* and his Introduction to *Critical Essays of the
Seventeenth Century.* He argued that "stage representation can
never circumscribe the poetic power or establish its conditions."[33] It is clear that his main point was the same in 1913
when he wrote "Dramatic Criticism and the Theatre." But in
the later essay, bent on dealing with an actual condition of the
American theater,[34] he went to un-Crocean extremes. He said,
for example, that "for criticism the theatre simply does not exist." He explained that, "when . . . artistic souls appear, theatres
will spring up like mushrooms to house them, and the humblest
garret will serve as an eryie for their art."

A. B. Walkley had objected (in "Criticism and Croce," the
London *Times,* March 20, 1911) to some of Spingarn's un-
Crocean exaggerations about the theater in "The New Criticism." But Walkley's rebuttal seemed to conceive stage production to be a method of adapting the dramatic intuition to the
exigencies of externalization and not to be a part of intuition
itself. He did not seem to understand that in the Crocean view
the artist could not conceive an intuition without conceiving
also the means of externalization.

When Walkley took up the problem again in 1926 in a rebuttal to Spingarn's "Dramatic Criticism and the Theatre," he seemed to have resolved his own confusion (to which he made oblique reference) and also to have defined the reason for Spingarn's confusion:

Spingarn is on the side of the angels, all for the spirit and against the material. . . . And the irony, I had almost said the pathos, [is] that fate has decreed him to be an apostle of Croce *in partibus,* I mean among the Americans, whom I take to be by temperament and traditions, the most un-Crocean or anti-Crocean of all the nations of the earth. In a society where the practical has long held the field of letters, from Benjamin Franklin to Dr. Frank Crane, Mr. Spingarn has remained impenitently academic. . . . Truth to tell, the zeal of the new convert at first outran his discretion.

And so Spingarn has become "plus Arabe que l'Arabe" in "narrowing the Crocean theory of art" so as to exclude a consideration by the critic of the expressive medium. Walkley then cited Croce's statement, in *Problemi di Estetica* (1910), that "artistic intuition . . . *takes account* of the materials to be used," and of "determined conditions and presuppositions; among which are [the artist's] own practical needs and those of the people to whom his work is addressed." Thus Walkley concluded that "Questions about the shape of the stage, the capacities of the actors, the psychology of the audience are *not,* in the Crocean theory, irrelevant to the question of dramatic art. The dramatist, like any other artist, produces his work of art by the process of pure intuition, but in the field of his intuition he takes care to include the practical conditions which affect his work."[35]

Walkley's point is well taken. In "Dramatic Criticism and the Theatre" Spingarn was attacking the heresy of "external form" and so he understandably enough remembered Croce's statement that "*there is no passage* from the physical fact to the aesthetic." But he forgot that "in each particular case certain given artistic intuitions have need of definite physical means for their reproduction and other artistic intuitions of other means."[36] He forgot what he would remember in "The American Critic": "the technique of art is part of the material out of which the artist fashions his creations." He often seemed to forget also that in the disputed essay itself he had written: "dramatic criticism . . . is concerned with externals, including the theatre, . . . in so far as they appear in dramatic literature itself." He emphasized that "these external conditions are merely dead material which has no aesthetic significance outside the poet's soul" and forgot to discuss their significance *in* the poet's soul—or the critic's.

Spingarn later saw the error of his ways. In "The Growth of a Literary Myth" (1923), he referred to "the obvious weaknesses of my . . . essay on 'Dramatic Criticism and the Theatre' " and admitted that Walkley was "perhaps . . . right." And in the draft of a personal letter to Walkley in April, 1926, he confirmed Walkley's guess about the reasons for his "error":

> if you will recall the condition of literary and dramatic criticism in America twelve or fifteen years ago, you will understand why a challenge and a stimulus seemed more necessary than a careful statement of aesthetic theory. My purpose, I suppose, was more practical then theoretical in Croce's sense of "la practica." . . . The dramatic essay was not so much to interpret him or even to convert people to his views as to use him for the benefit of American literature.

However concerned Spingarn was with "la practica" as a part of the spiritual life, his concern for the "theoretical" nature of art discouraged an interest in practical criticism. He wrote to Bradley (March 11, 1932): "my enthusiasm for Croce . . . was a theoretical and not a practical ardor, the enthusiasm of a man who had discovered a new theory in his chosen field and wanted to expound it to all who would listen." As we have noted, he thought Americans needed first of all education in esthetic theory;[37] and, though his expounding of theory was, ironically, compromised by practical conditions, Spingarn's interest was still in the theory of art and not in the practice of criticism. Croce himself had said, in *Ariosto, Shakespeare, and Corneille*, that practical analysis "will be of use in schools, to promote good reading, and outside them, it may assist in softening those hard heads which belong sometimes to men of letters."[38] But Spingarn was unwilling to play the schoolmaster, however much the children of criticism might have needed his instruction.

IV   *The Schoolmaster and the Critic: The Problem of Language*

Croce was more willing than Spingarn to admit the importance of the schoolmaster's job. Echoing Croce, Spingarn had admitted that more or less blind experimentation with his medium might help the artist to bring his intuition to clarity, that a non-esthetic action (taking a walk or smoking a cigarette) might act as a stimulus to esthetic activity, even that experimentation was the very life of art. But Croce conceded that for the critic the rules of "kind" and "class" might have a kind of pragmatic value. So also the "rules" of grammar, rhetoric, and prosody; and the "classification" of literary genres might after all become useful to critics—even to artists. But there is nothing inevitable or final, he said, about the help they can give to either: "Everything depends upon not confounding hints with reality, and hypothetic warnings or imperatives with categoric imperatives."[39]

Spingarn's approach to the question of the practical aids available to the critic was not so careful as Croce's. He had early set the tone of his emphasis when he wrote in "The New Criticism": (1910) "There are not . . . only three, or ten, or a hundred literary kinds; there are as many kinds as there are individual poets." How far he was willing to go along the road to nominalism he made clear in his essay on "Prose and Verse" (1917), in which he denied the relevance of metrical scansion in critical discussion: "All we can say is that out of the infinite variations of rhythm, we may conveniently classify the more irregular as prose and the more regular as verse." The convenience of metrical labels was, for Spingarn, little more than the convenience of a reference filing system. And thus, even the pragmatic value of such classifications was, for criticism, almost nil: "a classification intended merely for convenience can never furnish a vital basis for criticism; and for criticism the question of versification, as something separate from the inner texture of poetry, simply does not exist."[40] Few critics would argue with Spingarn's condemnation of the discussion of versification *separated* from poetry. What we miss, however, is the definition of a method of discussing that versification which is *integral* with "the inner texture of poetry."

Spingarn said, in "Prose and Verse," that "what is true of metre is also aesthetically true of language itself. To speak of 'learning a language' is to risk the danger of . . . confusion, for we do not learn a language, we learn how to create it." Thus, "figures of speech" cannot be learned as guides to linguistic meaning; "style" is an intellectual construct after the fact of ex-

pression, and esthetically it is not separate from expression but
"part and parcel of its inner being. If 'lion-hearted' be only another way of saying 'brave,' why use one rather than the other?
Or if they mean something different, however slight, why say
that one is used for the other at all?"[41] The pragmatic answer
to Spingarn's query is that we must have some way of talking
about what are, admittedly, theoretically incommensurate units;
and that tentative, conditional categories of similitude, "abstract" though they be, are one such means.

Spingarn's view of language was, of course, derived from
Croce's idea of language as expressive intuition. Croce rejected
the view that language is primarily a set of conventional signs
employed according to conventional lexicographical, grammati-
cal, and rhetorical rules; for such a system of reference is possible only after the significances that it deals with have come into
being. And, strictly speaking, there is never any such "after,"
because each utterance, though it "uses" old forms, "dislocates"
them, as T. S. Eliot would say, into new meanings. Thus, "language is no longer conceived as a sign, but as an image which is
significant—that is, a sign in itself, and therefore coloured,
sounding, singing, articulate."[42] As E. F. Carritt asserted in *The
Theory of Beauty,* "Language only has a meaning for me when
in hearing it I express myself in it." Carritt quoted R. L.
Nettleship, " 'We say what *we* mean . . . ,' " and then he added:
"the most plausible explanation of a parrot's inability to
converse is that he has really nothing to say. . . ."[43]

Croce, of course, admitted to a kind of conventional relationship between the word and the concept; but he pointed out that
the conceptual significance of language is only a partial use
of words:

The concept, the universal, considered abstractly in itself, is *inexpressible.*
No word is proper to it. So true is this that the logical concept remains the
same, notwithstanding the variation of verbal forms. In respect to the concept, expression is a simple *sign* or *indication.* There must be an expression, it cannot be absent. . . . [But] The quality of the expression is not
deducible from the nature of the concept. There does not exist a true
(logical) sense of words. The true sense of words is that which is conferred
upon them on each occasion by the person forming a concept.[44]

Croce's view is not new, for Coleridge perhaps hinted at the
problem: "A man of Genius using a rich and expressive language

. . . is an excellent instance and illustration of the ever individualizing process and dynamic Being, of Ideas. What a magnificent
History of acts of individual minds, sanctioned by the collective
Mind of the Country, a Language is. . . . How rightly shall we
conceive this marvellous Result, a Language? A chaos grinding
itself into compatibility."[45]

Because Coleridge is not committed to Croce's separation of
image and concept, he seems to offer the critic a balance between the "individualizing process" and "the collective Mind,"
between "chaos" and "compatibility." George Santayana insisted upon the need to emphasize the *second* of the terms in
these pairings, as a prerequisite for getting any critical work
done at all. Addressing himself to Croce's theory of language,
Santayana agreed that a word is, theoretically, "a synthesis
reached by creative genius" and not a sign. But, practically
speaking, it is never used without conceptual reference:

it may ultimately become a sign; and its destiny in that respect is precisely
what renders language steadily and usefully articulate and different from
music. If speech never became symbolic it would remain in that region of
irrecoverable scintillations and dreams which is still haunted by the music
and vague suggestions of poetry; it would not have become an instrument
for practical communication and rational discourse. Though prose may be
an afterthought, prose fortunately exists, and we cannot very well deny
that to communicate ideas is a function which even "aesthetic" language
occasionally subserves. Discourse without concepts . . . may be momentari-
ly sufficient for that contemptible entity, the abstract poet, whose mind is
a barren kaleidoscope for the endless intuition of everything, but [it] is
nevertheless singularly tedious to the sensitive, political, and thinking
animal properly called man.[46]

Santayana reversed Croce's emphasis and thus enfranchised
the critic. In Spingarn's occasional remarks about language, we
sense a super-Crocean emphasis that may, at the very outset of
his literary speculations, have fixed his fear of abstractions so as
virtually to debar the critic from talking at all: "there is no
equivalent," he said, "for [any] expression except itself."[47]
Under these circumstances, it would be nearly impossible to
provide a practical guide to help the critic "create" his own language or re-create that of the artist: esthetic "meanings," being
always individual and untranslatable, would tend to remain
outside the categories of practical criticism.

In Spingarn's approach to the problem of distinguishing prose
from verse, concept from intuition, and sign from symbol, he
was obviously dogged by his old fear that the age in which he
lived was "giving itself up more and more to abstractions and
classifications rather than realities." To an idealist, who found
reality only in the fiery core of personality, where the job of
making arbitrary divisions (even that between theory and practice) is notoriously hazardous, such a surrender was death. Thus
it was that, for Spingarn, "the ever-recurring malady of critics"
was "to formulate new abstractions on the basis of a dead art,
and to 'wish them' on the artists of a day still living."[48] Though
Spingarn certainly enjoined the critic to make value judgments,
though he acknowledged, in his calmer moments, the esthetic
significance of the artistic medium in judging works of art, he
seemed, in his suspicion of abstract thought in the realm of
esthetic judgment, almost to recommend the abandonment of
articulate practical criticism in favor of the silent exercise of
"taste."[49] Almost, but not quite—for in the next chapter we
shall see how Spingarn hoped to combine Impressionist sympathy, scholarly learning, taste, and judgment in a criticism which
was, in a special Crocean sense, "historical criticism."

CHAPTER *8*

Criticism and History

IT SEEMS UNKIND, even unjust, to emphasize Spingarn's failure to provide a guide to practical criticism. For, as he said, such guides can inhibit rather than encourage insight. Before dogma comes understanding; before conviction, imagination; before judgment, experience. This realization prompted Spingarn to use a sentence of Goethe's as a motto for the 1931 edition of *Creative Criticism*: "If you read a book and let it work upon you, and yield yourself up entirely to its influence, then, and only then, will you arrive at a correct judgment of it." In his essay on "Prose and Verse" (1917), Spingarn's own words had been: "we must subdue our minds to every new expression, before we can hope to rise above it, and explain . . . its real meaning and the secret of its power." And in "Scholarship and Criticism" (1922), he called for "a more complex submission to the imaginative will of the artist."

Spingarn's conviction that all critical judgment was vain without this enabling act of submission was perhaps sufficient justification for his persistently negative approach. But he was aware that the act of submission was not the whole of the critical performance. He wrote in the opening paragraph of "Scholarship and Criticism":

When I wrote the essays which a few years later were collected in a volume bearing the subtitle of "Essays on the Unity of Genius and Taste," the pedants and the professors were in the ascendant, and it seemed necessary to emphasize the side of criticism which was then in danger, the side that is closest to the act of the creator. . . . But now the professors have been temporarily routed by the dilettanti, the amateurs, and the journalists, who treat a work of the imagination as if they were describing fireworks or a bullfight (to use a phrase of Zola's about Gautier); and so it is necessary now to insist on the discipline and illumination of knowledge and thought —in other words, to write an "Essay on the Divergence of Criticism and Creation."

If we look carefully at Spingarn's early writings, we discover that he had always acknowledged the importance of "knowledge and thought."[1] From his submission to the spirit of the work of art, disciplined by a scholarly knowledge of the empirical circumstances in which it is born, and guided by his thought in the field of esthetics, the critic is to elaborate a judgment of whether the particular is a true instance of the general. But, because the category against which any given work is measured is, by definition, a category of individual non-conceptual intuitions, of discrete, unanalyzable spiritual phenomena, and because these phenomena cannot be referred to anterior premises (there is no passage from impression to expression), nor to subsequent empirical discriminations, the critic seems reduced, again, to unarguable assertion. Spingarn's problem was to describe how the critic can use "knowledge and thought" as a guide for taste.

I   Croce and the Art of Historical Criticism

The answer to the problem lies in Croce's idea of criticism as history. For history is, to the Crocean, "intuition placed in contact with the concept." That is, history is first of all art, a formal act directed toward the expression of an individual, non-repetitive vision. But history is also a special kind of art in regard to the "content" with which it deals: an order of "impression" that admits the relevance of certain concepts, "the concepts of external and internal, of what has happened and what is desired, of object and subject, and the like." The historian "does not construct the concepts of the real and the unreal, but makes use of them"—in the way that the sculptor makes use of, or takes into account, the special nature of the stone with which he may have to work. The historian, like the sculptor, expresses his own individual vision "in determined conditions and presuppositions," to use A. B. Walkley's phrase. Among these presuppositions of the historian are the various historical laws of evidence. Thus, history is "art receiving in itself philosophic distinctions [as part of its material], while remaining concrete and individual."[2]

Because the historian is not determined in the formal interpretive act (except in the sense that, like any artist, he works with determined material), his "expression" has not the certain-

ty of a mathematical equation or a philosophic syllogism, where
the manipulation of the material is rigidly prescribed by a synthetic system and can be criticized by that system. For history
"is directed *ad narrandum, non ad demonstrandum.*" Thus the
"certainty" of the historian is "the certainty of memory and of
authority, not that of analysis and demonstration. . . . The conviction of the historian is the undemonstrable conviction of the
juryman, who has heard the witnesses, listened attentively to the
case, and prayed Heaven to inspire him." So, too, the case of
the literary critic. Thus the historian-critic "cannot do otherwise than *represent*" his material, "in the sense in which logi-
cians use the word . . . when they say that one cannot have a
concept of the individual, but only a representation."[3]

The aim of the literary critic is to create "a historical work of
art founded upon one or more works of art." Using the methods
of scholarly research in much the same way in which the artist
uses the pedagogic devices of his craft, the critic first reproduces
the art work and then re-presents it. "There is this difference,
then, between the man of taste and the historian: the first merely reproduces in his spirit the work of art; the second, after
having reproduced it, represents it historically. . . ."[4] Such
representation is, like all art, judgment in the sense described at
the outset of Chapter 7. To attempt one more rephrasing, the
job of the historian-critic is to *characterize* his material by ab-
sorbing into his expression various conceptual distinctions, "to
say [or express]," for example, "whence comes [a] particular
form of enchantment, to determine . . . the character of the
inspiration that moved Ariosto, his dominant poetical motive,
the peculiar effect which became poetry in him."[5]

Such historical criticim merges quickly "into a criticism of
life, since it is not possible to judge—that is, to characterize—
works of art without at the same time judging and characterizing
the works of the whole life."[6] Croce's criticism of Sir Walter
Scott as an "industrial producer, intent upon supplying the mar-
ket with objects for which the demand was as keen as the want
was legitimate" is a case in point. Croce concluded that Scott's
"facile fiction" and his verse were not art, but interesting examples of the reaction in his time against "eighteenth-century rationalism . . . and . . . the Jacobinism of the French Revolution,"
and appeals to the contemporary taste for "antiquarian and

touriste lore."[7] The criticism of art, Croce said, cannot stop at the boundaries of art, "because it knows that what is not artistic yet is something else";[8] and, like anything else, that "something else" may be esthetically or historically represented.

Spingarn made the same point in his New School lectures, where he charged the critic with dealing with the non-poetic passages of literature. For, although these passages "do not exist" esthetically, they obviously have "some other kind of reality." And thus part of the critic's job is to differentiate "between what is art, what is pure theory, and what is some contamination of the practical spirit."[9] The instrument of this differentiation will be the resourcefulness of the critic's style, his ability to "characterize" his subject. His "proof" will be in the stylistic success with which he enforces the relevance of whatever categories he is working with, and not in an ability to demonstrate the matter "logically" or "mathematically." Spingarn offered as examples, as we have already noted, the need to characterize certain bits of unassimilated religious doctrine or Thomistic philosophy in Dante's *Divine Comedy,* or the need to gloss some of the allegory of Spenser's *Faerie Queene* in terms of Elizabethan Protestant partisanship. And he concluded with Croce that "all [literary] criticism fundamentally becomes in the end not merely a criticism of art but a criticism of life."[10]

In various places Croce described the "concepts," the "points of view,"[11] of which the literary historian might make legitimate expressive use. Most important, of course, was the critic's understanding of the category of art itself as individual intuition. But, after insisting that "every true work of art is incomparable and contains in itself its proper perfection,"[12] Croce allowed that a sensitive critic might discern degrees of "complexity" among certain works of a single author or of a given period. He might notice that some works are more "mature" than others, that one author may seem to "dominate" a wider range of impressions than another, and he might thus conclude that some works are "major" and some "minor," that some are culturally sophisticated and some culturally primitive.

Or the critic might notice in certain works an "affinity" "as regards quality of artistic inspiration" and thus construct synthetically historical "cycles," in which "similar" artistic solutions for similar spiritual problems are grouped together. Although

such a "mode of presenting the history of poetry and art contains . . . something of the abstract, of the merely practical, and
is without strict philosophical value," it may serve metaphorically
"as a useful aid to the accurate description of an artist's character." Everything depends, of course, on the recognition that the
"concepts" used by the critic are an integral part of his own
expression and are not independent of it as are true philosophic
concepts. Everything depends on recognizing that the judgments
made in the critical process are expressive structurings and not
immutable fact, that they will be, as Spingarn said, "ever
new and changing."[13]

Such criticism as has been outlined will not only yield com-
prehension and appreciation of individual works, but also,
through the expressive comparison and contrast of many works,
will be broadly educative in the life of the spirit. Because the
history of art deals with individual creations, it must be a
"monographic" history; but good criticism will also implicate
"the whole history of the human spirit." Croce did not deny
that, to a European or American of the twentieth century, some
artistic worlds will seem uninteresting, even incomprehensible.
But the high function of the critic is to contribute to "the ever-
increasing accumulation of our historical knowledge" and so
make us "able to sympathize with all the artistic products of all
people and of all times, or, as they say, [make] our taste
more catholic."

If it be objected that such a program for the critic does not
make literary criticism very practical, the Crocean answer might
well be that the practice of this "art" is no more amenable to
rational formulation than is any creative act. "Hints" can be
given and "rules" may be suggested, but abstract rules can never
determine the final theoretical synthesis. Believing that Americans of the twentieth century had forgotten the "language of
thought"—that is, the language of theory, of idealism [14] —
Spingarn concentrated on demolishing "grocer shop criticism"
and never made explicit in his published essays the positive critical program just described. But his constant emphasis on the
interdependence of meaning and expression, and his insistence
that knowledge, thought, and taste are integral in critical judgment and in the writing of history, make clear that he understood
that program.[15] And his discussion of history in the unpub-

lished New School lectures confirms this conclusion.

II *Spingarn's Adaptation of Croce*

Convinced that "tradition is a state of the soul," that "there is no past except the past that we love or hate,"[16] that the historian, like the poet, can only deal with his own contemporary vision of the past, and that to circumscribe that vision with empirical abstractions that are not absorbed by the vision itself is to impoverish one's spiritual life—believing these things, Spingarn was committed, as he explained at length in the New School lectures, to a continuing war against the notion of external "causes" in history. An emphasis on material causes led to a mechanistic and infinite regression; such causes left out the mind of man:

> All life is a process of the inner urge of men acting on the external conditions. . . . [History] is not the condition, it is not the urge; it is the unity of the condition and the urge.
>   . . . conditions generate nothing. They are dead until they come in contact with the generating power of the mind. . . . the condition produces nothing. It is inert until man's power gives it force.[17]

Thus, Spingarn concluded that no philosophy of history is intellectually adequate; no external scheme can solve the historian's or the critic's problems, which are the same problems. Such a scheme as the Marxian scheme may be an important practical force in the world; but intellectually it is "dead as a doornail." For "you cannot bind the creative rhythm of life by a fixed scheme which defines what is going to happen."[18] Although Spingarn repeatedly insisted that "the history of imaginative literature presents a quite different problem from the history of social ideals," the difference he had in mind was mainly the difference in "material," the difference between the history of the work of Walter Scott and that of the poetry of Dante. The writing of any kind of history will always be an intuitive interpretation, a theoretic or speculative act, not a scientific or practical one. The difference in material is important only, as Spingarn said in "The New Criticism," because the "historian . . . may legitimately consider a work of art, not as a work of art, but as a social document";[19] he may consider its practical effects; his historical intuition may be "in contact with" different concepts from those used by the critic of art. But the result of any historical labor is expression. Perhaps the literary historian's is the harder problem, because the category of art does not admit of conceptual interconnections between its various original intuitions as readily as do sociological "facts," which are much later in the life of the spirit— the result, as it were, of intuition, concept, and practice. "How can you give a history of a series of creations, . . . each of which is a thing in itself and has no relation to another thing in itself?" This difficulty is, as Spingarn admitted in the New School lectures, a special difficulty of the Crocean view of the doubleness of the theoretic mode. It is a difficulty which even the "Romantic historians of art" had not solved. The large free-wheeling Romantic emphasis on spirit had sometimes encouraged a preoccupation with biography or with *zeitgeist*. But, on the other hand, the idea of Romantic "genius" had stimulated a reaction in favor of more "scientific" criteria. Either way, new emphases hardened into the application of external, mechanical, or "positivistic" methods, as in the criticism of Taine.[20]

And, so as early as Spingarn's article on comparative literature in *A Cyclopedia of Education* (IV, 48) in 1913, he had attempted to substitute for Taine's environmental interest in nationality Matthew Arnold's "dictum that 'that criticism which alone can much help us for the future is a criticism which regards Europe as being for intellectual and spiritual purposes one great federation bound to a joint action and working to a common result.' " Thus the literary study of the future will "not concern itself with each national literature as a separate and sporadic fact of history, but rather with the great international movements or types of literature, with the great literary periods, or with the interrelations of one literature with another." Here are Croce's common spiritual problems, his "cycles" of literary production, which, though "without strict philosophical value" in an esthetic theory, nevertheless aid in the attempt to organize and dominate groups of individual expressions. Whether the interrelations suggest "causal" connection or "parallel" phenomena is irrelevant to the critic interested in *art,* however much it may concern cultural historians like Maurice Magendie and Daniel Mornet.

Spingarn admitted, in the New School lectures, that the

Crocean solution to the problems of the practical critic was, from the point of view of those seeking for certainties, "not wholly satisfactory"—it was, in fact, "virtually a surrender, a refusal." For even the comparative method retains something of the extrinsic about it, and is partial. Partial approaches are not enough when the aim is to give "the history of [the] poet's soul as found in his poetry, not in his life, but in his poetry." "Soul" has a kind of independence from concept and from the practical life which seems to require a radical discreteness in critical expression. And so "a history of literature would be merely a series of monographs, a series of essays."[21]

But if criticism is thus fragmentary, it is also disconcertingly inclusive:

In every judgment as to the spiritual development of the poet, [the historian-critic] will have the whole universe in his mind. Before he makes a judgment on every point he will be thinking of the history of the period. He will be thinking of the various philosophies of the poet . . . ; in fact, everything that he knows will be present consciously or unconsciously to form that judgment which he makes of the poet's development, of the criticism which he gives. . . . there would be in a sense . . . , if the historian had a large enough mind, . . . implicit a history of humanity.

As an example of such a history, Spingarn cited Francesco De Sanctis' *History of Italian Literature.* Although he recognized a certain irrelevant nationalism and libertarianism in De Sanctis' work, Spingarn praised it for being "more than a history of literature," for being "a history of the spiritual life of the Italian people, their religious life, their moral life, their political life, their poetic life," and for containing "some of the noblest criticisms of poetry that have ever been written."[22] If De Sanctis' work was not wholly adequate, and if Croce's theory was not quite conclusive, it is because in the life of the spirit there are no final answers, only provisional answers called forth by particular problems and made inadequate by new problems—all of which are perpetually re-created by the critic's own expressive "vision."

Spingarn knew that value judgments are not wholly matters of empirical evidence, but depend also on the critic's election of a "system" of measurement. He rejected easy "scientific" formulas which overemphasize the "empirical" side of critical judgment; for the problems of judgment are, he insisted, theoretic problems; and, insofar as literary critics presume to judge, their first need is philosophic sophistication. Their second need was historical sophistication, and that in turn implied the need of stylistic sophistication, or even inspiration. Especially were these needs pressing, said Spingarn, in America in the 1920's, where a naïve empiricism and pragmatism had deluded critics into the assumption that scientific method or moralistic formula were substitutes for the "convicted imagination" of the historian, who must also be an artist.

CHAPTER *9*

Conclusion: Influences and Cycles

SPINGARN may have begun with an old-fashioned, even naïve, Romantic sympathy for the "heart." But Romantic philosophers since Kant had developed a pretty sophisticated critique of the head. It was this tradition which Spingarn fell heir to in his discovery of Croce. The combination of Woodberry's intuitive sympathy with Croce's philosophical sophistication enabled him to see the subtle difficulties of value judgments more clearly than many of his crudely "empirical" or sloganeering contemporaries.

I Literature and the National Culture

But Spingarn was also very much a part of an American polemical tradition which characteristically merges literary criticism quite quickly with cultural criticism, whether in the provincial patriotism of Emerson and Melville and Lowell, or in the urbane cosmopolitanism of Santayana. Whether in the academic moralism of Babbitt or the scholarly journalism of Van Wyck Brooks and Edmund Wilson, whether in the simple partisanship of the Marxists or the elegant concern of Lionel Trilling, whether in the Freudian sermons of Ludwig Lewisohn or in the neo-traditionalism of Allen Tate, twentieth-century American critics have continued to worry about the national culture and the artist's relationship to it.

The tradition includes also those scores of writers who, in the nineteenth and twentieth centuries have been concerned with such problems as the "great American novel," or indeed with that ubiquitous will-o'-the-wisp "the American dream." One persistent way of formulating many of these concerns in the first half of the twentieth century was to talk of the alienation of the American artist from his society. As examples, we may

[142]

cite Van Wyck Brooks' interest in a "usable past" as a means of
bridging the gap between "highbrow" and "lowbrow"; Babbitt's
interest in *Literature and the American College,* or for that matter, Lionel Trilling's interest in *The Liberal Imagination.* Finally,
we may cite Spingarn's belief that the "chief duty" for "the
critics of America" was "to justify the ways of artists to
Americans."[1]

It is against this background that Spingarn wished to "use"
Crocean doctrine ("for the benefit of my countrymen") rather
than to "expound" it; in the precise historical moment in which
he found himself, he wished to advance the claims of the urgent
Romantic heart of the artist against the "empirical" claims of
American "pragmatism" and "materialism," which he repeatedly
named as the great enemies, or, on the other hand, against the
genteel passivity of "an audience that read with respect if not
with pleasure the work of Hamilton Wright Mabie and Richard
Watson Gilder."[2] Croce's idealistic conception of the artist
spoke to America's need. His idealism and the provocative
swordplay of his dialectic made him a "seminal" power for
twentieth-century American criticism.[3]

For in the United States in the twentieth century, as Spingarn
explained at the New School (I, 8), "the very conception of
speculative heights [had] been lost." To regain this conception
—the concept of ideas as a function of thought, of meaning as a
function of expression, of the world as a function of spirit—
Spingarn had early (in "The Younger Generation") recommended the Italian idealists: "not because I dreamt that [they]
had found the final solutions of the problems that haunt the
minds of men," but because "they might teach us again the
language of thought, which we have forgotten." As he wrote to
Croce (September 21, 1931), this idealism was just "what the
pragmatic mind of America needs most to learn." For this
reason, though we may have " 'passed beyond' Croce," all who
would understand modern criticism must have "passed through"
Croce.[4] In a real sense, then, Spingarn's enrolling himself in
"The New Criticism" "under Croce's banner" was, as John
Chamberlain has said, more a soldier's pledge of allegiance to
the regimental standard than a disciple's simple confession of
faith.[5]

II *Art, Knowledge, and Emotion*

Spingarn's relation to those who followed him is a difficult subject, but a few general observations are possible. John Crowe Ransom, the leader (perhaps now retired) of the "new critics," has written that the esthetic attitude "aims at a kind of cognition which is unknown to pure science and which grows increasingly difficult for us in practical life. It wants to recover its individuals. . . ." This Crocean idea of art lies behind Ransom's theory of the poem as "a *logical structure* having a *local texture.*" For the poem's textural embellishments are simply "excursions into particularity. They give . . . a sense of the real density and contingency of the world in which arguments and plans have to be pursued. They bring out the private character which the items of an argument can really assume if we look at them."[6] Always Ransom contrasts "qualitative density" with the quantitative knowledge of science arrived at by "a technique of universals." In fact, Ransom's comparison of poetic knowledge and scientific knowledge bears more than superficial resemblance to Croce's distinction between art and philosophy: "There are two ways of transcribing nature, and between them they exhaust the possibilities of formal cognition . . . the scientist knows how to interest himself strictly in the universals. . . . The artist interests himself entirely in individuals. . . ."[7] We may compare this statement with Croce: "Knowledge has two forms: . . . knowledge of the individual or knowledge of the universal. . . ." "The cognitive spirit has no form other than these two. Expression and concept exhaust it completely." "Science" for Croce is "nothing but . . . a system of concepts."[8]

If Ransom's esthetic is Croce-esque, there is nothing to show that he got his Croce through Spingarn. Spingarn had repeatedly differentiated science and art, emphasizing, for example in "The Younger Generation," that, though the concepts of scientists are of enormous practical value, "they must be left behind when we enter the realm of spiritual values; on the ideal plane of art and thought thay have no place." But such distinctions were, in Spingarn's case, and probably also in Ransom's, as much a response to a generally felt cultural situation as a matter of specific indebtedness. They were for Spingarn a "lesson America must learn if it would free itself from the bondage of its restless and homeless life. It must learn once more to speak and to think in terms of ideal values."

Allen Tate shares the view that literature is a form of knowledge, and in his idea that the abstract "quantitative" knowledge of science must be balanced by an imaginative or "religious" recovery of the "qualitative" contingency of experience, with all the "unique possibilities of the particular" that such recovery implies, he may be echoing Ransom's views. Tate specifically rejected Spingarn's esthetic, but he recognized Spingarn's importance as a diagnostician of America's cultural situation.[9] Perhaps Ransom and Tate came by their versions of the cognitive theory through a species of reaction against "art for art's sake," the very doctrine some thought Spingarn preached. Or perhaps all three, and others whose sympathy for cognitive theories of literature is very different from theirs (the neo-Humanists, the Marxists, Yvor Winters), offer, in the vocabulary of Spingarn's dispute with Mornet and Magendie, examples of "parallel" interests and not of direct "influences."

These matters of "influence" are tangled. Spingarn, for example, argued at length against what he took to be T. S. Eliot's wish to suppress the poet's "personality" in favor of his "medium," having in mind, apparently, Eliot's statement in "Tradition and the Individual Talent," which Spingarn had reprinted in his own anthology of modern criticism, that "The progress of an artist is a continual self-sacrifice, a continual extinction of personality." But Spingarn also conceded that Eliot's position was a healthy reaction against the excesses of Romantic self-expression and the indulgence of "temperament." And Eliot's further statement, also in "Tradition and the Individual Talent," that "the more perfect the artist, the more completely separate in him will be the man who suffers and the mind which creates," is very close to Spingarn's insistence that, in the passage from impression to expression, it is the poet's "theoretical, that is his creative and artistic, personality" that is important—"not the whim, not the eccentricity, which he must get rid of if he would . . . rise from practice to theory."[10] When Eliot argued that "Poetry is not a turning loose of emotion, but an escape from emotion," he was emphasizing that the poetic talent must digest and transmute the passions which are its material."[11] His point is very close to Spingarn's idea that raw emotion must be transformed into serene theory.

Both Eliot and Spingarn sought some way to explain how emotion could appear in poetry purged of its practical and biographical origins. Even the attacks of other critics on Eliot's theory of the "objective correlative" and on his use of an affective vocabulary in describing the poetic act are similar to the charges of emotionalism brought against Spingarn and Croce and against the vocabulary of Expressionism.[12] But these are very general similarities and hardly sufficient evidence for Robert Spiller's statement in the *Literary History of the United States* that "Spingarn did more than anyone else of his generation to supply rationale and method for the analytical criticism of Eliot and the critics of the thirties and forties."[13] It is better perhaps simply to assume the existence of "cycles" in the growth of the human spirit, cycles in which the interaction of the spirit with its conditions (to use Spingarn's language) generates certain problems and may, in some spirits, tend toward similar solutions. Thus Spingarn may be seen as one of the very earliest among the twentieth-century critics who—reacting against the practical spirit of modern technology and post-Freudian notions of Romantic self-expression—began feeling their way toward the view that poetry was a theoretical and, in some sense, cognitive activity more or less distinct from philosophy, different from practical morality, and superior to psychological conditioning.

III   *Environmentalism and the Historical Consciousness*

Spingarn also led the modern critical attack on the environmentalist assumptions of Taine which lay behind much of the factual historical scholarship of his time. The *locus classicus* of this attack as it applies to the inadequacies of biographical study in the criticism of literature is the article by E. K. Wimsatt and M. C. Beardsley on "The Intentional Fallacy" in *The Sewanee Review* (Summer, 1946), but Yvor Winters gives a more general statement of the position, one widely shared by other modern critics: "A poet is conditioned by his time to this extent, that it offers him most of his subject matter; but what he does with

that subject matter . . . is very largely the result of his own intelligence and talent."[14] For Wimsatt and Beardsley, for Winters,
and for many other modern critics,[15] the poet must, as
Spingarn repeatedly said, "transcend" his own personal history
and his sociological environment even while making use of them.

Spingarn's own scholarly work in the *History of Literary Criticism in the Renaissance* was, as Bernard Weinberg has pointed
out, less a chronological narrative about demonstrable "influences" causally related than "a free organization and discussion
of a basic body of ideas belonging to a central theme."[16]
Spingarn's goal was an imaginative synthesis rather than a scientific reconstruction of the empirical record. And the synthetic
principles governing his scholarly work were, as we have seen,
often reflections of his own developing esthetic rather than that
of his "sources." Weinberg attributes this situation to the rudi-
mentary state of scholarly knowledge of the Renaissance at the
time Spingarn was writing. But Spingarn himself offered another
justification: the past, he said, exists only in "our very selves";
even as the poet cannot "deal with anything but contemporary
material," so the historian, who is also an artist, cannot "deal
with any subject but the life of his own time, except in the most
external and superficial detail."

Spingarn's Emersonian, or Crocean, view of the past was *not*
intended to denigrate historical consciousness. On the contrary,
Americans above all needed to cultivate a true consciousness of
the past as a means of expanding their awareness of the world of
the spirit: "To limit our knowledge of [the past] is . . . to circumscribe not the past but the present, to limit life itself in its
deepest and richest sense." Our knowledge, however, must not
be of "an abstraction . . . which we vaguely label 'the past,' "
but a re-creation of felt experience. "For there is no past except
the past that we love or hate. . . ."[17]

T. S. Eliot has written that the "historical sense . . . is a sense
of the timeless as well as of the temporal, and of the timeless
and the temporal together," and he has explained that the literatures of the past were for him "systems" or "organic wholes"
which qualified, and were in turn modified by, individual works
of art, past and present, thus composing a "simultaneous order."
Eliot's "systems" seem to emphasize more than Croce's "cycles"
"something outside of the artist to which he owes allegiance, a

devotion to which he must surrender and sacrifice himself,"[18] but they also seem of a piece with Spingarn's Arnoldian sense of large international movements in literary history and with his effort to distinguish erudition and pseudo-scientific analysis of "externals" from expressive history. Allen Tate, in discussing the possibility of a fruitful merger between history and criticism, has stated the problem succintly enough:

> We must judge the past and keep it alive ourselves; . . . we must judge the past not with a method or an abstract hierarchy but with the present, or with as much of the present as our poets have succeeded in elevating to the objectivity of form. For it is through the formed . . . experience of our own time that we must approach the past, and then by means of a critical mastery of our own formed experience we may test the presence and the value of form in works of the past. The critical activity is reciprocal and simultaneous.[19]

In "Miss Emily and the Bibliographer," in "The Present Function of Criticism," and in "Liberalism and Tradition" (all collected in *Reason in Madness* [1941]), Tate repeatedly emphasized that "pattern," which is the historian's own judgment "more or less articulate," is inevitable in all written history.[20] Perhaps in these essays he is echoing Croce or Eliot, but he is surely in agreement with Spingarn's idealistic rejection of the idea that the past can be "objectively" perceived merely as a succession of "facts." Tate's interest in the Southern past is largely an interest in history as a field of values for the sensibility to operate in, as is evidenced by his biography of *Stonewall Jackson: The Good Soldier* (1928), in which the contrasting portraits of Lee and Lincoln and the treatment of Calhoun and Jackson himself suggest the methods of the novelist, as does his biography of *Jefferson Davis* (1929).[21]

Tate's ideas about the uses of history may be similar to Spingarn's; certainly both men, as Tate himself recognized,[22] were passionately concerned with the relation of artists to contemporary society and with the different relations between earlier artists and *their* societies. But the uses to which Spingarn and Tate put their sense of the relationship of past and present are not peculiar to them; they are rather a common property of many critics of the twentieth century. Certainly the Marxists saw history as material useful for the definition of a contemporary point of view; and, as Frederick Pottle has pointed out, "the standards of . . . [the new] criticism are not really derived from a study of seventeenth-century literature. They are [instead] the definition of [a] modern sensibility"[23] —which is attempting to explain itself through historical metaphor.[24]

Eliot, of course, worked in this way, and so did Van Wyck Brooks, although to a different end. The neo-Humanists likewise, in such a book as Babbitt's *Rousseau and Romanticism,* to cite only one example, quite openly hoped to redefine the past for contemporary uses. And Vernon Louis Parrington's *Main Currents in American Thought* (1927-1930), which Van Wyck Brooks recommended to Harcourt, Brace and Company, is a notorious example of the effort to define a "usable past" for twentieth-century America. Richard Ruland, in his *The Rediscovery of American Literature,* cites James Harvey Robinson's work in history and John Dewey's work in philosophy as important influences in encouraging a relativistic attitude toward the past; and he cites the work of Lewis Mumford, Spingarn's close friend, as an example of "the conception of the past as storehouse, as arsenal."[25] But Ruland might also have cited Croce's work on history as both general influence and concrete example. The truth seems to be that in noting such relations as those between Eliot, Spingarn, and Tate described above, we are noting a general cycle or a pervasive atmosphere which encompassed a great variety of critics, rather than a network of demonstrable influences.[26]

IV   Criticism and the Inexpressible

The network of connections linking Spingarn to the critics who followed him is, nevertheless, surprisingly detailed. When Allen Tate argues, for example, that in these latter days "Both politics and poetry, having ceased to be arts, are cut off from their common center of energy" and are trying to nourish each other "on a diminishing diet,"[27] we are reminded of Spingarn's essay on "Politics and the Poet" and of his notion that the failure of the sense of *civitas* is reflected in poetry's failure any longer to celebrate heroes. R. P. Blackmur's eloquent statement on the near-identity of creation and criticism[28] could have been

derived from Spingarn's championship of the unity of genius
and taste, though it could also have come from Eliot or from a
generalized sense of Croce's pervasive influence, or from some
other source, if a "source" is required.

Similarly, Blackmur's idea that the "enabling act of criticism"
is an "act of submission" to the authority of the work in hand
echoes Spingarn's doctrine, and Blackmur's idea that the best
criticism ends in a stylistic re-enactment of the work criticized [29]
echoes Spingarn's and Croce's idea of historical re-presentation
in which evaluation is a function of the critic's style. Blackmur,
like Spingarn, knew that the act of the "convicted imagination"
(the "leaping over," as Spingarn called it) meant that the critic
must pass "beyond the realm of ideas" into artistic expression,
and further that the consequences of the passage were a "loss of
faith: seen in critical practice as the constantly increasing in-
credibility of any given intellectual bridge-work." [30] Spingarn
rehearsed most of the problems of modern criticism and thus no
doubt helped to generate a critical "cycle," even though he
was probably not a first cause.

And yet there is a difference in emphasis between Spingarn
and the others. Blackmur spoke for many modern critics when
he insisted, as did Spingarn, that a resolute critical candor re-
quires that the interest in the work criticized must never be sub-
ordinated to interests external to the work. And he agreed with
Spingarn that the critical act, as well as the creative act, "is imaginative." But then Blackmur asked "a crucial question": "do
we in fact ever understand literature only by literary means?"
And he spoke for most modern critics when he answered,
"no." [31] Whereas Spingarn suggested that poetic and critical
"transcendence" were matters almost of "inspiration," which is
always integral, Blackmur pointed out that without partial analyses we shall have to forego criticism entirely. Norman Foerster
agreed with Blackmur that without some point of purchase
more or less "inept," the critic is doomed to silence. [32] And, if
Foerster's argument sounds like an apology for the sins of the
fathers of neo-Humanism, Eliot's remarks on the criticism of
Ramon Fernandez may serve as a reminder that the "appreci-
ators" themselves were sometimes apologetic. Fernandez' ethical
bias was legitimate, because "if we should exclude from literary
criticism all but purely literary considerations, there would not

only be very little to talk about, but actually we should be left without even literary appreciation."[33]

Spingarn would perhaps not contradict Eliot or Foerster; but he was certainly less confident than they that such pluralism could really help the critic, except negatively. T. E. Hulme had stated Spingarn's dilemma—and Blackmur's and Foerster's and Eliot's—by insisting that "in all these matters the act of judgment is an instinct, an absolutely unstatable thing akin to the art of the tea taster," but he went on to recommend a combination of esthetic and rhetorical "metaphors" which, though they "cannot state the essentially unstatable intuition, can yet give you a sufficient analogy to enable you to see what it was and to recognize it on condition that you yourself have been in a similar state."[34] Yvor Winters, too, recognized that "the final act of judgment is in both life and art a unique act," but he has also written: "any critical definition is merely an indication of a unique experience which cannot be exactly represented by any formula, though it may be roughly mapped out; and it is frequently of greater importance to discover something of the nature of the experience than to reduce the more or less expert formula to something simpler and still less veracious and then to demolish it."[35]

The difference between the "new criticism" of Spingarn and the criticism of the "new critics" is most clearly evident in matters of practice rather than in matters of theory; it is evident especially in the matter of dealing with the details of language. Blackmur's description (in "Notes on E. E. Cummings' Language") of the "origin" of language and his discrimination of the two functions it may perform (imaginative and conventional) could, with some revision, be accepted as neo-Crocean. But Blackmur will not, practically speaking, "credit . . . words . . . with immaculate conception and . . . hold them unquestionable."[36] Questioning words is, for him, one of the most important tasks of the critic; and it provides him with a basis for criticizing E. E. Cummings' poetry, even as the poetry provided him with an illustration of his theory.

Cleanth Brooks, too, endorses the Crocean conclusions of Louis Urban (in *Language and Reality* [1939]) that a poem "is strictly untranslatable," that "what it 'says' can be rendered only by the poem itself";[37] but Brooks goes on to develop his idea of "irony" and "paradox" as a means of getting at the untranslatable poem. Allen Tate has agreed with Spingarn that in a poem "subject and language [are] one," and that every poem is "absolute" and "unique." But Tate developed his idea of "tension" as a tool for handling practically the fused subject and language of the theoretically unique poem.[38]

Spingarn's attitude toward such solutions of his dilemma was diffidently negative; but the attitude of many of his successors is assuredly (sometimes dogmatically) positive. Spingarn's approach was determinedly idealistic where that of the "new critics" is provisionally empirical, or even "pragmatic." Though Spingarn conceded, in "Prose and Verse," that "it is possible to approach [poetry] from many angles, to study it from many points of view,"[39] he emphasized the partiality of all these points of view rather than their practicality. His failure, for example, in his controversy with Walkley, to exploit the Crocean identification of intuition and expression as a sufficient explanation of how technique could become an aperture through which the critic might get "inside" a work of art seems to leave the critic with almost no method of representing, and so criticizing, the object of his attention. Spingarn seemed unwilling to admit that we have not only perceptions, but apperceptions as well.

V   *The Uses of Criticism*

Hypersensitive to what Foerster called the ineptitude of critical discussion, the "mechanical inadvertence of abstractions" (to use Blackmur's phrase),[40] Spingarn was not at all sanguine about the benefits of practical criticism. He had said in "The New Criticism" that "Criticism . . . can be of small service" to poets; and at the New School he repeated that "criticism can't help the poet really." In his later years he was even skeptical about the idea, prevalent among modern critics at least since Matthew Arnold and implicit in his own early work, that one of the jobs of criticism was to create a suitable atmosphere for the poet to work in.

In America E. C. Stedman had endorsed this notion before the turn of the century; and in Spingarn's day W. C. Brownell had also argued for an elite literary "remnant" as a means of developing higher standards and a more discriminating taste. Van Wyck Brooks, hardly a disciple of Stedman or Brownell, had emphasized the need for an intellectual elite in such essays as "The Unacknowledged Legislators," "The Remnant," and "The Literary Life."[41] Sinclair Lewis publicized the problem as a peculiarly American one in his address to the Swedish Academy on the occasion of his acceptance of a Nobel Prize in 1930. Though Spingarn could agree with Lewis' indictment of the "materialism" of the American environment, he was not confident that material circumstances explained intellectual sterility or that intellectual analysis could bring about the reform that was needed. Real reform was a matter of spiritual regeneration, for which there were no easy prescriptions.

While Van Wyck Brooks was intent on discovering a "usable past," while the neo-Humanists were lecturing on the need for an "inner check," while the Marxists were working for a usable present or future, and while some of the "new critics" were professing to discover in Southern agrarianism a model of the civilized society,[42] Spingarn was repeating his warning that the gap between sociology and creative effort was all but unbridgeable. In "Scholarship and Criticism" he had admitted that critics may offer tentative suggestions about areas and subjects suitable for imaginative exploitation; but he added that such "incursions into the geography of the imagination are incidental to the critic's main duty of interpreting literature and making its meaning clear to all who wish to love and understand it." Literature is a spiritual matter. A country's failure to produce "instant literature" cannot be remedied by critical exhortation. The belief that a national literature can be willed into existence is only another example of "mechanical optimism." For the "fervor of sociological obsession . . . is no substitute for the faculty of imaginative sympathy which is at the heart of all criticism."[43]

Spingarn was passionately interested in the whole spiritual life of America, but this very concern made him skeptical about such fashionable interests as that of the neo-Humanists in Buddhism, which he felt could lead seekers after the exotic into an unhealthy alienation. Instead, he said, we must remain "immune to momentary fashions of thought and . . . think of things in the light of eternal history" (VI, 36).[44] For, as Spingarn ex-

plained in "Creative Connoisseurship" (1913), "Nothing outside
of art seems really to help or hinder; out of its own life it mus-
ters the mysterious power that helps it to speak or be silent."
The best that the critic can do, then, is to try "to come to grips
with actual works of art and make us understand them, and,
perhaps, even though that is more difficult, to love them."[45]
The task was difficult and Spingarn himself never undertook to
give a practical demonstration of how it might be managed. Perhaps his thoroughgoing devotion to an idealism tending toward
solipsism or nominalism precluded such a demonstration. And
perhaps such tendencies are a useful simple for critics hot for
methodological certainties in this our time. As Spingarn himself
said in 1931, echoing his advice to Geroid Robinson five years
earlier, perhaps what a world enamored of the new *this* and
the new *that* needs most is the "New Humility."[46]

VI   *The Unity of the Spirit*

Spingarn's criticism was often one of denial (but much of the
best criticism of our time has been negative, a deflation of cliché, a clearing of the critical underbrush). It was also, however,
a sustained idealistic affirmation of the primacy of spirit which
attempted to transcend partisanship. Perhaps the two characteristics taken together account for its having "seeped" into
American critical thought (to borrow Bernard Smith's term),[47]
despite its failure to enlist disciples. Certainly a great number of
critics undertake to refute Spingarn's work even though they
may deny it any real standing. Gorham Munson (In "Our Critical
Spokesman") and Bernard Smith (In "Huneker and the Tribe")
are examples of this procedure. The special urgency, even the
defensiveness, of the arguments of Spingarn's detractors suggests
that they do not feel they are debating dead issues; and we
might imagine that Smith's and Munson's criticism was more
sophisticated as a result of their having to confront the issues
Spingarn raised.

Clearly Spingarn *was* important as an introducer of Croce.
Norman Foerster wrote Spingarn twice (August 1, 1922, and
June 13, 1925) that his advocacy of Croce had prompted
Foerster's own study of Croce and had encouraged him to deal

at length with Croce's esthetic in his university courses in critical theory. Spingarn's notices of Croce's work in *The Nation* must have reached another audience; and his editorship of the European Library for Harcourt, Brace probably helped spread European idealism among readers who never acknowledged indebtedness to Spingarn himself.

Spingarn was certainly responsible, as he himself somewhat sadly noted in "The Growth of a Literary Myth," for the popularization of those famous two questions, "What has the poet tried to do, and how has he fulfilled his intention?" Edith Wharton seems to have been paraphrasing Spingarn in her use of the questions in "The Criticism of Fiction" (*The Living Age*, April 25, 1914). Sometimes paraphrase gave way to direct quotation, and in the most unlikely places—for example, in Eden Phillpotts' novel, *The Joy of Youth* (1913).[48] In 1943 Spingarn's two questions and Goethe's third formed the basis of the general article on "Criticism" in Joseph Shipley's *Dictionary of World Literature*.

If we accept the Crocean dictum that nothing that has happened in the life of the spirit is ever lost, we may guess that some of the sophistication of recent American criticism (when it *is* sophisticated) may derive from Spingarn's repeated attacks on critical naïveté. The point cannot be proved, but recent critical attitudes toward the connections between literature and morality or literature and politics may derive in part from Spingarn's indefatigable war on the naïve didacticism of the neo-Humanists and the Marxists alike. How far on the defensive, for example, the neo-Humanists had moved in 1941 may be gauged by Norman Foerster's essay, "The Esthetic Judgment and the Ethical Judgment," in Donald Stauffer's *The Intent of the Critic* (1941). Foerster, who had read Spingarn's strictures on Babbitt, reprimands Babbitt for his crude didacticism and seems to concede that morality gets into poetry through the formal elements of the writing. It is true that Foerster is not talking to Spingarn; he is talking instead almost directly at the *new* "new critics" who are sandwiched in uncomfortably close to him between the covers of Stauffer's anthology. Spingarn is *not* there, and *these* "new critics" are not *his* disciples. But Foerster's defense against their voices, at times as strident as those which had trained *him*, seems to suggest that, if the precepts of Babbitt's creed will not serve against the new heresy, he can at least remember the breviary of Spingarn's esthetic.[49]

The new "new critics," despite what Foerster may have thought of their "esthetic" bias, knew, too, that the artist must be a whole man. Allen Tate, who credited Spingarn with having been the first to diagnose the plight of the American artist in the twentieth century,[50] echoed Spingarn's call for renewal in the "Preface" to his *Reactionary Essays.* William Van O'Connor also saw the importance of Spingarn's "Politics and the Poet" for both critic and artist,[51] and perhaps it is not too much to say that this aspect of Spingarn's thought has "seeped" into the thought of others and helped to guard the new "new critics" as well as the new neo-Humanists from some of the narrowness of their predecessors.

Spingarn labored mightily to distinguish art from other things, but his effort in this regard was simply part of a dialectical, or "speculative," effort to order the primary flux of experience. Finally, it was the indivisible unity of life that interested him. And so perhaps it is right and just that he started no school of criticism. His stubborn Romantic suspicion of formula has a kind of defiant exaggeration about it that may even yet challenge complacency and dogmatism. If, in his special sense of the term, "manliness is the basis of all art,"[52] perhaps it is also the basis of criticism.

Manliness was for Spingarn both a moral and an esthetic virtue, even as his long polemic on criticism was both social and literary—a plea, as he put it, for "personality" and "style" "in the battle against the benumbing chaos and the benumbing monotony of American art and life."[53] Manliness could not be legislated into existence by party platforms and manifestos; it was a matter of spiritual regeneration, defined in practice as well as theory, in life as well as in art. Such quaint Emersonian echoes must have seemed at best irrelevant in the hustling 1920's. In the Orwellian 1970's, they may be more arresting—if we can listen carefully enough to hear them at all.

Notes and References

Preface

1. See Spingarn's "Scholarship and Criticism," in *Civilization in the United States: an Inquiry by Thirty Americans*, ed. Harold Stearns (New York, 1922), p. 100; Mencken's "Footnote on Criticism," *Prejudices, Third Series* (New York, 1922), p. 102; Brooks' "Our Critics," *Letters and Leadership* (New York, 1918), p. 64; Peyre's "The Criticism of Contemporary Writing," *Lectures in Criticism*, Bollingen Series, XVI (New York, 1949), 120; and O'Connor's *Sense and Sensibility in Modern Poetry* (Chicago, 1948), p. 250.
2. Allen Tate, "American Criticism," *Dictionary of World Literature*, ed. Joseph T. Shipley (New York, 1943), p. 27.
3. John Chamberlain, "Mr. Spingarn Puts His Critical Fences in Repair," *New York Times Book Review*, October 18, 1931, p. 2.
4. Lewis Mumford, "Scholar and Gentleman," *Saturday Review of Literature*, XX (August 5, 1939), 8.

Chapter One

1. Gates' critical position is best summed up in his *Studies and Appreciations* (New York, 1900).
2. See Robert E. Spiller, "The Battle of the Books," *Literary History of the United States* (New York, 1948), II, 1154; and Morton D. Zabel, "Summary in Criticism," *ibid.*, pp. 1359, 1365, 1367. See also Bernard S. Oldsey and Arthur O. Lewis, "Introduction," *Visions and Revisions in Modern American Literary Criticism* (New York, 1962), p. xiv.
3. In the spring of 1931 Spingarn delivered six lectures on *Literature and the New Era* at the New School for Social Research. The fourth has been edited by Lewis Mumford and published in the *Atlantic Monthly*, CLXX (November, 1942), 73-78, under the title of "Politics and the Poet." The others exist only in the rough form given them by the stenotypist. The quotation above is from I, 16.
4. See George Edward Woodberry, "Two Phases of Criticism: Historical and Esthetic," *The Heart of Man and Other*

Papers (New York, 1920).

5. All of Spingarn's letters cited in this work, unless otherwise indicated, are unpublished. They and all other unpublished material cited were made available to the author by Mrs. Spingarn.

6. See John Macy, "George E. Woodberry," *The Critical Game* (New York, 1922), pp. 216-23. Typical of Macy's jibes was his observation that the Woodberry Society was the only literary society dedicated to a writer still living: "Mr. Woodberry was old when he was young, and he is an institution before he is dead."

7. See *Life and Letters of Stuart Sherman*, ed. Jacob Zeitlin and Homer Woodbridge (New York, 1929), II, 581.

8. John Garrett Underhill, in the "Preface" to his *Spanish Literature in the England of the Tudors*, Vol. III of *Columbia University Studies in Literature* (New York and London, 1899), p. vii, acknowledged that Spingarn had made available "the results of his unpublished research upon John Lyly and the origins of his style." Underhill was also a student of Woodberry's, as was Frank Wadleigh Chandler, whose *Romances of Roguery* was published in 1899 as Vol. II of the Columbia series.

9. In the "Preface to the Fifth Impression" Spingarn wrote that the second edition "merely reproduced the first except for a few trifling corrections and the addition of a new 'Conclusion' [based on his article on "The Origins of Modern Criticism," *Modern Philology*, I (April, 1904), 477-96].... It is only fair to state ... that the Italian translation of this book ... contains much important material ... not included in any of the editions in English. ... I virtually rewrote the book from beginning to end for ... my translator ... ; ... every serious student of the subject is advised to consult the Italian edition."

10. Some description of this feud may be found in Hartley Davis and Clifford Smith, "The Land of the Feuds," *Munsey's Magazine*, XXX (November, 1903), 161-72; R. L. M'Clure, "The Mazes of a Kentucky Feud," *The Independent*, LV (September 17, 1903), 2216-24; O. O. Howard, "The Feuds in the Cumberland Mountains," *The Independent*, LVI (April 7, 1904), 783-88; and Charles G. Mutzenberg, *Kentucky's Famous Feuds and Tragedies* (New York, 1917).

11. See Mumford's "Introduction" to "Politics and the Poet," p. 73.

12. For an account of Woodberry's political and social ideas and of his religious radicalism, see Joseph Doyle, "George Edward Woodberry," an unpublished dissertation, Columbia University, 1952, esp. Chap. VI. See also Woodberry's "Democ-

racy" in *Heart of Man* and "The Salem Athaneum," *The Torch*
(New York, 1905).
13. "Politics and the Poet," pp. 75, 76.
14. Spingarn had four children: Stephen J. (né Joel Elias,
Jr.), Hope Judith, Honor Edith, and Edward David Woodberry.
15. Mumford, "Scholar and Gentleman," p. 8.
16. See Spingarn's review of *La politesse mondaine et
l'honnêté en France au XVIIIe siècle . . . ,* par M. Magendie
(Paris, 1925?), in *The Romanic Review*, XVII (January-March,
1926), 71-73.
17. See "Politics and the Poet," pp. 75, 76.
18. Letter to William Aspenwall Bradley, March 11, 1932.

Chapter Two

1. See above, p. 29.
2. See *Modern Philology*, II (April, 1905), 451-60.
3. See "Scholar and Gentleman," p. 8; also Mumford's
'Introduction" to "Politics and the Poet," p. 73.
4. Letter to J. E. Spingarn, January 28, 1919.
5. Marjorie Nicolson, "Richard Foster Jones," *The Seventeenth Century: Studies in the History of English Thought and
Literature,* by Richard Foster Jones and others writing in his
honor (Stanford, 1951), p. 5. But see the dissenting view of
Bernard Weinberg in his "Introduction" to the Harbinger edition of *Literary Criticism in the Renaissance* (New York, 1963).
6. Gay's reference is to Spingarn's graduate courses. Spingarn wrote Croce, March 6, 1906: "I have planned a course of
lectures for under-graduates next year, to which I am looking
forward with great interest as a relief from the more specialized
lecture-work designed for maturer students."
7. See Spingarn's review of Croce's edition of De Sanctis'
Saggio critico sul Petrarca, The Nation, LXXXVI (April 16,
1908), 355; and his review of Farinelli's *Dante e la Francia, The
Nation,* LXXXVI (December 31, 1908), 656.
8. J. E. Spingarn, *American scholarship: les belles lettres et
l'érudition en Amérique du point de vue académique* (Macon,
1901), pp. 5-6.
9. Letter to Croce, March 7, 1900.
10. "Scholarship and Criticism," p. 108.
11. See John Herman Randall, Jr., and George Haines IV,
"Controlling Assumptions in the Practice of American Historians," *Theory and Practice in Historical Study* (New York,
1948), pp. 22-23.
12. Chester MacArthur Destler, "Some Observations on
Contemporary Historical Theory," *The American Historical*

Review, LV (April, 1950), 503-29.

13.. See "Extract from Introduction to the First English Edition, 1909," Benedetto Croce, *Aesthetic as the Science of Expression and General Linguistic*, 2d ed., trans. Douglas Ainslie (London, 1929), p. xxiii.

14. "The Younger Generation: a New Manifesto," *The Freeman*, V (June, 1922), 297.

15. William A. Nitze, "Modern Language Scholarship," *PMLA*, XXXVIII (March, 1923), lxxi-lxxiii.

16. Stuart Sherman, "Disinterested? No!" *The Main Stream* (New York, 1927), p. 1.

17. See *America's Coming of Age* (New York, 1915).

18. "The American Scholar," pp. 150, 149, and 160-61.

19. See Spingarn's "Prefatory Note" to *Creative Criticism* and Alfred Kazin, *On Native Grounds* (New York, 1942), p. 197.

20. Harold E. Stearns, "America and the Young Intellectual," *The Bookman*, LIII (March, 1921), 48. This article was an answer to Sherman's "The National Genius," *Atlantic Monthly*, CXXVII (January, 1921), 1-11; Stearns modified his tone of martyrdom when he reprinted his essay in *America and the Young Intellectual* (New York, 1921).

21. Stuart Sherman, "The Belligerent Young," *New York Evening Post*, January 14, 1922, p. 346. This essay includes the discussion of "personalities" which Ellery Sedgwick apparently forced Sherman to withdraw from his "What Is a Puritan?" *Atlantic Monthly*, CXXVII (September, 1921), 342-56. (See Zeitlin and Woodbridge, I, 493.) Elizabeth Sergeant summarized the whole exchange between Sherman and Stearns in "A Tilt With Two Critics," *The Bookman*, LIII (June, 1921), 289-93.

22. Daniel Mornet, "Philosophie de la littérature ou histoire de la littérature," *The Romanic Review*, XVIII (April-June, 1927), 107.

23. Bernard Faÿ, "Doutes et réflexions sur l'étude de la littérature," *The Romanic Review*, XIX (April-June, 1928),112.

24. Daniel Mornet, "La véritable méthode historique de la critique littéraire," *The Romanic Review*, XIX (October-December, 1928), 325.

25. Paul Van Tieghem, "Influences et simultanéités en histoire littéraire," *The Romanic Review*, XX (January-March, 1929), 140.

26. Philippe Van Tieghem, *Tendances nouvelles en histoire littéraire* (Paris, 1930), p. 55.

Chapter Three

1. See Horace Coon, *Columbia: Colossus on the Hudson* (New York, 1947), pp. 93-133.
2. See above, pp. 39-40.
3. See Doyle, Chap. IV.
4. Printed in full in *A Scholar's Testament: Two Letters from George Edward Woodberry to J. E. Spingarn*, with an Introduction by Lewis Mumford, no. 1 of *Troutbeck Leaflets*, second series (Amenia, N. Y., 1931), pp. 5-6.
5. Whatever the cause of Peck's dismissal, the results were sure—and swift: libel, social and professional ostracism, the wreckage of his marriage, mental collapse, bankruptcy (1913), and suicide (1914).
6. This resolution and the quotations which follow are taken from Spingarn's collection of documents relating to his dismissal, privately printed in New York, 1911, "for distribution among the alumni," under the title *A Question of Academic Freedom.*
7. Upton Sinclair, *The Goose Step, A Study of American Education* (Pasadena, 1923), p. 15. Doyle suggests (pp. 497-99) that friction between Matthews and Woodberry helped bring about Woodberry's resignation.
8. Erskine speaks of his feelings in a letter to Spingarn, January 28, 1919.
9. Mumford, "Introduction," "Politics and the Poet," p. 74.
10. Mrs. Amy Spingarn, Letter to the author, January 26, 1952.
11. W. E. B. Du Bois, *Dusk of Dawn: An Essay Toward an Autobiography of a Race Concept* (New York, 1940), p. 290.
12. The Department of Comparative Literature had, according to Doyle, been established by President Seth Low to help keep Woodberry's war with the English professors (especially Brander Matthews) under control. But Butler placed severe restrictions on the operation of the department; and, when Woodberry grew restive, he was told he could join the English Department; he refused, and then resigned. (See Doyle, pp. 497-99.)
13. See *A Question of Academic Freedom* for the full text of Butler's and Spingarn's letters and for the other quotations which follow.
14. See Sinclair, p. 53.
15. The stories of Fraser, Cattel, H. W. Dana, Charles Beard, and James Harvey Robinson are told in Coon, pp. 125-31, and Sinclair, pp. 45-57. Sinclair (pp. 56-57) also tells the story of Leon Ardzrooni, who was anonymously accused of being a

member of the International Workers of the World and of carrying a red card.

16. See Cattel's description of Columbia as a department store with Butler as "proprietor and floor walker to the faculty" and "errand boy to the trustees," as quoted in Sinclair, p. 55; Beard's description of conditions of employment at Columbia in a letter to Butler quoted in Sinclair, p. 55; and Beard's letter to *The New Republic*, December 29, 1917.

17. See *Literature and the New Era*, VI, 37 and *Time Magazine*, XXVII (March 23, 1936), 43, and XXXIV (August 7, 1939), 37.

18. Mumford, "Scholar and Gentleman," p. 8.

19. See Spingarn's *Poems* (New York, 1924), pp. 39-40. In "The Fate of a Scholar," written after Peck's suicide in 1914, Spingarn described Peck's "slayer" as dressed "in scarlet with Oxford hood and sleeves" and then charged that "Seven hundred rats obeyed the fox's will;/ Another cast him out, another struck him dead,/ But never a word of protest the seven hundred said."

20. Woodberry, Letter to Spingarn, April 5, 1911, in *A Scholar's Testament*, pp. 7-8.

21. *Ibid.*

22. *Ibid.*

Chapter Four

1. Chief of these was the story of how Myron Benton first introduced John Burroughs to Whitman's *Leaves of Grass* at Troutbeck. See Burroughs' account in his *Notes on Walt Whitman as Poet and Person*, 2d ed. (New York, 1871), and Spingarn's mention of the incident in the "Prefatory Note" to the second *Troutbeck Leaflet*.

2. Doyle quotes a moving passage from a Woodberry letter to Harry Harkness Flagler, September 19, 1905, about his "love [for] this little spot of earth" as "refuge" between his venturings-forth into the world. See Doyle, pp. 51-54, *et passim*, and Woodberry's *Selected Letters*, with an Introduction by Walter De La Mare (Boston and New York, 1933), p. 32. For Spingarn's echo of Woodberry's phrase, see the colophon to nos. 4, 5, 6, 8, or 10 of *The Troutbeck Leaflets*.

3. W. E. B. Du Bois, *The Amenia Conference: An Historic Negro Gathering*, no. 8 of *Troutbeck Leaflets* (Amenia, N. Y., 1925), pp. 3-4.

4. Sherman wrote Spingarn at Troutbeck, June 18, 1923: "I am able to think of you as a stout Tory squire riding on errands of benevolence among your contented tenantry—and excogitating an aesthetic theory in vital correspondence with the setting."

Under the banter of these words Spingarn sensed other implications. His objections brought from Sherman this reply (July 1, 1923): "I have a dictionary which gives me the first sense of *Tory*: 'brave, bold'!"

5. Charles E. Benton, *Troutbeck, A Dutchess County Homestead*, with an Introduction by John Burroughs (Dutchess County Historical Society, 1916), pp. 27-28. To Benton's bibliography on "the history of Troutbeck and its neighborhood" should be added Clara Barrus' *The Life and Letters of John Burroughs* (Boston and New York, 1925), and F. B. Sanborn's edition of Thoreau's *Familiar Letters*, Vol. VI in *The Writings of Henry David Thoreau*, Walden Ed. (Boston and New York, 1906).

6. Oswald Garrison Villard, "Issues and Men," *The Nation*, CXLIX (August 12, 1939), 174.

7. See Doyle, pp. 58, 79; and also Woodberry's essay on Wendell Phillips (1912), reprinted in *The Heart of Man*.

8. Du Bois, *Dusk of Dawn*, p. 255.

9. Charles Flint Kellogg, *NAACP: A History of the National Association for the Advancement of Colored People*, Vol. I (Baltimore, 1967), p. 155.

10. *Ibid.*, pp. 140-42.

11. Du Bois, *Dusk of Dawn*, p. 243.

12. In addition to Spingarn's tact in handling the invitations, Du Bois praised his arrangement of the daily menu: "let us confess that one thing helped everything else: we were gloriously fed." See *The Amenia Conference*, pp. 9-10, and *Dusk of Dawn*, p. 256.

13. Kellogg, pp. 101-4, 110-11.

14. Du Bois, *The Amenia Conference*, pp. 12, 17-18. See also Kellogg, pp. 87-88, 292.

15. For some sense of the vigor and variety of Spingarn's activities, see Kellogg, *passim*. A much fuller account of Spingarn's work in the field of race relations and civil rights should soon be available in Barbara Joyce Ross' book on these aspects of his career.

16. For a good summary of these ideas, see Spingarn's presidential address on *Racial Equality*, delivered at the twenty-third Annual Conference of the NAACP, Washington, D. C., May 17, 1932 (New York, 1932), pp. 2-5. See also below, pp. 69, 72.

17. See below, p. 99 and Chap. 6, note 5.

18. During the week of November 20, 1916, he gave a brief course in literary criticism for advanced students at the University of North Carolina, and the following week he repeated it at the University of South Carolina.

19. See Doyle, pp. 51-54, 58, *et passim*.

20. See Kellogg, pp. 250-56.

21. Du Bois, *Dusk of Dawn*, pp. 256-57, 249-50.

22. Reprinted as "Tradition," in *Americans* (New York, 1923).

23. Letter of 1918, as quoted by Mumford in his "Introduction" to "Politics and the Poet," p. 73.

24. See the "Appendix" to Spingarn's edition of *Goethe's Literary Essays* (New York, 1921), p. 291.

25. Villard, p. 174.

26. See Alfred Harcourt, *Some Experiences* (Riverside, Conn., 1951), p. 41.

27. One may recall Spingarn's definition of race in his article on Woodberry in the *Dictionary of American Biography*: it was "not so much an ethnic entity as a spiritual quality of mind made up of imaginative memories and experiences." For Spingarn's idea of cultural pluralism and his objections to the idea of an American "melting-pot," see his *Racial Equality*.

28. See *The Arizona Daily Star*, February 13, 1930, p. 2.

29. See Mumford's "Introduction" to "Politics and the Poet," pp. 73-74.

30. Du Bois, *Dusk of Dawn*, pp. 290-91.

31. *Literature and the New Era*, III, 12, 2-4.

32. Du Bois, *Dusk of Dawn*, p. 291.

33. Spingarn, *Racial Equality*, pp. 2-7. The subordination of economic affairs in *Racial Equality* (1932) and in the New School lectures (1931) was not a new emphasis. Kellogg (p. 132) mentions Spingarn's reluctance to involve the NAACP in various economic programs proposed in 1916.

34. Du Bois, *Dusk of Dawn*, p. 299.

35. Mumford, "Introduction" to "Politics and the Poet," p. 74.

36. *Ibid.*, and "Scholar and Gentleman," p. 8.

37. Mumford, "Introduction," "Politics and the Poet," p. 74, and Gay, Letter to Mrs. Amy Spingarn, November 6, 1942.

38. See above, pp. 19, 21.

39. See above, p. 71.

Chapter Five

1. "The Younger Generation," *The Freeman*, p. 297.

2. Santayana had voiced a similar fear in "Croce's Aesthetics," p. 195, and Spingarn had had to defend (in a letter to Croce, May 25, 1903), against Croce's objections, Santayana's right to differ, though in "The Rich Storehouse of Croce's Thought," *The Dial*, LXIV (May 23, 1918), 485-86, he called Santayana's view "blind." In two letters in 1907 (October 30 and December 23) Spingarn wrote Croce that whatever their

differences, he remained loyal to Croce's general doctrine.
   3. Woodberry's influence on Spingarn was, as Spingarn himself recognized, of a similar kind. Alongside his statement in 1931 in the New School Lectures (I, 6) that "Benedetto Croce gave me a philosophical explanation for those things which have been implicit in the thought of Woodberry," one may put his suggestion to Croce in a letter of February 18, 1900, that "you would find it worth while, in writing the theoretical portions of your *History of Aesthetics*, to consult Pr. Woodberry's recent Heart of Man."
   4. Harry Hartwick, *The Foreground of American Fiction* (New York, 1934), pp. 144, 307; Sherman, *Americans*, p. 25, and *The Genius of America* (New York, 1923), pp. 9-10, 17, 25; Ludwig Lewisohn, *Expression in America* (New York and London, 1932), p. 422; Gorham Munson, "Our Critical Spokesmen," in *Humanism and America: Essays on the Outlook of Modern Civilization* (New York, 1930), pp. 239, 242; Cornelius Blum, "Journalist Critics," *The Dial*, LXXVI (June, 1924), 554; Bernard Smith, *Forces in American Criticism* (New York, 1939), pp. 282-83; James Farrell, *A Note on Literary Criticism* (New York, 1936), p. 21; George E. DeMille, *Literary Criticism in America: a Preliminary Survey* (New York, 1939), p. 254; Irving Babbitt, "Genius and Taste," *The Nation*, CVI (February 7, 1918), 140-41; Randolph Bourne, "The Suicide of Criticism," *The Columbia Monthly*, VIII (March, 1911), 188; Woodberry, *Heart of Man*, p. 262; Horace Kallen, "What Is an Elephant? A Fable for Critics," *The New Republic*, XLI (December 10, 1924), 3-4.
   5. "Scholarship and Criticism," p. 100.
   6. *Ibid.*
   7. *Literature and the New Era*, V, 23.
   8. Ainslie, "Extract from Introduction . . . ," p. xxiii.
   9. See "The Younger Generation," *Creative Criticism*, 1931, pp. 118-21.
   10. See *Literature and the New Era*, I, 9. See also "The American Critic," *Creative Criticism*, 1931, p. 146; "the modern critic has learnt to distinguish clearly between art, philosophy, history, religion, morals, not for the purpose of denying but of establishing their essential unity in the life of the spirit. Those who deny this unity and those who would substitute for it a muddle-headed if well-meaning confusion are alike the Enemy."
   11. Van Wyck Brooks, *America's Coming of Age* (New York, 1915), p. 27.
   12. *Literature and the New Era*, II, 1.
   13. Benedetto Croce, *The Breviary of Aesthetic*, trans. Douglas Ainslee, *Rice Institute Pamphlets*, II (1915), 237.

14. *Literature and the New Era*, II, 25-26, and V, 12, 21. In 1900, in his review of *Interpretations of Poetry and Religion*, Spingarn had rebuked Santayana for his tendency to merge poetry and religion.

15. See *Biographia Literaria, with Aesthetical Essays*, ed. J. Shawcross, 2 vols. (London, 1907), I, 12.

16. Except for his exemption of "Dr. Jung of Zurick," whom he praised in a letter (March 11, 1932) to his friend Bradley as "the only philosophical mind that psychoanalysis has yet produced," Spingarn's anathema on the psychologists was complete: "You cannot have," he said at the New School, "both psychology and philosophy; that is, a philosophical interpretation of literature and a psychological interpretation of literature at the same time."

17. See the *Aesthetic*, p. 96.

18. "Criticism in the United States," *Criticism in America, Its Function and Status*, ed. J. E. Spingarn (New York, 1924), pp. 288-89. For Spingarn's relationship to Gates, see above, p. 18.

19. *Biographia Literaria*, II, 241.

20. Babbitt, "Genius and Taste," p. 141.

21. "The Growth of a Literary Myth," *Creative Criticism*, 1931, p. 173. Also see below, note 33.

22. See *The Arizona Daily Star*, February 13, 1930, p. 2, and *Literature and the New Era*, III, 3-4.

23. See *Literary Criticism in the Renaissance*, pp. 71-72, 86, 155, 239.

24. *Literature and the New Era*, VI, 1. The language here is very close to that in "Scholarship and Criticism" (1922).

25. "The New Criticism," in *Creative Criticism*, 1931, pp. 13-14.

26. Garland's *Crumbling Idols* was published in 1895. Thompson was editor of *M'lle New York* from 1895 to 1898 and published *French Portraits* in 1900. Huneker wrote for the *New York Sun* from 1900 to 1917 and published *Iconoclasts* in 1905, *Egoists* in 1909, and *Promenades of an Impressionist* in 1910. Gates' *Studies and Appreciations* appeared in 1900, and Matthews' *The Development of the Drama* in 1903.

27. "The New Criticism," p. 16.

28. See "The New Criticism," "Creative Connoisseurship," "The Seven Arts and the Seven Confusions," in *Creative Criticism*, 1931, pp. 23, 98, 212, 218, and *Literature and the New Era*, III, 23.

29. See "The New Criticism," "The Younger Generation," "The American Critic," in *Creative Criticism*, 1931, pp. 15-16, 112, 135, 141, and "Jacobean and Caroline Criticism," *The*

Cambridge History of English Literature (Cambridge, 1911), VII, 302.
   30. *Literary Criticism in the Renaissance*, pp. 71-72, and *Literature and the New Era*, I, 24.
   31. *Literature and the New Era*, VI, 10-14.
   32. Croce, *Aesthetic*, p. 1.
   33. *Ibid.*, p. 11. Croce explained as follows: "On the hither side of the lower limit is sensation, formless matter, which the spirit can never apprehend in itself as simple matter. This it can only possess with form and in form, but postulates the notion of it as a mere limit. Matter, in its abstraction, is mechanism, passivity: it is what the spirit of man suffers, but does not produce. . . . mere matter produces animality, whatever is brutal and impulsive in man, not the spiritual dominion, which is humanity." Repeatedly Croce emphasized that intuition is not "impression" or "simple sensation," but instead "something cut off and standing out from the psychic basis of the sensations. . . . Every true intuition . . . is also *expression*. That which does not objectify itself in expression is not intuition . . . , but sensation and mere natural fact." (See *ibid.*, pp. 5-8, 11.)
   34. Croce, *Breviary of Aesthetic*, pp. 257-58.
   35. Croce, *Aesthetic*, p. 16.
   36. *Ibid.*, pp. 22, 23-26. "What intuition reveals in a work of art," said Croce, "is not space and time but *character, individual physiognomy*." Or more formally: "Independent and autonomous in respect to intellectual function: indifferent to later empirical discriminations, to reality and unreality, to formations and apperceptions of space and time, which are also later: intuition or representation is distinguished as *form* from what is felt and suffered, from the flux or wave of sensation, or from psychic matter; and this form, this taking possession, is expression." (*Ibid.*, pp. 5, 11.)
   37. But see Croce's answers to such criticisms below, pp. 91-92, 135.
   38. See George Santayana's trenchant denial of this idea in "What Is Aesthetics?" in *Obiter Scripta*, ed. Justus Buchler and Benjamin Schwartz (New York, 1936).
   39. Croce, *Aesthetic*, p. 96.
   40. *Ibid.*, p. 103.
   41. R. A. Scott-James, *The Making of Literature* (New York, n.d.), pp. 325, 331-32; A. E. Powell, *The Romantic Theory of Poetry: an Examination in the Light of Croce's Aesthetic* (London, 1926), pp. 242-43; E. F. Carritt, *The Theory of Beauty* (London, 1923), p. 201; Horace Kallen, *Art and Freedom*, 2 vols. (New York, 1942), I, 526, and II, 740.
   42. See Croce's *Aesthetic*, p. 121.

43. Croce, *Breviary of Aesthetic*, pp. 299-300. See also *Aesthetic*, p. 127.
44. "Dramatic Criticism and the Theatre," *Creative Criticism*, 1931, p. 84.
45. Croce, *Aesthetic*, p. 114. See also *Breviary of Aesthetic*, p. 231.
46. Galsworthy's article and Spingarn's reply appeared, along with brief notes by Alfred Ollivant and Rockwell Kent on the nature of art, as "Letters on Criticism and Art," *The Columbia Monthly*, IX (January, 1912), 72-73.
47. Croce, *Breviary of Aesthetic*, p. 229.
48. Carritt, pp. 89, 296-99.
49. D. G. James, *Scepticism and Poetry: an Essay on the Poetic Imagination* (London, 1937), pp. 72-73.
50. Robert Shafer, *Paul Elmer More and American Criticism* (New Haven, 1935), p. 18.
51. See above, p. 29.
52. R. P. Blackmur, "A Feather Bed for Critics," *The Expense of Greatness* (New York, 1940), p. 302.
53. "The American Critic," pp. 136-37.
54. Blackmur, "A Feather Bed for Critics," p. 302.
55. All the foregoing quotations may be found in *Creative Criticism*, 1931, pp. 18, 19, 167.
56. *Literature and the New Era*, I, 18.
57. "The American Critic," p. 147.

Chapter Six

1. Smith, *Forces in American Criticism*, p. 285; Sherman, *Genius of America*, p. 9; Babbitt, "Genius and Taste," p. 140; Lewisohn, *Expression in America*, p. 422.
2. H. L. Mencken, "Criticism of Criticism of Criticism," *Prejudices, First Series* (New York, 1919), p. 18.
3. Brooks, "Our Critics," p. 87; Chamberlain, p. 2; Spiller, *Literary History of the United States*, p. 1137; Woodberry, "Two Phases of Criticism," p. 262.
4. Blum, p. 554, and Mencken, "Criticism of Criticism of Criticism," p. 10.
5. Spingarn had rejected in 1908 Thomas Rymer's identification of poetry with "the conditions of actual and contemporary life" ("Introduction," *Critical Essays of the Seventeenth Century*, I, lxix) and complained in "Jacobean and Caroline Criticism" (1911) about Hobbes' emphasis on the "manners of men."
6. *Literature and the New Era*, V, 28-29 and VI, 36.
7. Spingarn's review was published in *Journal of Philosophy, Psychology, and Scientific Method*, X (December 4, 1913), 693-95, and reprinted in *Creative Criticism*, 1931, as the first of two "Notes on the New Humanism."

8. Irving Babbitt, "The Modern Spirit and Dr. Spingarn," *Journal of Philosophy, Psychology, and Scientific Method*, XI (April 9, 1914), 215-18.
9. "The Ancient Spirit and Professor Babbitt," *ibid.* (June 4, 1914), 326-27.
10. "American Criticism Today," *On American Books*, ed. Francis Hackett (New York, 1920), pp. 8-9.
11. See Babbitt's "Reply to Dr. Spingarn," *The Journal of Philosophy, Psychology, and Scientific Method*, XI (June 4, 1914), 328-29.
12. "Creative Connoisseurship," pp. 95-98.
13. "The Growth of a Literary Myth," p. 171.
14. See *Literature and the New Era*, VI, 5-6. But Spingarn also said that he agreed "with the New Humanists, that today the chief duty of criticism is to defend . . . the theoretical and synthetical character of art, against the emotional element which is its material and which is now swamping the theoretical material" (*Ibid.*, pp. 7-8).
15. See Sherman, "Point of View in American Criticism," *The Genius of America*, p.225; Shafer, pp. 10, 15-16; Lewisohn, *Expression in America*, p. 421; Smith, *Forces in American Criticism*, pp. 282-85, and "Huneker and the Tribe," *Proletarian Literature in the United States*, ed. Granville Hicks, et al. (New York, 1935), pp. 373-74; Calverton, *The New Ground of Criticism* (Seattle, n. d.), pp. 47-48 ff., and *The Newer Spirit* (New York, 1925), pp. 156-59. See also Munson, pp. 239-42, and Bourne, p. 192.
16. See Shafer, p. 16n.
17. *Literature and the New Era*, V, 24.
18. *Ibid.*, III, 2.
19. See for example his review of Santayana's *Interpretations of Poetry and Religion*, in *East and West*, I (June, 1900), 261-63.
20. *Goethe's Literary Essays*, p. 291.
21. "Politics and the Poet," p. 75.
22. *Literature and the New Era*, V, 3-4.
23. Partisan politics "will not make poetry" as the "political novels of Disraeli and Wells show . . . only too well" ("Politics and the Poet," p. 78).
24. "Politics and the Poet," pp. 75-76.
25. "The idea . . . that our wide-flung power must inevitably flower . . . in the 'great American novel' is merely another example of our mechanical optimism" ("Scholarship and Criticism," p. 93).
26. "Politics and the Poet," p. 77.
27. Calverton, *The Newer Spirit*, pp. 51, 135-36. See also pp. 49, 158.

28. *Ibid.*, p. 156. Parentheses and italics are Calverton's.

29. See below, pp. 117, 121, 136, 138, 140-41.

30. Sherman, "The National Genius," pp. 7-8.

31. "The New Criticism," pp. 27, 29.

32. See Spingarn's review of Croce's *Vico* in *The Nation*, LXXIII (July 18, 1901), 60.

33. *Literary Criticism in the Renaissance*, p. 8.

34. "The American Critic," pp. 135, 130.

35. *Literature and the New Era*, VI, 4.

36. "Scholarship and Criticism," pp. 102-4.

37. See Sherman's *Americans*, pp. 25, 20, and *The Genius of America*, pp. 9, 10, 17.

38. Sherman, "The National Genius," p. 4.

39. He did, however, engage in a private exchange of letters with Jacob Zeitlin, a co-editor of Sherman's *Life and Letters*, about the nativist element in Sherman's essays. Zeitlin apologized (in a letter of February 21, 1921) for his colleague's excesses but argued that other critics were just as bad. See also Sherman's letters to Ellery Sedgwick (April 25, 1931), to his sister (January 5, 1922), and to Carl Van Doren, all quoted in Zeitlin and Woodbridge, pp. 491-92, 495. In a mildly conciliatory letter to Spingarn (January 26, 1922), Sherman implied that Spingarn, too, was occasionally unfair.

40. See "Non Credo," in *Creative Criticism*, 1931, pp. 182-83.

41. Croce, *Breviary of Aesthetic*, pp. 233-34.

42. Yvor Winters, *In Defense of Reason* (Denver, 1947), pp. 28-29, 372.

43. Certainly this view is not foreign to Romantic critics, as witness Shelley's statement in the *Defence*: "The great instrument of moral good is the imagination; and poetry administers to the effect by acting on the cause." Croce offers a qualified but moving version of Shelley's idea in *The Defence of Poetry: Variations on a Theme by Shelley* (Oxford, 1933), pp. 17, 27-31. See also Croce's "Dante and the World Today," in *The Literary Review* of the *New York Evening Post*, II (September 17, 1921), 17-18.

44. Lewisohn, *Expression in America*, p. 422. Again Spingarn made no public sign, though he complained of Lewisohn's "inverted Hitlerism" in a letter of March 11, 1932, to W. A. Bradley. It is interesting to remember Stuart Sherman's accusation in "Is There Anything to Be Said for Literary Tradition," *The Bookman*, LII (October, 1920), 108-12, that Lewisohn and the other contributors to Lewisohn's anthology, *A Modern Book of Criticism* (New York, 1919), were deaf to American "ances-

tral voices" and insensitive to the "national experience," however connected they might be "with the house of Jesse." Lewisohn at that time replied in "Tradition and Freedom," *The Nation,* CXI (December 8, 1920), 651-52, that he preferred "insurgent" voices to "ancestral" ones.

45. *Critical Essays of the Seventeenth Century,* I, lxxxi, and *Literature and the New Era,* II, 29.

46. *Literature and the New Era,* II, 24.

Chapter Seven

1. "Grocer Shop Criticism and Real Criticism," *The Dial,* LVII (August 16, 1914), 97.

2. "The New Criticism," p. 8.

3. Woodberry, "Two Phases of Criticism," pp. 253-64; Bourne, "The Suicide of Criticism," p. 189; Smith, *Forces in American Criticism,* pp. 278-85; Farrell, p. 21; Babbitt, "Reply to Dr. Spingarn," p. 328, "Genius and Taste," pp. 138-41, "On Being Creative," *On Being Creative* (Boston and New York, 1932), pp. 25-29; Paul Elmer More, *The Demon of the Absolute* (Princeton, 1928), p. 7; Norman Foerster, *American Criticism* (Boston and New York, 1928), p. 119n; Sherman, "Disinterested? No!" pp. 3-6; Hartwick, pp. 142-44, 307; Shafer, pp. 11-13.

4. Babbitt, "On Being Creative," pp. 28-29.

5. Shafer, p. 13.

6. "Grocer Shop Criticism," p. 97, and "Scholarship and Criticism," p. 103.

7. *Goethe's Literary Essays,* p. 140.

8. "The Growth of a Literary Myth," pp. 167, 171, 170. There was nothing evasive, however, in Spingarn's statement in "Notes on the New Humanism": "Professor Babbitt had asserted a fundamental, and to my mind valid, principle when he defended the value of judgment against impressionists in criticism and intuitionalists in philosophy."

9. Lewisohn, *A Modern Book of Criticism,* p. iii. Spingarn complained in a note to the reprinting of "The Seven Arts and the Seven Confusions" in *Creative Criticism,* 1931, that he had not been properly consulted (he was in the Army in Europe) about Lewisohn's use of this essay.

10. More, p. 7, and Farrell, pp. 16-17. Richard McKeon also misrepresents Spingarn by quoting the passage cited by Farrell in "The Philosophical Bases of Art and Criticism," in *Critics and Criticism,* ed. R. S. Crane (Chicago, 1952).

11. "The American Critic," pp. 143, 147. See also Spingarn's criticism of Saintsbury's "impressionism" in his review of Saintsbury's *The Earlier Renaissance,* in *The Nation,* LXXIV

(February 6, 1902), 116, and also "Non Credo," p. 181.
12. "American Criticism Today," p. 14.
13. Smith, *Forces in American Criticism*, pp. 278-80.
14. Woodberry, "Two Phases of Criticism," pp. 255, 257, 272; Granville Hicks, *The Great Tradition* (New York, 1935), pp. 248-51.
15. "American Criticism Today," p. 14.
16. See above, pp. 107-8, and below, pp. 121, 136, 138, 140-41.
17. *Literature and the New Era*, VI, 25.
18. Brooks, "Our Critics," p. 85; Mencken, "Criticism of Criticism of Criticism," p. 181.
19. Smith, *Forces in American Criticism*, p. 283; Peyre, "The Criticism of Contemporary Writing," pp. 230-31; Calverton, *The New Ground of Criticism*, p. 54; Sherman, "Disinterested? No!" pp. 5-6. See also Mencken's "Criticism of Criticism of Criticism," pp. 13-14.
20. Mencken, *ibid.*, p. 18.
21. *Literature and the New Era*, III, 23; "Prose and Verse," *Creative Criticism*, 1931, p. 47; and "The New Criticism," p. 38.
22. D. H. Lawrence has, of course, pointed to an early American preoccupation with Spirit in his *Studies in Classic American Literature* (New York, 1923), especially in the essay on Poe. Lionel Trilling, in "Reality in America" and "Manners, Morals, and the Novel," both reprinted in *The Liberal Imagination* (New York, 1950), and especially in "William Dean Howells and the Roots of Modern Taste," reprinted in *The Opposing Self* (New York, 1955), has suggested that even in the pêle-mêle industrial production of modern America one may see a pursuit of ideal system rather than a love of material objects. Christopher Isherwood has recently offered a brilliant comic defense of the American motel room as a triumph of the abstract over the actual in *A Single Man* (New York, 1964), pp. 90-92.
23. *Literature and the New Era*, VI, 37-41.
24. "The New Criticism," p. 38, and *Literature and the New Era*, I, 6.
25. *Literary Criticism in the Renaissance*, pp. vi, 59, 318.
26. Croce, *Aesthetic*, pp. 109, 117.
27. *Ibid.*, pp. 111, 103. For a good explanation of Croce's idea of technique, see *Breviary of Aesthetic*, pp. 259-60.
28. Croce, *Aesthetic*, p. 52. In regard to the "usefulness" of certain physical art objects, Croce points out that "the extrinsic purpose is not necessarily . . . a limit or impediment to the other purpose of being a stimulus to aesthetic reproduction. . . . not

only are the two purposes not necessarily contradictory, but . . . the artist always has the means of preventing this contradiction. . . . How? by simply making the *destination* of the object which serves a practical end enter as material into his aesthetic intuition and externalization" (*Aesthetic*, p. 102).

29. Allen Tate and John Peal Bishop, *American Harvest* (New York, 1942), p. 10, and Cleanth Brooks, *The Well Wrought Urn* (New York, 1947), p. 183.

30. "The New Criticism," pp. 25, 32, and "Prose and Verse," pp. 47, 50.

31. Farrell, pp. 17-18; Henry Seidel Canby, *Definitions*, 2d series (New York, 1924), p. 10; Lewisohn, *Expression in America*, p. 421; Sherman, "The National Genius," p. 17.

32. Edmund Clarence Stedman had complained about the problem in *The Nature and Elements of Poetry* (Boston, 1893), pp. 191-92, and Van Wyck Brooks was still complaining about it in "The Literary Life," in *Civilization in the United States*, p. 180, in 1922. For discussions of the "well-made play" and of the rise of the theatrical "syndicate," see Montrose J. Moses, *The American Dramatist* (Boston, 1911), pp. 154-68, 288-96, and Arthur Hobson Quinn, *A History of the American Drama from the Civil War to the Present Day* (New York, 1945), II, 2-3.

33. *Literary Criticism in the Renaissance*, pp. 56, 71-74, 97-100, and *Critical Essays of the Seventeenth Century*, pp. xii, lxix, lxxii-lxxiii.

34. Even in *Literary Criticism in the Renaissance* (pp. 56, 71) and *Critical Essays of the Seventeenth Century* (p. lxxiii) Spingarn connected the identification of theatrical appeal and dramatic art with "modern" tendencies, naming among others Brander Matthews.

35. A. B. Walkley, "An American Croce," *The Times*, March 24, 1926, p. 14.

36. Croce, *Aesthetic*, pp. 114, 115-16.

37. See "The American Critic," p. 143.

38. Croce, *Ariosto, Shakespeare, and Corneille*, trans. Douglas Ainslie (New York, 1920), p. 280.

39. Croce, *Breviary of Aesthetic*, pp. 270-71.

40. "Prose and Verse," pp. 44-45, 51.

41. *Ibid.*, pp. 49-50, and "The Seven Arts and the Seven Confusions," pp. 220-21. See also "The New Criticism," p. 26.

42. Croce, *Breviary of Aesthetic*, pp. 265-66.

43. Carritt, pp. 183, 22n, 34.

44. Croce, *Aesthetic*, p. 42.

45. As quoted in Alice D. Snyder, *Coleridge on Logic and*

Learning (New Haven, 1929), p. 138.

46. Santayana, "Croce's Aesthetics," *Journal of Comparative Literature*, I (April-June, 1903), 195. But see Croce's answer to such an analysis in the *Aesthetic*, p. 150.

47. "The New Criticism," p. 26.

48. See "The Younger Generation" and "Prose and Verse" in *Creative Criticism*, 1931, pp. 112, 41.

49. The preceding chapters explain, perhaps, why N. Giordano Orsini, in "Il caso Spingarn e il Crocianesimo in America," *Criterio*, I (July, 1957), 517-23, could accuse Spingarn of misrepresenting Croce by his emphasis on "taste." Theodore Stenberg probably had Spingarn in mind when he discussed a similar "misrepresentation" in his "Croce and American Criticism," *Sewanee Review*, XXXIII (April-June, 1925), 223.

Chapter Eight

1. See, for example, "Origins of Modern Criticism" (1904), p. 477, and the "Introductory Note" to *Sir William Temple's Essays on Ancient and Modern Learning and on Poetry*, ed. J. E. Spingarn (Oxford, 1909), as well as "Scholarship and Criticism" (1922), p. 107, and "Mr. Spingarn's Position," *The Nation*, XLV (January 14, 1925), 200-201.

2. Croce, *Aesthetic*, pp. 31, 28; also pp. 27, 29. For Walkley's phrase, see above p. 127.

3. Croce, *Aesthetic*, pp. 27, 29. Croce's idealistic belief in the "unity of the real" minimizes the problem of historical error in a manner that recalls Emerson's essay on "History." See *Breviary of Aesthetic*, pp. 299-300, and *Aesthetic*, p. 127. Also see above, pp. 91-92.

4. Croce, *Aesthetic*, pp. 130-31. Sometimes, as in the "idle times" of Emerson's scholar, synthesis does not succeed scholarship and "the historical student must . . . reconcile himself to the useful but inglorious function of a collector of facts," which "remain for the time being formless, incoherent and meaningless," but which may become "preserves or mines for the historian of the future." (*Aesthetic*, pp. 129-30.) Spingarn made the same point repeatedly in the New School lectures.

5. Croce, *Breviary of Aesthetic*, p. 307.

6. *Ibid.*, p. 308.

7. Croce, *European Literature in the Nineteenth Century*, trans. with an Introduction by Douglas Ainslie (New York, 1924), pp. 66-78.

8. Croce, *Breviary of Aesthetic*, p. 307.

9. *Literature and the New Era*, VI, 20, 29.

10. *Ibid.*, p. 21.
11. See, for example, *Aesthetic*, pp. 133-34.
12. The following summary of Crocean doctrine is taken from *Ariosto, Shakespeare, and Corneille*, pp. 221-22, 267-68; *Aesthetic*, pp. 73, 112-13, 130-31, 136-37; and "Condition of Criticism in Italy," in *Lectures on Criticism*, Bollingen Series, XVI (New York, 1949), 178.
13. "Prose and Verse," p. 41.
14. See "The Younger Generation," *Creative Criticism*, 1931, pp. 118-20.
15. See, for example, "Origins of Modern Criticism," p. 478, and "The American Scholar," pp. 153-54.
16. "The American Critic" and "The Younger Generation" in *Creative Criticism*, 1931, pp. 145, 113.
17. *Literature and the New Era*, III, 30.
18. *Ibid.*, I, 25, 35.
19. See "A Note on French Scholarship" and "The New Criticism," in *Creative Criticism*, 1931, pp. 200n, 27.
20. *Literature and the New Era*, III, 14-18.
21. *Ibid.*, III, 20, 21, 23.
22. *Ibid.*, pp. 23-24, 26.

Chapter Nine

1. Van Wyck Brooks, "On Creating a Usable Past," *The Dial*, LXIV (April 11, 1918), 337-41, and *America's Coming of Age;* Babbitt, *Literature and the American College* (New York, 1908); Lionel Trilling, *The Liberal Imagination: Essays on Literature and Society* (New York, 1950); and Spingarn, "The American Critic," p. 146.
2. "The Growth of a Literary Myth," p. 164. Also see above, p. 128.
3. *Ibid.*, p. 176.
4. "The Growth of a Literary Myth," pp. 173-74.
5. Chamberlain, "Mr. Spingarn Puts His Critical Fences in Repair," p. 2.
6. John Crowe Ransom, "The Mimetic Principle," *The World's Body* (New York, 1930), p. 206; "Criticism as Pure Speculation," *The Intent of the Critic*, ed. Donald Stauffer (Princeton, 1941), p. 109. See also "Wanted: an Ontological Critic," *The New Criticism* (Norfolk, Conn., 1941), p. 314; *God Without Thunder* (New York, 1930), p. 173; and "Art and Mr. Santayana," *The World's Body*, p. 326.
7. Ransom, "A Psychologist Looks at Poetry," and "The Mimetic Principle," in *The World's Body*, pp. 156, 205-6.

Though Ransom had written in *God Without Thunder*, p. 173, that the esthetic attitude was "the most objective and the most innocent attitude in which we can look upon the world," he elsewhere specifically rejected the Crocean view that intuition was prior to concept: "It can hardly be argued that the arts are constituted automatically out of original images, and arise in some early stage of innocence." For "Men become poets, or at least they read poets, in order to atone for having been hard practical men and hard theoretical scientists." Thus, "It is not as in a state of innocence, to receive the fragrance of the roses on the world's first morning that our moderns, the scarred veterans, may enact their poetry, but in the violence of return and regeneration. They re-enter the world, but it is the world which they have marked with their raids, and there is no other world they can enter." (But Croce, too, knew that intuitions included all the psychic material available, including concepts; he only insisted that this material be intuited.) See Ransom's "Poetry: a Note on Ontology" and "Preface," *The World's Body*, pp. 116-17, viii-xi. See also his "Wanted: an Ontological critic," p. 281, and "The Literary Criticism of Aristotle," *Lectures in Criticism*, pp. 15-42.

Santayana (who sometimes, in some matters, acts as an unofficial philosopher for the "new critics") thought that "Before prosaic objects are descried, the volume and richness needful for poetry lie in a blurred and unidentified chaos; but after the common world has emerged and called on prose to describe it, the same volume and richness may be recovered; and a new and clarified poetry may arise through synthesis." See *Reason in Art* (New York, 1934), p. 114. See also *ibid.*, p. 15, and above, p. 131.

8. Croce, *Aesthetic*, pp. 1, 26, 42. Cf. also *ibid.*, p. 31: "Intuition gives us the world, the phenomenon; the concept gives us the noumenon, the Spirit."

9. See Allen Tate, "Present Function of Criticism" and "Understanding Modern Poetry," in *Reason in Madness* (New York, 1941), p. 9; and "American Criticism," p. 27.

10. *Literature and the New Era*, III, 6-7.

11. T. S. Eliot, "Tradition and the Individual Talent," *The Sacred Wood*, 4th ed. (London, 1934), pp. 53, 58. See also "The Perfect Critic," *ibid.*, pp. 14-15.

12. See E. K. Wimsatt and M. C. Beardsley, "The Affective Fallacy," *The Sewanee Review*, LVII (Winter, 1949), 31-55;

Eliseo Vivas, "The Objective Correlative of T. S. Eliot," *American Bookman*, I (Winter, 1944), 7-18; and Winters, *In Defense of Reason*, pp. 463, 469-74. Wimsatt and Beardsley touch on some genuine difficulties in Eliot's vocabulary, but surely Eliot argues, in his famous essay on *Hamlet, against*, not for, "qualitative progression." Vivas, likewise, is sensitive to the problems of Eliot's affective vocabulary, but in making Eliot a defender of the "expression theory," an advocate of the idea of a "preestablished harmony . . . between the waiting feeling and its verbal grament," Vivas flatly denies the possibility that the "waiting feeling" is, like Croce's "impressions," posited for convenience of exposition, but never really known until clothed in its "verbal garment." For Spingarn's defense of Croce against similar criticism, see above, pp. 85-86.

13. Spiller, p. 1155.

14. Winters, pp. 498-99.

15. Despite Winters' efforts in his essay on Eliot in *In Defense of Reason* to make Eliot a determinist, Eliot seems largely to be on Winters' side, as indicated by his remarks on art and personality quoted above. See Eliot's "The Perfect Critic," and also "The Social Function of Poetry," *Adelphi*, XXI (July, 1925), 152-61. Also see Blackmur's "D. H. Lawrence and Expressive Form," in *The Double Agent.*

16. Weinberg, p. vii.

17. See "The Younger Generation" and "The Seven Arts and Seven Confusions," in *Creative Criticism*, 1931, pp. 113, 220. See also above, p. 147.

18. Eliot, "Tradition and the Individual Talent," p. 49, and "The Function of Criticism," *Selected Essays* (New York, 1932), pp. 12-13.

19. Tate, "Miss Emily and the Bibliographer," *Reason in Madness*, pp. 114-15.

20. See also Tate's "What is a Traditional Society?" in *Reason in Madness* for a description of the "historical imagination" as "the religious imagination manqué," only a little "lower" and a little less potent in its ordering of human experience than religion itself.

21. Tate's novel, *The Fathers*, has a strong historical tone, for all these works proceed from his conviction that fact and fiction may be fused in the creative imagination.

22. See his "American Criticism," p. 27.

23. Frederick A. Pottle, "The New Critics and the Historical

Method," *The Yale Review*, XLIII (Autumn, 1953), 15.

24. A brief sketch of the attitudes of the Marxists and the "new critics" toward the use of history can be found in "Criticism in the Thirties: the Marxists and the New Critics," *The Western Humanities Review*, XVII (Winter, 1963), 75-84, by the present author.

25. Richard Ruland, *The Rediscovery of American Literature: Premises of Critical Taste, 1900-1940* (Cambridge, Mass., 1967), pp. 5-6.

26. Some idea of the complication of viewpoints involved, as well as the importance of Croce's role, may be had in R. G. Collingwood's *The Idea of History* (Oxford, 1946), which is perhaps the culmination of the cycle in question. Collingwood translated Croce's *Autobiography* in 1927.

27. See Tate's "Preface" to his *Reactionary Essays on Poetry and Ideas* (New York, 1936).

28. Blackmur, "A Feather Bed for Critics," p. 302. Also see above, p. 94.

29. See Blackmur's "The Enabling Act of Criticism," *American Issues*, ed. Willard Thorpe, Merle Curti and Carlos Baker (Philadelphia, 1941); also "A Critic's Job of Work" and "The Critical Prefaces of Henry James," both in *The Double Agent*. Also cf. above, p. 133 and Chapter 8, *passim*.

30. See Blackmur's "A Feather Bed for Critics," pp. 279, 302, and Spingarn's "American Critic," pp. 136-37.

31. Blackmur, "The Enabling Act of Criticism," p. 879.

32. Foerster, "The Esthetic Judgment and the Ethical Judgment," in *The Intent of the Critic*, pp. 76-77.

33. Eliot, "Experiment in Criticism," *The Bookman*, LXX (November, 1929), 231.

34. T. E. Hulme, *Speculations*, ed. Herbert Read (New York, 1924), p. 129.

35. Winters, pp. 371, 75-76.

36. Blackmur, "Notes on E. E. Cummings' Language," *The Double Agent* (New York, 1935), p. 13. See also Blackmur's discussion of the "confusion of ideas with . . . words . . . and the worse confusion of words with ideas, which in fact exhaust only a fraction of the power of words," in "A Feather Bed for Critics," p. 292.

37. Cleanth Brooks, *The Well Wrought Urn*, p. 132. Brooks explained on pp. 68-69 of *The Well Wrought Urn* that "the poem itself is the only medium that communicates the particular

'what' that is communicated." Cf. pp. 131, 136 above.
  38. Tate, "Literature as Knowledge," *Reason in Madness*, p. 25, and "Poetry and the Absolute," *The Sewanee Review*, XXXV (January, 1927), 44. See also "Tension in Poetry," in *Reason in Madness*.
  39. "Prose and Verse," p. 48.
  40. Blackmur, "A Note on Yvor Winters," *The Expense of Greatness*, p. 173.
  41. See E. C. Stedman, "What Is Criticism?" *Epoch*, I (March 11, 1887), 131, and *Poets of America* (Boston, 1885), p. 25; W. C. Brownell, *Standards* (New York, 1917), pp. 37-43, 133-45. The Brooks essays are in *Sketches in Criticism* (New York, 1932) and Harold Stearns' *Civilization in the United States*.
  42. See *I'll Take My Stand: the South and the Agrarian Tradition*, by Twelve Southerners (New York, 1962). This collection was originally published in 1930.
  43. "Scholarship and Criticism," pp. 104-6, 93. See also *Literature and the New Era*, I, 6-7.
  44. *Literature and the New Era*, VI, 36. Some sense of Spingarn's impatience with "momentary fashions of thought" is in the following remark delivered during the question period at the fifth New School lecture: "I am afraid . . . that while I am going to welcome every question that you may ask as long as it remains a question, I don't think that it is worth while taking up . . . the time of the audience here as an outlet for the emotions of those whose emotions now find their favorite outlet in a religious devotion to Marxism."
  45. *Ibid.*, I, 6-7.
  46. See above, p. 72.
  47. Smith, "Huneker and the Tribe," p. 373.
  48. Eden Phillpotts, *The Joy of Youth* (London, 1913), pp. 119-20.
  49. For his part, Spingarn was willing, as we have seen, to make concessions to Babbitt. See Chap. 6, note 14, and Chap. 7, note 8.
  50. Tate, "American Criticism," p. 27.
  51. O'Connor, *Sense and Sensibility in Modern Poetry*, pp. 249-50.
  52. *Literature and the New Era*, VI, 2. Also cf. above, pp. 27-29, 105-9, 112.
  53. "Scholarship and Criticism," p. 106.

Selected Bibliography

PRIMARY SOURCES

(in order of publication)

None of Spingarn's letters has been published, except for those appearing in his pamphlet on *Academic Freedom* (see below) and a few excerpts in *Selected Letters of George Edward Woodberry*, with an Introduction by Walter De La Mare (Boston and New York: Houghton Mifflin Co., 1933). All the letters and other unpublished materials cited in this study were made available by Mrs. Spingarn, who has since donated many of her husband's books and papers to the New York Public Library.

"Lyly's 'Endimion'." *The Athaneum*, no. 3484 (August 4, 1894), p. 172.

A History of Literary Criticism in the Renaissance. Vol. I, *Columbia University Studies in Literature.* New York: published for the Columbia University Press by the Macmillan Co., 1899. Also published in London: Macmillan Co., Ltd., 1899.

Review. *Interpretations of Poetry and Religion.* George Santayana. *East and West*, I (June, 1900), 261-63.

Notice of *Tesi fondamentali di un' Estetica.* Benedetto Croce. *The Nation*, LXXI (November 15, 1900), 386.

"American Scholarship; Les Belles Lettres et l'Erudition en Amérique du Point de Vue Académique." *Proceedings of the Congress of Comparative History.* Paris, 1901. Reprinted at Macon by Protat Frères, 1901.

The New Hesperides. New York: printed under the auspices of the New York Delta of Phi Beta Kappa at the Laurentian Press, 1901.

Review. *Giambattista Vico, Primo Scropritore della Scienza Estetica.* Benedetto Croce. *The Nation*, LXXIII (July 18, 1901), 60.

Review. *The Earlier Renaissance.* George Saintsbury. *The Nation*, LXXIV (February 6, 1902), 116-17.

Review. Leonard Eckstein Opdycke's translation of Castiglione's *Cortegiano. The Nation*, LXXIV (April 24, 1902), 330-31.

Review. *Estetica.* Benedetto Croce. *The Nation*, LXXV (September 25, 1902), 252-53.

"Saintsbury's History of Criticism," *The Nation*, LXXVI (January 15, 1903), 56-58.

"Unpublished Letters of an English Humanist." *Journal of Comparative Literature*, I (January-March, 1903), 47-65.

A Note on Croce's journal of criticism, *La Critica. The Nation*, LXXVI (June 18, 1903), 497.

"Corneille and the Spanish Drama." *Journal of Comparative Literature*, I (July-September, 1903), 282-84.

English Literature, Elizabethan Period, Prose, in *The Encyclopedia Americana*, 16 vols. New York: Americana Company, 1903-4.

"The Origins of Modern Criticism." *Modern Philology*, I (April, 1904), 477-96. Later revised and included as the "Conclusion" to the second edition of *A History of Literary Criticism in the Renaissance.*

"The Sources of Jonson's 'Discoveries'." *Modern Philology*, II (April, 1905), 451-60.

La Critica Letteraria nel Rinascimento, Saggio Sulle Origini dello Spirito Classico nella Letteratura Moderna. Trans. into Italian by Antonio Fusco. Corrections and additions by the author, and a preface by Benedetto Croce. Bari: G. Laterza, 1905. The definitive form of Spingarn's *A History of Literary Criticism in the Renaissance.*

A History of Literary Criticism in the Renaissance, 2d ed., rev. and augmented. New York: The Columbia University Press, 1908.

Review. Croce's edition of Di Francesco de Sanctis' *Saggio Critico sul Petrarca. The Nation*, LXXXVI (April 16, 1908), 355.

Review. *Dante e la Francia dall' Eta media al Secola di Voltaire.* Arturo Farinelli. *The Nation*, LXXXVI (December 31, 1908), 656-57.

Critical Essays of the Seventeenth Century. 3 vols. Ed. J. E. Spingarn. Oxford: Clarendon Press, 1908, Vols. I and II; Vol. III, 1909.

Sir William Temple's Essays on Ancient and Modern Learning and on Poetry. Ed. J. E. Spingarn. Oxford: Clarendon Press, 1909.

"Literary Criticism." *Columbia University Faculty Lectures on Literature.* New York: Columbia University Press, 1911. The first published version of Spingarn's lecture on "The New Criticism."

The New Hesperides and Other Poems. New York: Sturgis and Walton and Co., 1911.

The New Criticism. New York: Columbia University Press, 1911.

"Jacobean and Caroline Criticism." *The Cambridge History of English Literature.* Vol. VII. Cambridge: Cambridge University Press, 1911.

A Question of Academic Freedom: Being the Official Correspondence Between Nicholas Murray Butler, President of Columbia University, and J. E. Spingarn, Professor of Comparative Literature and Chairman of the Division of Modern Languages and Literature, in Columbia University, During the Academic Year 1910-1911, With Other Documents. New York: printed for distribution among the alumni, 1911.

"Letters on Criticism and Art." J. E. Spingarn, John Galsworthy, Alfred Ollivant and Rockwell Kent. *The Columbia Monthly,* IX (January, 1912), 72-77. Spingarn's contribution included in the 1917 edition of *Creative Criticism* as "A Note on Genius and Taste."

["Creative Connoisseurship."] New York *Evening Post,* February, 1913, p. 9. Later revised and included in all editions of *Creative Criticism.*

"Note on Dramatic Criticism." *English Association Essays and Studies by Members.* Vol. IV. Oxford: Clarendon Press, 1913. Later revised and included in all editions of *Creative Criticism* as "Dramatic Criticism and the Theatre."

A Note on Dramatic Criticism. Oxford: Clarendon Press, 1913. See preceding entry.

"Literature, Comparative." *A Cyclopedia of Education.* Ed. Paul Monroe, Vol. IV. New York: The Macmillan Co., 1913.

Review. *The Masters of Modern French Criticism.* Irving Babbitt. *The Journal of Philosophy, Psychology, and Scientific Method,* X (December 4, 1913), 693-95. Included as the first of two "Notes on the New Humanism" in *Creative Criticism,* 1931.

"The Ancient Spirit and Professor Babbitt." *The Journal of Philosophy, Psychology, and Scientific Method,* XI (June 4, 1914), 326-28. Reprinted as the second of two "Notes on the New Humanism" in *Creative Criticism,* 1931.

"Introduction." Giovanni della Casa's *A Renaissance Courtesy-*

Book: Galateo of Manners and Behaviours. Trans. Robert Peterson. *The Humanist's Library.* Ed. Lewis Einstein. Vol. VIII. Boston: The Merrymount Press, 1914.

"Grocer-Shop Criticism and Real Criticism." *The Dial,* LVII (August 16, 1914), 96-99.

"The Seven Arts and the Seven Confusions." *The Seven Arts,* I (March, 1917), 507-14. Included in *Creative Criticism,* 1931.

Creative Criticism: Essays on the Unity of Genius and Taste. New York: Henry Holt and Co., 1917. Includes "The New Criticism," "Dramatic Criticism and the Theatre," "Creative Connoisseurship," "Prose and Verse," and "A Note on Genius and Taste."

"The Rich Storehouse of Croce's Thought." *The Dial,* LXIV (May 23, 1918), 485-86.

"American Criticism Today." *The* (London) *Nation,* XXVII (April 17, 1920), 82-84. Reprinted in *On American Books.* Ed. Francis Hackett. New York: B. V. Huebsch, Inc., 1920.

Goethe's Literary Essays. Ed. J. E. Spingarn. New York: Harcourt, Brace and Co., 1921.

"Scholarship and Criticism." *Civilization in the United States: An Inquiry by Thirty Americans.* Ed. Harold Stearns. New York: Harcourt, Brace and Co., 1922. An abridged version of this essay appeared in Walter Fischer's *Amerikanische Prosa* (Leipsig and Berlin: Verlag und Druck von B. G. Geubner, 1926). The part dealing with criticism was revised and reprinted in Spingarn's anthology, *Criticism in America, Its Function and Status,* as "Criticism in the United States"; it also appeared as "The American Critic" in *Creative Criticism,* 1931. The part dealing with scholarship was revised and reprinted in *Creative Criticism,* 1931, as "The American Scholar: A Lament."

Scholarship and Criticism in the United States. New York: Harcourt, Brace and Co., 1922. See preceding entry.

"The Younger Generation: A New Manifesto." *The Freeman,* V (June 7, 1922), 296-98. Reprinted as No. 4 of the *Troutbeck Leaflets;* this essay also appears in the 1931 edition of *Creative Criticism.*

"Foreword." "Tsang-Lang Discourse on Poetry." *The Dial,* LXXIII (September, 1922), 272-73.

"The Growth of a Literary Myth." *The Freeman,* VII (May 2, 1923), 181-83.

"The 'Quite Unintelligible' Emerson," *The Nation,* XCVII (August 8, 1923), 140.

Criticism in America, Its Function and Status. Essays by Irving Babbitt, Van Wyck Brooks, W. C. Brownell, Ernest Boyd,

T. S. Eliot, H. L. Mencken, Stuart P. Sherman, J. E. Spingarn, and George E. Woodberry. Ed. J. E. Spingarn. New York: Harcourt, Brace and Co., 1924. Spingarn's contributions include "The New Critic" and "Criticism in the United States."

Poems. New York: Harcourt, Brace and Co., 1924. Spingarn published verse in *Cosmopolitan* (May, 1899), *East and West* (November, 1899, January and August, 1900), *The Atlantic Monthly* (April, 1902), *The Masses* (February, 1914), *Commonweal* (October 21, 1925), as well as in *The Nation* and the *International.* His verses also appeared in E. C. Stedman, ed., *An American Anthology, 1787-1900* (Boston: Houghton Mifflin and Co., 1900); in Burton Stevenson's first *Home Book of Verse, American and English, 1580-1912* (New York: Henry Holt and Co., 1912), and in most editions of Stevenson's *Home Book of Modern Verse* (New York: Henry Holt and Co., 1923, 1926, 1937); in Upton Sinclair's *The Cry for Justice: An Anthology of the Literature of Social Protest* (Philadelphia: The John C. Winston Co., c. 1915, published by the author, 1921); in *Columbia Verse: An Anthology of Verse Published in Undergraduate Magazines of Columbia University from 1897-1924*, ed. Cargill Sprietsma, with a preface by John Erskine (New York: Columbia University Press, 1924); in Genevieve Taggard's *May Days: An Anthology of Verse from Masses-Liberator* (New York: Boni and Liveright, 1925); and in William Stanley Beaumont Braithwaite's *Anthology of Magazine Verse for 1926 and Yearbook of American Poetry*, Sesqui-Centennial ed. (Boston: B. G. Brimmer Co., 1926).

The Troutbeck Leaflets, ed. J. E. Spingarn, Amenia, N. Y.: printed for private distribution by the Troutbeck Press, 1924-1926.

1. *Poetry and Religion: Six Poems.* J. E. Spingarn. June, 1924.
2. *Criticism: An Unpublished Essay.* Walt Whitman. Christmas, 1924.
3. *Aesthetics: A Dialogue.* Lewis Mumford. February, 1925.
4. *The Younger Generation: A New Manifesto.* J. E. Spingarn. 1925.
5. *Thoreau's Last Letter.* With a Note on his Correspondent, Myron B. Benton, by Edwin Arlington Robinson. April, 1925.
6. *Four Days on the Webutuck River.* Charles E. Benton. With an Introduction by Sinclair Lewis. July, 1925.
7. *New Houses: Twelve Poems.* Amy Spingarn. 1925.

8. *The Amenia Conference: An Historic Negro Gathering.* W. E. Burghardt Du Bois. September, 1925.
9. *A Troutbeck Letter-Book, 1861-1867: Being Unpublished Letters to Myron B. Benton from Emerson, Sophia Thoreau, Moncure Conway, and Others.* Introduction by George Edward Woodberry. Christmas, 1925.
10. *John Burroughs at Troutbeck: Being Extracts from His Writings, Published and Unpublished.* Introduction by Vachel Lindsay. 1926.

"Mr. Spingarn's Position." *The New Republic*, XLV (January 14, 1925), 200-201. Reprinted in *Creative Criticism*, 1931, as "Non Credo."

Review. *La politesse mondaine et les théories de l'honnêteté en France au XVIIe siècle, de 1600 à 1660.* Maurice Magendie. *The Romanic Review*, XVII (January-March, 1926), 71-73. Reprinted in the 1931 edition of *Creative Criticism* as "A Note on French Scholarship."

"The Negro in Art: How Shall He Be Portrayed—A Symposium." Langston Hughes, J. E. Spingarn, Walter White, Alfred A. Knopf, William Lyon Phelps. *The Crisis*, XXXIV (April, 1926), 278-80.

A Spingarn Enchiridion: Being Passages from the Writings of J. E. Spingarn in Reply to Paul Elmer More's Charge That He Has Taught That "Criticism is Only Impression." Collected by Alain T. Peters. New York: The Minaret Press, 1929.

"Bibliographical Note on the Literature Available in English." Karl Vossler's *Mediaeval Culture, An Introduction to Dante and His Times.* Trans. William Cranston Lewis. Vol. IV. New York: Harcourt, Brace and Co., 1929.

Creative Criticism and Other Essays. New York: Harcourt, Brace and Co., 1931. Includes "The New Criticism," "Prose and Verse," "Dramatic Criticism and the Theatre," "Creative Connoisseurship," "The Younger Generation," "The American Critic," "The American Scholar," "The Growth of a Literary Myth," "Non Credo," "Notes on the New Humanism (1913-14)," "A Note on French Scholarship," and "The Seven Arts and the Seven Confusions."

A Scholar's Testament: Two Letters from George Edward Woodberry to J. E. Spingarn. Introductory Note by Lewis Mumford. *The Troutbeck Leaflets.* Second series. Ed. J. E. Spingarn. Amenia, N. Y.: The Troutbeck Press, 1931.

Racial Equality. An Address Delivered at the Twenty-third Annual Conference of the National Association for the Advancement of Colored People. Held at Washington, D. C., May 17, 1932. New York: The National Association for the Advancement of Colored People, 1932.

"Climbing Clematis." (London) *Gardeners' Chronicle*, XCIII (January 14, 1933), 29-30. Excerpts in *Garden Digest*, IV (March, 1933), 6-8.

"American Clematis for American Gardens." *National Horticultural Magazine*, XIII (January, 1934), 76-95.

"Proud Clematis Clan Unfurls Its Flag." *House and Garden*, LXV (February, 1934), 38-39.

"The Large-Flowered Clematis Hybrids." *National Horticultural Magazine*, XIV (January, 1935), 64-91.

"New Clematis Hybrids." *Horticulture*, XIII (May 1, 1935), 240-41.

"Clematis in America." *Clematis, the Large and Small Flowered, Their Cultivation in the Open Air, Including a Comprehensive List of Species and Varieties.* Ed. Ernest Markham. Introduction by William Robinson. New York: C. Scribner's Sons, 1935.

"Clematis in Old Japan." (London) *Gardeners' Chronicle*, XCIX (January 18, 1936), 67-68.

"Clematis." *The Garden Dictionary.* Ed. Norman Taylor. Boston and New York: Houghton Mifflin Co., 1936.

"Hybrids of Clematis Texensis and Other American Clematis Species." (London) *Gardeners' Chronicle*, C (September 5, 1936), 178-79.

"George Edward Woodberry." *The Dictionary of American Biography.* Vol. XX. New York: C. Scribner's Sons, 1936.

"Clematis for American Gardens and Where to Get Them." *Flower Grower*, XXIV (March, 1937), 130-31+.

"Clematis for the Northeastern States." *Arnold Arboretum Bulletin of Popular Information.* July, 1937.

"Henry Winthrop Sargent and the Early History of Landscape Gardening and Ornamental Horticulture in Dutchess County, New York." *Yearbook, Dutchess County Historical Society.* 1937.

"A Negro Gardener's Diary." *Bulletin of the Garden Club of America.* March, 1938.

"Politics and the Poet." *The Atlantic Monthly*, CLXX (November, 1942), 73-78. The fourth of Spingarn's six lectures at the New School for Social Research in 1931 on *Literature and the New Era.* The other five remain unpublished.

SECONDARY SOURCES

Heretofore there has been no substantial study of Spingarn, though Barbara Joyce Ross has announced the imminent publication of a book on his work in the field of race relations and civil rights. Many of the accounts of the literary scene in the

United States during the first thirty years of the twentieth century make brief mentions of his literary criticism, as do the introductions and notes to the numerous anthologies of criticism in which various of his essays have been reprinted. The following list provides a sampling of representative comment on his criticism and related matters.

Babbitt, Irving. "Croce and the Philosophy of the Flux." *The Yale Review*, XIV (January, 1925), 377-81.

——————. "The Modern Spirit and Dr. Spingarn." *Journal of Philosophy, Psychology, and Scientific Method*, XI (April 9, 1914), 215-18.

——————. "Reply to Dr. Spingarn." *Journal of Philosophy, Psychology, and Scientific Method*, XI (June 4, 1914), 328-29. This and preceding two articles detail Babbitt's neo-Humanist criticism of what he takes to be the irresponsible emotionalism of Spingarn's position and its Crocean assumptions.

Brown, Merle E. *Neo-Idealistic Aesthetics: Croce-Gentile-Collingwood.* Detroit: Wayne State University Press, 1966. Lively account of the idealistic philosophical basis of the Crocean esthetic.

Chamberlain, John. "Mr. Spingarn Puts His Critical Fences in Repair." *New York Times Book Review*, October 18, 1931, p. 2. Shrewd description of Spingarn's involvement in the guerilla warfare of criticism before and during 1920's.

Cook, George Cram. "The Third American Sex." *The Forum*, L (October, 1913), 445-63. Indictment of academic submissiveness in American universities.

Coon, Horace. *Columbia, Colossus on the Hudson.* New York: E. P. Dutton and Co., 1947. Summary account of Spingarn's firing as part of a semipopular narrative of the development of Columbia.

Du Bois, W. E. B. *Dusk of Dawn.* New York: Harcourt, Brace and Co., 1940. Sympathetic account of Spingarn's role in the National Association for the Advancement of Colored People by one who came to disagree with him.

——————. *The Amenia Conference: an Historic Negro Gathering*, no. 8 of *Troutbeck Leaflets.* Amenia, N. Y.: The Troutbeck Press, 1925. Affectionate memoir of the mood and setting of the conference by a leading participant.

Galsworthy, John. "Letters on Criticism and Art." *The Columbia Monthly*, IX (January, 1912), 72-77. Attacks Spingarn's failure to distinguish between the artist and the critic.

Goldberg, Isaac. "Joel Elias Spingarn: a Causerie." *The Stratford Monthly*, I (new series) (June, 1924), 240-47. Somewhat superficial praise of Spingarn as a prophet of progressivism.

Hughes, Langston. *Fight for Freedom: the Story of the NAACP.* New York: W. W. Norton and Co., 1962. Brief comment on Spingarn's role, including his latter-day concern over incipient Negro exclusivism.

Kellogg, Charles Flint. *NAACP: A History of the National Association of Colored People.* Vol. I. 1909-1920. Baltimore: The Johns Hopkins Press, 1967. Best history yet published.

Lewisohn, Ludwig. *Expression in America.* New York and London: Harper and Bros., 1932. Dubious socio-psychological speculation on Spingarn's weaknesses in the debate with Babbitt.

Mencken, H. L. "Criticism of Criticism of Criticism." *Prejudices, First Series.* New York: A. A. Knopf, 1919. A complaint that "creative criticism" puts too heavy a burden on the critic, whose approach must always be "empirical" and practical, not to say catch-as-catch-can.

Mumford, Lewis. "Aesthetics: a Palaver." *The American Mercury*, III (November, 1924), 360-65. Reprinted as no. 3 of *Troutbeck Leaflets* under title of *Aesthetics: a Dialogue.* An "imaginative reaction to conversations which took place at Troutbeck, in 1921, between Van Wyck Brooks, Lewis Mumford, Ernest Boyd, and J. E. Spingarn," largely centering on the relations between art and its environment. In an unpublished memorandum of June 8, 1951, Mumford made the fairly obvious connections between the fictional and the real characters: DeFiori and Spingarn, O'Malley and Ernest Boyd, Adams and Brooks. He then added: "I chose to assign most of the thoughts of the remaining member ["Percy Scott"] to an old friend of mine, Clarence Britten [an associate editor of the *Dial*] –all the more because, in the dialogue, I gave to Brooks many of my own thoughts, just as in fact, at the actual meeting, I had sided with him."

–––––. "Introduction." "Politics and the Poet." J. E. Spingarn. *Atlantic Monthly*, CLXX (November, 1942), 73-78. Contains personal testimony to Spingarn's growing disillusion with easy liberal optimism.

O'Connor, William Van. *Sense and Sensibility in Modern Poetry.* Chicago: University of Chicago Press, 1948. Perceptive comment on Spingarn's sense of "politics."

—————. *An Age of Criticism.* Chicago: Henry Regnery Co., 1952. Good critical summary of Spingarn's view of technique, connecting it with the idea of "organic form"; of morality in poetry; of Spingarn's idealistic assumptions; and of his anti-Marxian notion of the "generative forces in history."

Orsini, N. Giordano. "Il caso Spingarn e il Croceanesimo in America." *Criterio,* I (July, 1957), 517-23. Contends that Spingarn's overemphasis on "taste" distorts Crocean doctrine.

—————. *Benedetto Croce, Philosopher of Art and Literary Critic.* Carbondale: Southern Illinois University Press, 1961. Careful brief comment by a devout Crocean on Spingarn's interpretations and misinterpretations of the master's doctrine, especially the relation between drama and the theater and the relation between criticism and taste.

Record, Wilson. *Race and Radicalism: the NAACP and the Communist Party in Conflict.* Ithaca, N. Y.: Cornell University Press, 1964. Includes comment on Spingarn's opposition to Communism.

Smith, Bernard. *Forces in American Criticism.* New York: Harcourt, Brace and Co., 1939. Very good, well-informed Marxian analysis; concludes that Spingarn was insufficiently concerned with the "effects" of literature.

Walkley, A. B. "An American Croce." *The* (London) *Times,* March 24, 1926, p. 14.

—————. "Criticism and Croce." *The* (London) *Times,* March 20, 1911, p. 12. This and the preceding entry find Spingarn's neglect of the artist's medium to be a result of his overstating the idealist's position in "pragmatic" America.

Weinberg, Bernard. "Introduction." *A History of Literary Criticism in the Renaissance.* J. E. Spingarn. Harbinger ed. New York: Harcourt, Brace and World, 1963. Good analysis of Spingarn's synthetic scholarly method in this book.

Index

Adams, Henry, 119
Agrarianism, 153
Ahab (*Moby Dick*), 119
Aldrich, Thomas Bailey, 57
Amenia, N.Y., 58
Amenia Conference, 58, 60-61, 72
Amenia Field Day, 59
Amenia Times. See Harlem Valley Times
Ariosto, Lodovico, 135
Arizona, University of, 70
Arnold, Matthew, 35, 36, 139, 152
Art: Spingarn on distinctions between philosophy, religion, and, 82, 96; as expression, 83-90, 102-3; Spingarn on, 61, 76, 80, 83-90, 105, 107-8, 113-18 *passim*, 144-45, 154, 156; Crocean view of, 90, 92, 93; critics on Spingarn's concept of, 104; and professors of comparative literature, 121; mentioned, 154. *See also* Poetry
Atheneum (London), 17
Atlanta University, 73
Atlantic Monthly, 25, 65
Austen, Jane, 120

Babbitt, Irving: opposition to "genteel tradition," 57; criticism of Spingarn, 77, 85, 97-98, 100-105 *passim*; Horace Kallen on, 77; Spingarn on, 99, 100-105 *passim*; controversy with Spingarn, 100-105, 107; as merger of literary and cultural criticism, 142; and *Literature and the American College*, 143; and re-

definition of the past, 149; Norman Foerster on, 155-56; mentioned, 37, 113, 114, 115, 120
Bacon, Francis, 84
Baker, George Pierce, 18
Baker, Newton D., 64
Baudelaire, Charles, 118
Beard, Charles, 37, 38, 52-53
Beardsley, M. C., 146, 147
Benton, Charles E., 59
Benton, Joel, 59
Benton, Myron B., 58, 59
Bergson, Henri, 101
Biography, 117, 139, 146
Blackmur, R. P.: on criticism, 94, 149-50; on imagination, 94, 114; on language, 151; mentioned, 152
Blum, Cornelius, 98
Bond, R. Warwick, 17
Bookman, The, 65
Bourne, Randolph, 77, 114
Boyd, Ernest, 110
Boyesen, Bayard, 52
Brace, Donald, 67. *See also* Harcourt, Brace and Company
Bradley, William Aspenwall, 25, 99, 128
Brandl, Aloïs, 22
Bread Loaf School of English, 70
Brooks, Cleanth, 124, 151-52
Brooks, Van Wyck: on American thought and culture, 37, 81; on "genteel tradition," 57; on Spingarn's separation of literature and life, 98, 118; as merger of literary and cultural criticism, 142; and the discovery of a "usa-

ble past," 143, 153; mentioned, 40, 149

Brownell, W. C., 152, 153

Burroughs, John, 58, 60

Butcher, S. H., 22

Butler, Nicholas Murray: as president of Columbia, 46-53; and disputes with faculty of Columbia, 47-48, 52-53, and dismissal of Spingarn, 48, 49-51; on Harry Thurston Peck, 50-51; Spingarn on, 52; mentioned, 49, 73, 74, 79, 80

Calverton, V. F.: as Marxist critic, 104; criticism of Spingarn, 107-108, 118

Cambridge History of English Literature, 31, 33, 84

Canby, Henry Seidel, 125

Carducci, Giosuè, 22

Carritt, E. F.: on Crocean idealism, 91; on Crocean "expression," 93; on language, 130

Castelvetro, Lodovico, 86

Castiglione, Baldassare, 26, 27

Cattel, J. McKeen, 52, 53

Chamberlain, John, 98, 143

Child, F. J., 18

Churchill, Winston, 61

Cincinnati Post, 24

Cincinnati, University of, 24

Clematis, 72-73

Coleridge, S. T., 84, 85, 130-31

Collier's, 53

Columbia College, 17

Columbia Monthly, 17

Columbia University: Spingarn's attendance at graduate school of, 18; Woodberry's resignation from, 20-47; Society of Phi Beta Kappa at, 25; Nicholas Murray Butler's presidency of, 46-56 *passim*; Harry Thurston Peck's dismissal from, 47-48; Spingarn's dismissal from, 47-51 *passim*, 56; Spingarn's criticism of, 50-53, 79; mentioned, 30, 44, 74, 87

Comparative literature: Spingarn's study of in college, 18; Spingarn's speech on at University of Cincinnati, 24; Spingarn's conception of, 32, 33; Woodberry on, 35; Spingarn's article on in *Cyclopedia of Education*, 36, 139

Comparative religion: Spingarn's interest in, 68, 72

Cosmopolitan, 53

Crisis, The, 61, 64

Criticism: Impressionist, 76; battles of, 76-77; Marxist, 94; "historical," 132; "practical," 152-53

Croce, Benedetto: Spingarn on influence of, 18; Spingarn's discovery of, 19; preface to *A History of Literary Criticism in the Renaissance*, 22; Spingarn's reviews of, 30; influence on "new historians," 37-38; influence on Spingarn, 18, 37, 38, 43, 73, 74, 78, 87, 105, 128, 136, 139, 142, 143; as neo-Hegelian, 74, 81; Spingarn's interpretations of, 75; Spingarn's quarrels with, 75; on religion, 82-83; on philosophy, 82-83, 88, 89-90; *Aesthetic*, 88, 89, 90; on intuition, 89, 111; on expression, 89, 114; on art, 75, 89-92, 93, 104, 110, 123-24, 127, 144-45; on distinctions between art and philosophy, 89-90, 144; on morals, 111; on history, 113, 149; on practical criticism, 128-29; on language, 130; on criticism as history, 134-37; conception of artist, 143; idealism, 143; influence on critics, 144-56 *passim*; mentioned, 20, 23, 24, 33, 35, 66, 67, 68, 79, 85, 98, 103, 140, 146, 148

Cummings, E. E., 151

Cyclopedia of Education, 36, 139

Dana, Henry Wadsworth, 52

Dante, 136, 138